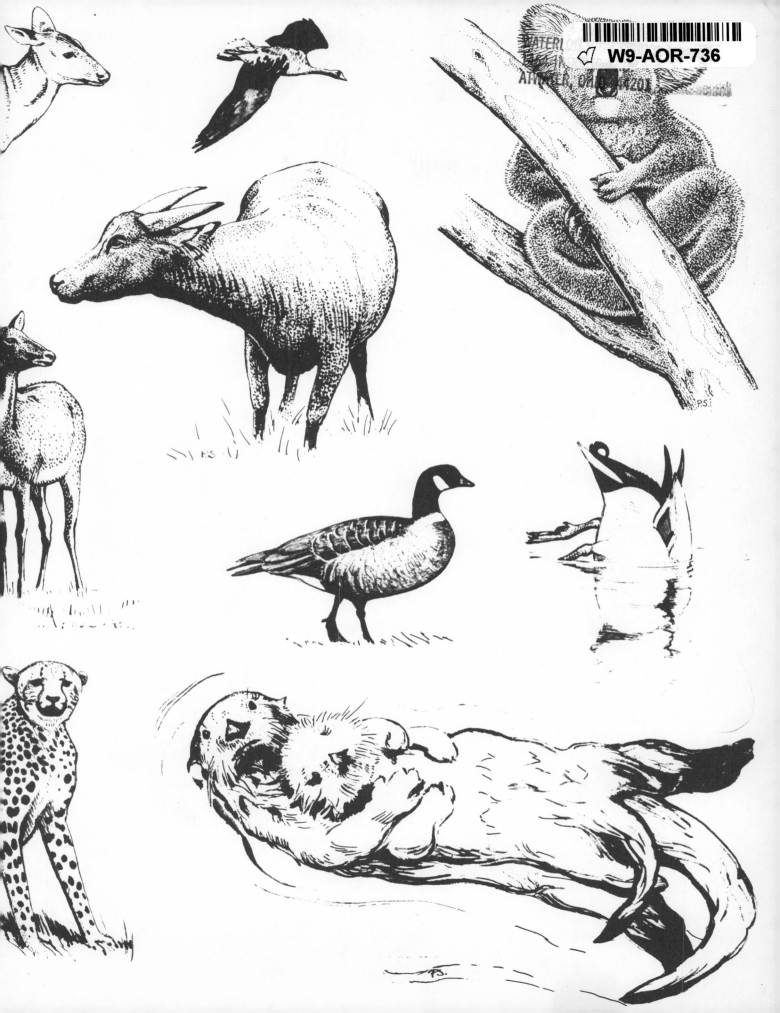

SAVING THE ANIMALS

 WORLD
WILDLIFE
FUND-US

MACMILLAN PUBLISHING CO., INC., NEW YORK

SAVING

The World Wildlife Fund Book of Conservation
By Bernard Stonehouse

Foreword by HRH The Duke of Edinburgh
Introduction by Sir Peter Scott

THE ANIMALS

Macmillan Publishing Co., Inc.
866 Third Avenue, New York, N.Y. 10022
Collier Macmillan Canada, Ltd.

Library of Congress Cataloging in Publication Data

Stonehouse, Bernard.
    Saving the animals.

    Bibliography: p.
    Includes index.
    1. Wildlife conservation. I. World Wildlife Fund.   II. Title.
QL82.S85 1981   333.95 416   81–4063
ISBN 0–02–614750–5   AACR2

First American Edition 1981
Printed in the United States of America

Designed by Allison Waterhouse for
George Weidenfeld and Nicolson Ltd.
91 Clapham High Street, London SW4 7TA, England

FOREWORD

In 1949 the International Union for the Conservation of Nature set up the Survival Service Commission (later the Species Survival Commission) under the Chairmanship of Sir Peter Scott. The Commission immediately set about compiling a Red Data Book of Endangered Species. There are separate sections for mammals, reptiles, invertebrates and fish, while a Red Data Book for birds is compiled by the International Council for Bird Preservation. At the latest count 321 species of mammals, 168 species of reptiles, 194 species of fish, 300 species of invertebrates and 437 species of birds are listed in these books and this is in spite of the fact that many of the lists are known to be incomplete, and the compilation of the book for fish has only recently been started.

This gives some idea of the scale of the problem, but what makes it even more depressing is that for every species 'saved' an average of another 10 are added to each list every year.

There is no simple formula for saving species threatened with extinction. Each case has to be treated according to its particular circumstances. But there is one common factor: unless wild animals – or plants for that matter – have somewhere appropriate for them to live and breed reasonably undisturbed by human activity, there is no hope for their survival in the wild.

Saving the Animals sets out clearly and dramatically why it is that the partnership between the World Wildlife Fund and the International Union for the Conservation of Nature is so vital to the future of the natural environment.

BUCKINGHAM PALACE 1981

CONTENTS

Author's acknowledgment

Many people have contributed to this book. I thank especially
Max Nicholson, who gave me material for chapter 1 from his
own files, and Guy Mountfort who checked and added
interesting detail to chapter 4. Peter Jackson, who has written
much for the World Wildlife Fund, contributed substantially
to chapters 12 and 13, and was helpful both in commenting on
other chapters and in selecting photographs from WWF
archives in Switzerland. Many field biologists involved in
WWF projects have contributed indirectly; I have been able to
use only a fraction of the splendid archival material available at
WWF headquarters in Gland. Four have made more direct
contributions. I thank Tony Whitten who helped with
chapters 3, 6 and 11, Robert Lamb who added some of his
special knowledge of Madagascar to chapter 8, Paul Munton
who contributed to chapters 14 and 15, and Tim Inskipp, of the
Wildlife Trade Monitoring Unit, Cambridge, who helped me
with chapter 17.

 World Wildlife Fund gave me access to its archives; Julia
Tucker of IUCN kindly found me a place to work and ensured
that none of my time in Gland was wasted. My main link with
WWF has been through Janet Barber, of WWF(UK), who has
contributed substantially to chapter 2 and the postscript,
commented usefully on every other chapter, and advised
unstintingly in a dozen ways; I am most grateful to her. I thank
Heather French and Jean Mellors, who typed – often in
unsocial hours – to get the manuscript out on time. Finally I
thank Barbara Mellor and her editorial colleagues at
Weidenfeld for their help and support; their contribution to
the book is apparent – and they were always very good
company.

Bernard Stonehouse, April 1981.

INTRODUCTION
BY SIR PETER SCOTT

My involvement with conservation began one day in 1935, when 'Chips' Ezra, the distinguished aviculturist, invited me to his Surrey home to show me a group of pink-headed ducks, newly arrived from India. 'They are very rare,' he said, 'indeed they may soon become extinct. But I'm hoping to breed from them.' They were strange-looking ducks – large, chocolate-coloured birds with long thin necks, their brilliant pink heads and bills pointing downward to give them a comically deprecating look.

I fervently hoped they would breed at Foxwarren. To me even then the extinction of a species was something to be deeply deplored, particularly if, with a little effort, it could be averted. Brought up as a naturalist at the express wish of my father, I had trained first as a biologist and then as a painter. I had a small collection of live waterfowl at my home (a disused lighthouse on the shores of the Wash), and I had read about Labrador ducks that became extinct in 1875, and the many other species, including dodos, great auks and passenger pigeons, that man in his remorseless spread across the globe had brought to extinction.

As it turned out, the ten pink-headed ducks never bred. The last one died during the Second World War, and the species has never been seen since. It was, I believe, the sight of those ducks that led me to a sharp awareness of the finality and irrevocability of species extinction.

Another of my early experiences has a curious link with the present. In the pre-war years I visited Woburn Park, where the Eleventh Duke of Bedford maintained a fine collection of waterfowl and also a herd of Père David's deer. These, I learned, had an extraordinary history. They had become extinct in northern China some three thousand years ago, but a population had been maintained in the Imperial Hunting Park on the southern outskirts of Peking. As Bernard Stonehouse tells in Chapter 15 of this book, in 1865 the missionary naturalist Père Armand David first saw them when he peeped over the park wall, and recognized them as a new species.

The Duke of Bedford received a pair of these large deer in 1898, shortly before the last remnants of the captive herd were destroyed in the Boxer Rebellion. He brought together all the Père David's deer he could acquire from zoos around the world – ten stags and eight hinds – and bred from them successfully. These are the ancestors of all the Père David's deer (about 870 is the present population) now existing in the world. Just a few months ago, when I was in China with a World

Saved from extinction, the néné, or Hawaiian goose.

Wildlife Fund delegation, I was told about a proposal to create an extensive reserve in which these splendid animals could once again run wild – or almost wild – in their homeland. It is doubtful if the Eleventh Duke of Bedford ever dreamed of such a possibility, but I knew he would have deemed it the best possible climax to his far-sighted efforts to save a species from extinction.

Shortly before the war I became involved in the fortunes of another threatened species – the Hawaiian goose or néné. In 1936, in my book *Wild Chorus*, I had written of '. . . another species which has reached the danger mark. It is said that the introduction of the mongoose onto the islands is partly responsible. Whatever the cause it would be a major tragedy if such an interesting and striking bird were to disappear. . . . Perhaps there are just enough left for its impending doom, like that of Europe, to be averted at the eleventh hour.'

But war came to Europe and to the rest of the world too, and by the end of it the nénés had almost gone. By 1950 there were believed to be only forty-two left, ten of them in the wild and the rest in the garden of Herbert Shipman, a naturalist who lived at Hilo on the 'Big Island' of Hawaii. Before the war Shipman had promised me a pair of his geese. In 1948, having established the Wildfowl Trust at Slimbridge, we could offer them a good home and a chance to breed in peace and safety. Shipman sent us a male and two females, and after initial difficulties they began to breed in 1951.

The rest of the story is told in Chapter 2 of this book, for the newly formed World Wildlife Fund was later to play a part. After eight years we needed fresh blood in the stock, and two more males were flown from Hilo; later we asked for and received a further two. From these birds – seven in all – we bred over 1,400 Hawaiian geese. We began shipping them back to repopulate their native islands, and sent others to form breeding stocks in zoos and waterfowl collections all over the world. Now there are probably some 2,500 altogether, and for the time being the species seems safe.

Fifteen years after my encounter with the pink-headed ducks I became involved in the activities of IUCN – the International Union for Conservation of Nature and Natural Resources. I was naturally drawn to the work of its Survival Service Commission, created by Harold Coolidge, one of the most dynamic international conservationists of the last forty years. I became Chairman of the SSC, now renamed the Species Survival Commission, in 1961 and retired from it in 1980. It is one of IUCN's six commissions, with special responsibility for guarding endangered and vulnerable species of flora and fauna. Its Specialist Groups draw on the knowledge and experience of more than a thousand scientists on a voluntary basis, and it is the primary source of the scientific and technical information needed in planning the conservation of species at risk. It was involved in every one of the campaigns for conservation mentioned in this book.

IUCN's work was subject to financial constraints from the moment of its inception in 1948. To provide it with adequate money was one of the objectives of the World Wildlife Fund when we brought it into existence in 1961. Through the Fund, with the help and advice of IUCN, naturalists and biologists all over the world have been able to save species and habitats at risk. This book tells some of the stories behind the campaigns. It is important that these stories should be told, for they are stories of successful conservation, and we need to know what has been achieved as well as what still has to be done.

All the animals and plants alive today are the end-products of a continuum of evolution, which has lasted something like four billion years since life began on earth . . . four thousand million years . . . forty million centuries. The evolutionary tree is like some gigantic Lombardy poplar, growing ever upwards with advancing time, the tips of its still-growing branches at the very top. Lower down are the dead branches – the species that have become extinct. Some die out because they are not adaptable enough to survive, and new branches are all the time being formed as local races becomes species in their own right, filling ecological gaps in the habitat.

But whereas the time scale of evolution is very long indeed, the time scale of extinction is often short and sharp. Recently the human species seems directly or indirectly to have increased the rate of extinction of other species at least four-fold, and maybe much more. I find this saddening, and that is why I feel motivated to try to reverse the trend.

Man has evolved as part of nature and remains subject to her laws. Those of us who were brought up to understand and enjoy unspoiled countryside, wilderness and wildlife believe passionately that these things must not be swept away for ever by ignorant and careless people. They seem to us to be essential for human health and happiness. However, future generations may think quite differently; our species is unbelievably adaptable, and already there are activities that fully occupy the human mind while relying hardly at all on contact with nature.

Research scientists, mathematicians, astronomers, even some artists and musicians may be able in the future to live full and contented lives without any contact with wildlife or wilderness. If we believe that generations of human beings will, in the long run, live their lives in space stations, or travelling through the galaxy for hundreds of light-years, it is quite possible that those lives will be perfectly fulfilling and rewarding without earthly environments.

But I believe the responsibility remains with us today to keep the options open for these future generations, so that as much as possible of the wonder of this planet, with its amazing diversity of living creatures, is handed on to them intact.

In 1980 IUCN and WWF, in collaboration with the United Nations Environment Programme (UNEP), produced a World Conservation Strategy; Bernard Stonehouse discusses it in the final chapter of this book. The World Strategy shows clearly that development programmes cannot succeed without taking conservation principles into account, any more than conservation can be implemented without the money that economic development can supply. Development and conservation must go hand in hand if we are to save anything of our natural heritage – even, perhaps, if we ourselves are to survive.

IUCN, WWF, UNEP – the jungle of these international organizations often seems dense and impenetrable. Having wandered in it for more than twenty-five years I have been able to reach a number of conclusions. I have discovered that conservation anywhere in the world is impossible to implement without engaging the interest of the local people, and that education is by far the most important single thing for conservationists to be doing. Whereas the importance of preventing extinctions of animal and plant species is easy to convey to people (including decision-makers), trying to explain the significance of habitats and ecosystems, whose disappearance is often the principal cause of extinction, is virtually impossible at present levels of awareness.

Sadly, I have discovered that there is no hope whatever of saving *all* that I or any other conservationist would like to save, but if we can work together without internecine strife and keep working hard without losing heart, we shall save a great more of our natural world than if we had never tried.

Peter Scott
Slimbridge, March 1981

Muddy hippos amble off across the African savanna.

WWF AND ITS WORKS

THE WORLD WILDLIFE FUND

THE WORLD WILDLIFE FUND comes of age in 1982. From its inception in September 1961 WWF has held an unrivalled position as the world's best-known, most widely acclaimed organization for the support of wildlife and wild habitats. After two decades and more of strenuous activity, in which it has raised and spent well over US $50 million in the cause of conservation, it can claim an extraordinary record of achievement, covering over one hundred countries on all the inhabited continents. WWF receives no government funding and is not, as many suppose, a protégé of the United Nations. It is an international charity, one that works on a vast, worldwide scale, collecting funds from many sources and disbursing them all over the globe in a wide range of conservation programmes.

The main business of WWF is to marshal money and public support for practical conservation work, often on a large scale, wherever it is needed. Its chief concerns are animals and their habitats, especially those threatened by man. More often than not the threats that put animals at risk arise from man-made changes in their habitats (the natural areas where they live); from the outset the World Wildlife Fund has concerned itself with both.

This book is not primarily about the politics of international wildlife management, nor even in the main about WWF itself. It is mostly about animals and their habitats, and the hazards both natural and man-made that beset them. Its subjects are creatures and places at risk that have been helped toward survival by WWF, from orang-utans and rhinoceroses of Sumatra to monk seals and seabirds of the Mediterranean – from the rainforests of Nepal to the Marismas of Spain and deserts of Arabia.

'In Africa's wild lands we have a surviving sector of the rich natural world as it was before the rise of modern man.' (Julian Huxley)

The World Wildlife Fund grew in association with an older and lesser-known organization, the International Union for the Conservation of Nature and Natural Resources (IUCN), with which it still works in close everyday cooperation. IUCN began in 1948 as the International Union for the Protection of Nature, which in turn arose from a pre-war, privately funded Belgian foundation based in Brussels. Set up on Swiss initiative (and with the early blessing of UNESCO) during the post-war international honeymoon of peace and goodwill, IUCN reflected the concern of naturalists and scientists over technological and other threats to natural resources, and their interest in planning for conservation of wildlife.

IUCN moved in 1961 to new headquarters in Morges, on the shore of Lake Geneva, Switzerland. To the conservationist-in-the-street today it is probably known best for its Red Data Books on endangered species, which list plant and animal species currently at risk and likely to be lost to the world by extinction. Now, as a union of governments, government agencies and conservation groups representing 109 countries, IUCN 'determines the scientific priorities for conservation action and harnesses the scientific resources needed to investigate conservation problems throughout the world, and to recommend and help implement appropriate action.'

IUCN developed as a scientific body, investigatory, opinion-forming and advisory, without major financial resources of its own: it was soon identifying conservation problems far bigger than it could cope with on its own, and its small hard-working executive had neither time nor capability to go out and raise the vast sums needed for the work it was advocating. With responsibility for world conservation on its shoulders, IUCN had an annual income less than that of many provincial natural history societies, and no mandate to raise more. That is where WWF began – not specifically to help IUCN (though it has done so in many ways since its inception) but to raise the massive funds needed to carry out the kinds of work that IUCN was advocating.

Toward the end of the 1950s several organizations and concerned individuals had felt the need for fund-raising, and small-scale schemes were afoot. But the idea of a new, larger-scale fund body did not arise from any existing conservation body. WWF began with a letter, written on 6 December 1960, from a Sunday newspaper reader to an eminent biologist. The writer was Mr Victor Stolan, a London businessman and naturalized Briton who read the *Observer*, one of Britain's two Sunday 'heavy' newspapers. The biologist was Sir Julian Huxley, a former Director of

'To see large animals going about their natural business in their own natural way, assured and unafraid, is one of the most exciting and moving experiences in the world.'
(Julian Huxley)

'Many elephants are slaughtered by poachers to satisfy the demands of white men for ivory ornaments.'
(Julian Huxley)

London Zoo, and well known in Britain as a writer and broadcaster. As first Director-General of UNESCO Huxley had helped to launch IUCN back in 1948, and he was one of several biologists of international standing – and certainly one of the most articulate – currently expressing concern about conservation on a world scale.

Recently returned from a UNESCO visit to East Africa, Huxley had written three articles for the *Observer* on growing threats to African wildlife, particularly the spectacular game animals threatened by the spread of man. The captions accompanying some of the photographs in this chapter are quotations from his articles, which were among the first to express deep concern about environmental problems in Africa. 'Many parts of Kenya and Tanganyika and the Rhodesias', he wrote, 'which fifty years ago were swarming with game are now bare of all wildlife ... cultivation is extending, native cattle are multiplying at the expense of wild animals, poaching is becoming heavier and more organised, forests are being cut down or destroyed – large areas are being overgrazed and degenerating into semidesert, and above and behind all this, the human population is inexorably mounting, to press even harder on the limited land space.' 'African wildlife is a major resource', he wrote in his final article, and went on to spell out the need for a campaign to set up more wildlife parks and urgently needed reserves.

Deeply moved by the Huxley articles, Victor Stolan wrote rather hesitantly to the author ('Only reluctantly, I add mine to the large number of letters which you must

Soil erosion: Julian Huxley was one of the first to point out the permanent damage done to pastures by the overgrazing of domestic cattle.

have received'), putting the case for a worldwide campaign to raise money quickly on behalf of threatened animals in Africa and elsewhere. 'I have some ideas as to how to collect substantial donations,' he wrote, 'but nobody of sufficient importance to speak to. Would you care to put me in touch with somebody with whom such ideas can be developed and speedily directed towards accumulating some millions of pounds. . .?'

Victor Stolan's idea was engagingly simple and direct – tackle the very rich. 'There must by a way', he wrote, 'to the conscience and the heart and pride and vanity of the very rich people to persuade them to sink their hands deeply into their pockets . . . If . . . what is left of wildlife in Africa (and elsewhere for that matter) is to be saved, a blunt and ruthless demand must be made to those who, with their riches, can build for themselves a shining monument in history . . .' From this germ of an idea grew the World Wildlife Fund, with a speed that might well have taken Victor Stolan's breath away.

Huxley discussed Stolan's letter immediately with E.M. ('Max') Nicholson, a dynamic ecologist and Director-General of Britain's leading conservation organization, the Nature Conservancy. Nicholson was sure that there was a case for a single, large-scale international effort to raise very substantial funds, and moved with characteristic energy to start one up. He discussed it with Peter Scott, well known as an artist, ornithologist and broadcaster and currently a Councillor of IUCN, who shared his enthusiasm and was already thinking along similar lines. He sounded out opinion in the United States, but was disappointed to find little interest or support at that time. Returning to Britain he discovered a strong ally in Guy Mountfort, director of a large international advertising agency and prominent amateur ornithologist; Mountfort's backing was especially significant because of his wide circle of contacts in the international business community. There were further discussions in London and Switzerland. Then early in April, just four months from the date of Stolan's letter, Max Nicholson drew up a paper under the title 'Saving the World's Wildlife' and sent it to a circle of conservation-minded friends and colleagues for comment.

His paper was discussed at a meeting held in the London offices of the Nature Conservancy on 25 April 1961. It was a small gathering including Sir Julian Huxley, Victor Stolan, Guy Mountfort, and several others prominent in conservation matters in Britain – Aubrey Buxton, Lord Hurcomb, Lt-Col C.L. Boyle, Ambrose Appelbe and Teresa Sexton. Max Nicholson took the chair, and Peter Scott, Phyllis Barclay-Smith and Dr E.B. Worthington sent apologies for absence. This group, with very few changes, formed the steering committee that launched the World Wildlife Fund, for Max Nicholson's paper – the subject of their discussion on that spring day in 1961 – was effectively the blueprint for the Fund we know today.

More than twenty years later, 'Saving the World's Wildlife' makes remarkable reading; all the major concepts of WWF are contained within it, and many of the details as well. Nicholson started with the subtitle 'Conservation Must Command Money', stressing the need for effective and large-scale action to safeguard both wildlife and wilderness against imminent destruction. There was no prime need for further research – the facts were well known. So were many of the remedies; danger to wildlife quite simply lay in lack of funds to carry them out. 'The threat of defeat', argued Nicholson, 'is primarily

a question of resources and above all of money. With money, large reserves and refuges could still be bought and safeguarded. With money, experts and leaders could be sent out and maintained in action at danger spots.'

From there on he outlined a scheme for a new organization 'needed only to raise, manage and allocate large sums of money, largely to enable existing bodies to pull their proper weight.' Nicholson's scheme included four elements:

1 A *'Save the World's Wildlife' Trust* or Foundation, registered in Switzerland with a governing body of six to ten leading conservationists and supporters, responsible for receiving and handling funds.

2 An international *Operations Group* to prepare and maintain a world map showing the main current threats to wildlife and wilderness, and pinpointing the projects and campaigns aimed at countering them; the group would

also be responsible for allocating funds and submitting statements of future requirements.

3 A *Supporters' Club* of wealthy members able to provide substantial sums of money immediately, in return for certain privileges of membership.

4 A number of *National Appeals*, to be launched simultaneously in several countries, to raise further funds by successive campaigns for particular conservation programmes – tapping the support of millions of people throughout the world whose deeply felt concern had no other effective means of expression.

The minutes of that first meeting record blandly an agreement that 'the project in the circulated paper by Mr Nicholson be accepted as a basis for further consideration and action.' They also set out the group's determination to regard themselves as an action committee, to start listing possible candidates for the Club (whose contributions were essential to finance all subsequent activities), to ask IUCN in Morges to begin organizing the Operations Group, and to develop a publicity campaign ready to move into action later in the year.

Other meetings followed rapidly through the late spring and summer. In mid-May the name 'World Wild Life Fund' was chosen for the Trust, with the slogan 'Save the World's Wild Life'. In late May firm links were forged with IUCN, which had recently issued a 'Morges Manifesto', signed by sixteen eminent ecologists, setting out the need for just such a fund; it was no coincidence that some of the phrases in the Manifesto had a familiar ring to them, or that Max Nicholson's name appeared at the bottom, together with those of Julian Huxley, Peter Scott and E.B. Worthington.

In June the Fund opened its first bank account with a float of £3,000 from anonymous donors. At the same meeting – the fifth – it received its first urgent request for funds: £60,000 was needed to buy a precious remnant of the Guadalquivir River marshes – the Marismas – of Spain, under threat of drainage and conversion to agriculture by the Spanish government. The July meeting saw the panda symbol adopted. Based on London Zoo's Chi-chi, it was to become one of the world's most widely recognized logos. In late July the group laid plans for the British National Appeal – first of all the national appeals. HRH Prince Philip, agreeing to become its President, took a vigorous hand in revising and simplifying the draft World Wildlife Charter. He also enlisted the support of HRH Prince Bernhard of the Netherlands, who agreed to become first Patron and later President of WWF.

The Fund came into existence officially on 11 September 1961, when it was legally constituted under Swiss law and registered as a charity at Zurich. Announcements about it followed a carefully timed sequence of events. At a Pan-African wildlife conference held that same month in Arusha, Tanganyika, the Prime Minister of Tanganyika, Mr Julius Nyerere, read a declaration affirming the support of prominent Africans – leaders in several of the newly independent countries – for wildlife conservation. Shortly afterwards IUCN issued a reply, pledging its own support for African conservation, and incidentally establishing its own credentials as a key organization in the field. Now at last came the cue for the World Wildlife Fund to appear. In a blaze of well organized publicity, at the Royal Society of Arts meeting rooms in London, the Fund was finally launched on 26 September 1961.

Earlier on the same day Max Nicholson had chaired the ninth and final meeting of the steering committee. Laconic as ever, the minutes record that 'Mr Nicholson thanked the Committe for their help and effective action in setting in motion the World Wildlife Fund' – a near-miracle

accomplished in exactly five months.

The British National Appeal came into being in November of that year, raising £40,000 and providing funds for eighteen projects during its first twelve months. The first handful of projects sponsored by WWF were in many ways indicative of how the Fund would work in the years to come. Project 1 was a substantial grant to IUCN, to help it establish the Operations Intelligence Centre, launch a special African Project, and meet some of its annual running costs. Projects 2, 3 and 4 helped three other hard-pressed organizations, the International Youth Federation, the International Wildfowl Research Bureau (IWRB) and the International Council for Bird Preservation (ICBP) to cover their expenses and extend some of their conservation activities; IWRB and ICBP have continued in a special relationship with WWF over the years. Project 5 was a small grant toward the work of the Charles Darwin Foundation on the Galapagos Islands, a token of more substantial help to come.

Project 6 was the first of WWF's major grants toward the conservation of a species – US $56,000 to the East African Wild Life Society to pay for and equip two mobile anti-poaching teams for the protection of the white rhinoceros in Uganda (chapter 5). Here the newly-fledged Fund overextended itself, running into a cash-flow problem that almost stopped the field teams in their tracks. The problem was solved at the last moment by a subsidy from the British National Appeal. Project 7 was a much smaller donation for a small but appealing project – a grant to the Water for Wild Animals Fund of Kenya that provided boreholes and piped water supplies for game animals in drought-stricken areas.

Later grants in 1961 helped to subsidize the running and maintenance costs of the Congo National Parks, which were suffering severe disruptions during the civil wars that plagued Zaïre's early years of independence (chapter 3), to extend a National Park in Tanganyika, to protect the néné or Hawaiian goose from extinction, to support an ecological survey of the mid-Atlantic island of Tristan da Cunha, where there had been a volcanic eruption, and to investigate the status of two further populations of rhinoceros on Java and Sumatra (chapter 5). A major grant of over £60,000 was set aside for a reserve and biological station on the Guadalquivir Marismas (chapter 9) and the first of several grants was made toward 'Operation Oryx', a widely-publicized programme to catch some of the few remaining specimens of the rare and beautiful Arabian oryx and establish a breeding herd in the United States (chapter 14).

The United States National Appeal was registered in December 1961, and other countries followed quickly – Switzerland in the same month, the Netherlands in 1962, and Germany and Austria in 1963. At the tenth

Wild animal skins, mounted and unmounted, on sale in a Munich sports store.

anniversary celebrations of the Fund in 1971 eighteen National Appeals were in existence; today there are twenty-five (plus two WWF National Committees), with promise of more to come.

How does WWF work? Much as Max Nicholson determined that it should in his paper of April 1961. Its aim is conservation of nature in all forms – landscape, water, air, soils, flora and fauna – on a worldwide scale, and for this aim it raises money. It distributes funds for conservation projects, and makes representations on behalf of wildlife at the highest levels of government. For this latter purpose it has always included among its trustees a number of influential public figures, who from time to time may be able to further a conservation cause by making a direct approach to a head of state or minister of government.

The parent body, World Wildlife Fund International (WWFI), was originally established with IUCN in Morges, but the two moved in 1979 to new headquarters in Gland, on the northern slopes overlooking Lake Geneva. WWFI is governed by a board of thirty-six trustees, including businessmen, financiers, scientists and the public figures mentioned above. That there are few ecologists or biologists among the Board is sometimes cited as a weakness of the organization, but only by those who misunderstand its functions; the Board is mainly a promotional body, not a scientific one, responsible for encouraging the fund-raising efforts of the national organizations, and ensuring the proper spending of the money. Lively, commercially-minded trustees probably serve it far better in promoting the aims of WWF – fund-raising and publicity – than would an equivalent number of scientists.

Responsible to the board of trustees is an Executive Committee and a small permanent staff under the management of a Director-General. The first Director-General, Dr Fritz Vollmar, joined the Fund in 1962 after several years with the Red Cross, establishing the efficient organization that was soon coping with cash flows of millions of dollars in a dozen world currencies. His successor, Charles de Haes, took over in 1978. WWF's executive is grouped in Divisions of Conservation, Development, Finance and Administration, and Public Affairs; WWF shares responsibility with IUCN for a Project Management Department, ensuring maximum efficiency in organizing and administering the field work. Their unity expresses the close liaison existing at every level between IUCN, the scientific and conservation body, and WWF, the money-raisers.

Requests for help come both to WWFI and to the National Organizations (which were formerly called National Appeals). Every request accepted for consideration is vetted by specialists, through national screening committees and IUCN.

The National Organizations work in close collaboration with WWFI, fund-raising for conservation projects at home and abroad. Precise relationships between WWFI and the National Organizations vary, but in general the national bodies seek funds for WWF's projects, sending about two-thirds of their net takings to WWFI for the funding of international projects, and keeping about one third for national projects. The National Organizations raise money in a dozen different ways – through membership, gift catalogues, by direct requests to both private and corporate sponsors, through press advertisements, by licensing use of WWF's name and logo to manufacturers, and with the help of hundreds of voluntary fund-raisers.

And Victor Stolan's principle of tackling the very rich has not been forgotten. The Founder President of WWF, Prince Bernhard of the Netherlands, who worked hard in promoting the Fund during his fifteen years in office, invited 1,000 wealthy people to join him in contributing US $10,000 each to provide a capital endowment. Income from the '1,001 Club' capital now looks after most of the running costs of WWF; the Fund will soon be able to claim with truth that all of the money collected by the National Organizations goes directly for conservation work.

SAVING THE BIRDS

THOUGH PROBABLY best known for its major projects on behalf of mammals, WWF has a long and lesser-known record of support for bird conservation. This is hardly surprising: several of its founders were committed professional or amateur ornithologists with strong ecological interests on a worldwide scale, who between them were only too well aware of the need for conservation of birds and their habitats on every continent. Each year since its launching World Wildlife Fund has supported many individual bird-oriented projects, and each year it has given substantial support to the International Council for Bird Preservation (ICBP), the Cambridge-based organization that coordinates bird conservation work internationally. In its turn ICBP advises WWF on ornithological topics, screening and often originating applications for grants involving birds.

While elephants, rhinos and tigers can rightly command immediate international public sympathy, birds too have an immense following of devotees, especially in western Europe and the United States, where there are long traditions of bird-watching as a hobby, and of good amateur research. More prominent in everyday life than mammals, more colourful and tuneful, birds may be the only wild creatures that city-dwellers see in the course of a day. Because they are mostly diurnal and relatively easy to study, we know more about their life histories and behaviour than is known of most mammals, and they have become useful biological indicators whose warnings we do well to heed. First indications that the natural world is suffering disturbing changes are often given by birds. The decline in numbers of songbirds, particularly white-throats, returning to Britain to breed in spring 1969, was

Gannets nesting in a Scottish colony. Seabird colonies, monitored for numbers and breeding success over several years, often give useful indications of changes in the local environment.

Guillemots (centre) and kittiwakes, nesting at high density in a cliff colony. Feeding in surface waters, these birds suffer severely when oil slicks drift close to their breeding areas.

an early indication of serious drought in their wintering grounds in the West African Sahel: we are gradually learning to read such signs and take note of them.

Birds too gave us some of the early indications that the polychlorinated biphenyl (PCB) effluents were cumulative poisons for vertebrates. Detected first in the eggs of British auks, shags and terns, they were then found in high concentrations in great skuas, fulmars, kittiwakes and other pelagic seabirds. On land, pesticides were estimated to have killed 200,000 birds of fifty-five different species in the Netherlands in 1960. One of their sinister effects was to upset the calcium metabolism of predatory birds whose diet exposed them to high dosages: peregrine falcons, golden eagles, kestrels and sparrow-hawks began laying thin-shelled eggs that broke during incubation, and the species affected began gradually to disappear from agricultural land.

These birds did not die entirely in vain: their deaths alerted us all to the dangers of pesticide abuse, and led to restriction in the use of agricultural chemicals, at least in the developed countries. In poorer countries where laws are less stringent, problems caused by their widespread use are still far from being solved, and may indeed be intensifying. The World Wildlife Fund is about to start an

Elegant terns: a breeding colony. Terns dip for tiny fish at the surface, seldom resting on the water. However, one local oil slick may destroy a whole colony.

Red kites, once common in Britain, Europe and North Africa, are now much reduced in numbers: hunters are their main enemy.

investigation in India on the decline of the grey pelican, in which DDT is likely to be implicated.

Typical of the problems that face modern birds are those affecting the hermit ibis, a rare species numbering no more than 1,000 individuals that nest in two populations at opposite ends of the Mediterranean, in Morocco and Turkey. The Turkish group clusters on cliff ledges above the small town of Birecic, returning to breed each February. Sombre birds with bare face, long bill and black plumage, they are gradually being ousted from their cliffs as the human population of the town grows. Children throw stones at the nests, lines of flapping washing disturb the incubating birds, and the pigeons kept by local fanciers flap noisily past, further upsetting their peace of mind. Flying down to the Euphrates marshes to find food, they encounter another hazard: the small crustaceans they seek are probably contaminated with chemicals that impair breeding performance. None of these is a natural hazard, and none is overwhelming, but together they may well destroy the breeding colony – half the world's population of hermit ibises. World Wildlife Fund is supporting an

ecological project that, among other remedies, is persuading some of the birds to breed on ledges away from the bustle of the town, and encouraging the folk of Birecic to take a more friendly interest in this rare and unusual species that nests with them.

Birds very clearly reflect ecological changes. As Stanley Cramp has pointed out in his book *Bird Conservation in Europe*, draining the East Anglian marshes of Britain caused us to lose bitterns, avocets, ruffs, black-tailed godwits and Savi's warblers as breeding birds, and northern Europe has lost pelicans, egrets and other herons and ibis for a similar reason. Only by providing suitable wetland reserves (chapter 9) do we get these species back. Not all man-induced changes are against the interests of birds. Starlings winter warmly in cities, gulls grow fat on refuse tips, and kittiwakes nest contentedly on warehouse windowledges. A Swedish study estimates that their modern forestry methods have favoured twenty species but brought dis-benefits to twenty-five: most of the ecological changes we induce probably bring similar ratios of good to some birds, harm to many more.

Over the years WWF has been involved in studies of a wide range of species, with waterfowl (chapter 9) and seabirds (chapter 18) well represented in their lists: this is not surprising, for wetlands and the sea are currently high-risk environments, and their birds are especially vulnerable. But landbirds too have had their share of trouble, and WWF has helped many threatened species toward recovery. Because birds live together in mixed communities, saving one species from extinction has often helped others out of trouble. Among early projects supported during WWF's first five years were the purchase of reserves in Texas and Mexico for two species seriously threatened by loss of habitat to agriculture – white-winged doves, that live in dry brushland, and Attwater's prairie chickens of the southern tall-grass prairies. Buying reserves for the last breeding stocks of these species saved them from certain extinction, and also gave protection to local stocks of tree-ducks, green jays, kiskadees, rose-throated becards, pigeons, woodpeckers, and other local species, some of which might soon have been at risk themselves.

The landbirds most severely affected by man's activities are undoubtedly the raptors – hook-billed birds of prey including eagles, vultures, hawks, falcons and harriers. Their numbers are declining all over the world, and it is not difficult to see why. Hunters and scavengers, they incur the enmity of man by taking his game or domestic stock, and so are themselves the most heavily hunted of birds. The wild places they prefer are becoming harder to find as man, his farming and his industry spread far and wide. Prey species of raptors, often insects, small mammals and birds, are in many cases agricultural pests that man is

A raven attacks a Himalayan griffon at 4,000 metres in Khumbu, Nepal. Griffons sail on upcurrents among the mountains, searching out the weak and fallen animals that are their prey.

decimating by poisoning. And by taking prey that may carry sub-lethal doses of toxins, the raptors stand seriously at risk from the cumulative effects of DDT and other poisons.

In 1966 ICBP, at its Fourteenth World Conference in Cambridge, drew attention to the drastic decline in numbers of birds of prey, and from its concern came a succession of surveys and species studies, funded by WWF and other conservation groups, to examine the ecological needs of the hunting birds and give them protection where possible. WWF was an early supporter of EUREL (the European Association for Free Nature Reserves), which established conservation programmes for birds of prey in France and Germany. In special reserves set up in Schleswig-Holstein the rare white-tailed sea eagle, reduced in western Europe to no more than eight nesting pairs, was given special protection during its breeding season: relays of volunteers guarded the nests against egg thieves, and while breeding the birds received special rations of meat uncontaminated with DDT. WWF is now funding further research in an attempt to save this splendid bird in Norway, Sweden, Finland and Greenland. Several lesser species of raptors – honey buzzards, black and red kites, marsh and hen harriers and goshawks, for example – have been given sanctuary in other small

reserves which EUREL has organized, with WWF help, in Belgium and Luxemburg.

With its abundance of wild country, mountainous and relatively unspoiled by man, Spain is well endowed with raptorial birds. Over the years her naturalists have made strenuous efforts to protect them, along with other wildlife, against a rising tide of commercial development brought about by increasing prosperity. Home of the imperial eagle, black vulture and many other species, it has since the early 1970s developed a conservation programme based mainly on newly established parks and reserves, with long-term support and backing from WWF. Several important sites have now been brought under the wing of ICONA, the Spanish government body responsible for conservation.

WWF's first involvement was in northern Spain, where eagles and vultures were in rapid decline. Their difficulty was traced to lack of food in winter, due to a fall in the number of animals living (more precisely, dying) on farms. Horses and donkeys were becoming especially scarce in the countryside, while in towns, where they were still used as draught animals, disposal of their carcasses was something of a problem. Spanish practicality, backed by WWF money, brought the two problems together and solved both. In Navarre dead animals were transported from the towns and set out on prepared areas of open country – 'Vulture Restaurants', they came to be called – where the birds of prey could find them and eat their fill. Clientele of the restaurants included Egyptian and griffon vultures, red kites, ravens, Bonelli's and golden eagles, and possibly lammergeyer, which were seen flying overhead. Some of the raptors brought their young ones, giving them a chance of learning how to feed at a crowded table in competition with other species. The restaurant experiment was voted a great success, not least by the raptors, and a chain of Vulture Restaurants is now being considered for other Spanish raptor resorts where winter and spring feeding is a problem.

Spain's most recent development, again with WWF help, is the Monfragüe National Park, a reserve of 18,000 hectares (45,000 acres) of mountain, crags, cork oak forest and maquis in the valley of the Tagus. This is reported to be a breeding centre for endangered black, Egyptian and griffon vultures and imperial and golden eagles, and many other species of raptors breed in or visit the park from time to time. Like all the best reserves it supports a wide range of interesting animals: other birds include eagle owls, black storks and kites, with a wide selection of smaller Mediterranean upland species.

In Majorca special protection is being given to a small population of black vultures which nest in wind-blown trees on the north-western cliffs of the island. A census of 1973 reported about thirty birds present; since then, however, over a dozen have been shot or poisoned, and nest disturbance by poachers and skin-divers has increased. Of thirty-one eggs monitored since 1972, only eleven hatched, though all but one of the chicks survived to fledging. As the eight-week incubation period is clearly a critical time, the local natural history group, with help from ICONA, is taking steps to protect the birds from nesting disturbance. WWF's contribution is a motor launch, based at Pollensa, that will allow the group to patrol the cliffs and keep intruders away.

Greece has an important centre for birds of prey in its forested north-eastern mountains; at least twenty-two species, several of them on the endangered list, are reported to breed there. Hitherto a peaceful though economically backward area, it has now become the subject of a forestry development plan, involving substantial felling and replanting with quick-growing timber. The scheme will bring work to the area, but could well destroy the habitat for raptors. A reserve of 5,000 hectares (12,000 acres), quite inadequate for conservation,

was built into the plan. With WWF backing, and after considerable discussion with the Greek government and World Bank, IUCN has now negotiated a more adequate reserve of almost twice the area, with buffer zones to minimize disturbance. This should itself help to bring work to the region by attracting visitors, besides maintaining ecological diversity and interest in a fascinating area of southern Europe.

Italy too has a range of raptors in its wild mountain lands, all very much at risk from sportsmen with shotguns for whom birds of any kind are challenging targets. 'Don't kill me, I'm useful' proclaims a short-toed eagle on a poster produced by an Italian bird conservation organization: the poster reminds marksmen that the species hunts snakes, but the tradition of bird-slaughter dies hard in many Mediterranean countries.

Another Mediterranean raptor at risk is Eleanora's falcon, an attractive species that nests mainly on Greek,

Spanish and Moroccan islands. Named for a Sardinian princess, it can often be seen darting after insects in the summer twilight, as many as twenty or thirty hunting together close to their breeding grounds. Eleanora's falcons nest in late summer, hatching their young just as migrant birds from Europe start to head south toward their African wintering grounds. Catching the migrants over the sea ensures a good supply of food for the nestlings. When breeding is over, the falcons themselves head southward across Africa to winter in Madagascar. Their population is estimated at about 12,000, and WWF is currently sponsoring a study of their breeding ecology in Morocco.

The Philippine eagle, one of the world's largest birds of prey, is threatened both by hunting and by loss of its home forests. It nests on four of the Philippine Islands which, like many other tropical islands, are rapidly being shorn of trees, both for the value of the timber and to clear the ground for agriculture and other developments. This is a species that nests high in the mountains and hunts over mountain forest, soaring to 3,000 metres and more (9,000 to 10,000 ft). Known also as the monkey-eating eagle, it has the reputation of swooping low to snatch monkeys and other living prey from the treetops.

A survey of Philippine eagles by a WWF-backed team in the late 1960s suggested that only a few dozen breeding birds remained, and that they were seriously at risk from an ever-expanding and well-armed human population. Later surveys sponsored by the Philippines government with strong WWF support now indicate a total population of about 500. Though rigorously protected by legislation, the species is still felt to be endangered, and

Griffon vultures with an Egyptian vulture (foreground) feeding at a carcass. Like all birds of prey vultures accumulate DDT and other poisons from their food.

WWF is sponsoring a further conservation study which will include a search of other islands in the group, and a full enquiry into the status, ecology and requirements of this magnificent bird.

Parrots are another group of birds that suffer severely at the hands of man. Colourful, lively and sociable creatures, with a knowing eye and a gift for mimicry, they have for long been popular as household and aviary pets. Though it is fast becoming a point of honour for fanciers to breed from their own stock, there is still a worldwide trade in parrots, parakeets, lories and related species. About one million parrots, most of them taken from the forests, enter international trade every year. This represents only a fraction of the birds actually caught. It is estimated that, for every ten thousand live parrots brought into the United States each year, half a million die as a result of stress and injury during capture and transit.

Not surprisingly, several species of parrots are now endangered, and WWF-sponsored research has helped them, often as part of wider studies, to maintain or build up their numbers. Examples include small island stocks of Amazon parrots on St Lucia, St Vincent, Dominica and Puerto Rico in the Caribbean, and endemic parakeets on Mauritius. Capture for the live bird trade is only one of their problems; numbers have been affected also by massive deforestation and the introduction of rats and other rodents that steal eggs and young from the nests. WWF is currently funding an expedition to the Molucca Islands of Indonesia to decide conservation priorities for seventeen species of lories and lorikeets, and assisting ecological studies in the coastal forests of Brazil, where macaws and other parrots are among the many species of tropical birds seriously affected by deforestation and live trading.

However, WWF's most effective help for parrots and other species under threat from the market is given through its support for more effective legislation, both national and international, to control trading in threatened wildlife species. This is done mostly through grants to IUCN, both general and specific. One important development for which IUCN was largely responsible is CITES, the Convention on International Trade in Endangered Species of Wild Fauna and Flora, which was drawn up in 1973, came into force in 1975, and has steadily been gaining international credibility and support since then. The main objective of the convention is to control or completely stop international trading, not only in hundreds of threatened species of plants and animals, but also in products derived from them.

IUCN first prepared the ground for international controls on wildlife trading at the historic Nairobi meeting of 1963, and continued lobbying actively for a decade. It provided the first draft of the convention, and assisted at the Washington conference of 1973 when the final version was signed by twenty-one nations. By the third biennial meeting of delegates in February 1981 there were sixty-seven parties, including most of the major consumer countries and many important wildlife-exporting countries.

The Convention recognizes in its preamble that 'wild fauna and flora in their many beautiful and varied forms are an irreplaceable part of the natural systems of the earth', and that 'international cooperation is essential for the protection of certain species of wild fauna and flora against over-exploitation through international trade.' It consists of twenty-five Articles that cover the working of the Convention, and important Appendices listing endangered species of plants and animals in three categories of urgency.

Species listed in Appendix I are threatened with extinction and may not be traded at all. Those in Appendix II are less at risk but could be endangered by unbridled trading. Appendix III species have protected status in their home country, and should not be imported by other countries that support the Convention. Currently only forty species of parrots appear in one or other of the Appendices; some of them are in Appendix I, in company with raptors, cranes, flamingos, pheasants, hornbills, curassows and other attractive species that for one reason or another are seriously endangered. CITES has a watchdog called the Wildlife Trade Monitoring Unit (formerly known as TRAFFIC), with a full-time staff that monitors international trade in wildlife. Financially supported by World Wildlife Fund grants, it contributes substantially to the effectiveness of the Convention.

So do IUCN's Red Data Books of endangered species, which also receive financial backing from WWF; the Birds volume is of prime importance in notifying CITES and other organizations of the changing status of species. The CITES lists of endangered birds, already depressingly long, receive additions from time to time as our awareness of threatened species grows. Though CITES itself has loopholes and imperfections, its existence is generally regarded as a great step forward in controlling trade in birds and other wildlife. So illegal trading continues today, but increasing support for the Convention ensures that it will become progressively less profitable, and more difficult to pursue, as time goes on. And species of birds that previously seemed doomed to extinction may now stand a chance of recovering their numbers in peace.

Giant marabou or adjutant stork – a long-legged scavenger of the open plains, prized for its white tail feathers.

The Rutshuru river and its rainforest, Zaïre.

THE RAINFORESTS

RAINFORESTS FOR SALE

VIEWED from a satellite, the tropical rainforests form a girdle about the earth – a green, irregular girdle that weaves in turn across South America, Africa and Asia. Over half of it lies in the vast river basins of the Amazon and Orinoco; about a quarter covers the islands and mountain chains of south-eastern Asia, and almost a fifth forms a solid block of green in Central and West Africa. There are patches of tropical rainforest in Australia and New Guinea, on the New Hebrides, Solomon and Philippine Islands, Fiji, and several islands of the Caribbean, and tattered remnants of a former green mantle still cover parts of India, Pakistan and Bangladesh.

Seen from within, tropical rainforest is a splendour of soaring trees and dense green undergrowth, of tangled vines, moss-draped branches and rioting flowers. Dripping wet from the latest shower (half an inch of rain *every* day is not unusual), oven-warm and humid, it has an atmosphere that reeks of growth – of plants competing silently and intensely for their right to space. No other kind of forest is quite like it, for in no other forest is the density of plants so high, their variety so rich, or their growth so uninhibited.

Not everyone likes tropical rainforest. Death and decay are present too among the teeming life – they must be, to keep it teeming. It is an ancient forest, older than the hills it stands on, and aeons older than man. And it quickly covers the works of man – swallowing villages, felling temples, forts, monuments and every other human vanity as soon as our backs are turned. Only pygmies live at peace with it: the rest of us are cutting it down as fast as we can.

To naturalists brought up in temperate regions the exuberance of the tropical forest is astonishing. The canopy reaches up to well over 40 metres (130 ft), with

The dense rainforests of the Ivory Coast, West Africa. The tallest trees stand 40 metres high; space between them is filled with lianas and tangled undergrowth.

37

individual super-trees poking through the tops. In the dim green wonderland below stands a dense understorey of shrubs, often brilliant with flowers, and of smaller, spindly trees awaiting their chance to leap upward when a forest giant falls. It is a thick, three-dimensional forest with growth at every level. Epiphytes (plants growing upon plants) cover the stems and branches – curtains of trailing mosses and ferns, brilliant upstanding orchids, strange plants perched like birds on the boughs, with roots drawing moisture directly from the wet air. Vines and lianas crisscross between the trees; strangling vines and creepers struggling upward to reach the light. With little or no seasonal control, fruits and flowers, seedlings and

new shoots flourish side by side – an ever-ready table for the multitude of animals that haunt the forests.

At first glance there are few animals. Casual visitors sometimes complain that rainforest is empty of everything but plants. But the animals are there; first light and evenings are the best times for seeing and hearing them, for many of the bigger ones lie up during the heat of the day. Leeches are often the first to make their presence known, leaning out to catch the passer-by and fondly sucking his blood. Insects are the most prominent animals. There are languid butterflies as big as dinner-plates and far more colourful, bustling beetles, busy weevils, ants and wasps, hoverflies buzzing in shafts of sunlight, noisy

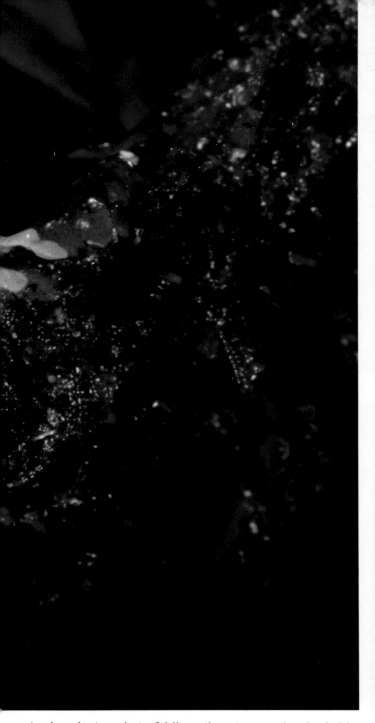

cicadas playing their fiddles, silent insects that look like twigs, leaves or bird-droppings – all going about their everyday business of keeping the forest moving. There are rats, mice, monkeys, bats and insectivores, most of them using the trees as thoroughfares; in rainforest it pays to keep off the sodden ground if you can, and nearly all the smaller mammals are tree-living. There are larger ground-living mammals, strong enough to push their way through the undergrowth and keep the forest tracks open – pigs, tapir, wild oxen and rhino are good examples. And there are birds by the thousand, often noisy, unusually colourful, always busy in search of food for themselves and their families.

Above left A red-legged tree frog, tiny amphibian of the Costa Rican rainforest. The expanded toes and fingertips help the frog to cling to wet vegetation.

Top A rufous-breasted hummingbird feeds its tiny young in a nest held together with cobwebs.

Above The common eggfly butterfly – one of the many species found in the rainforests of south-east Asia.

Everyone's first impressions of tropical rainforest are of exuberance and variety, and statistics bear them out. In sheer bulk of living material no other kind of forest can match tropical rainforest; in productivity it beats temperate forest by a factor of two to three, and grassland by three to four. The variety of species is extraordinary; while a hectare (2½ acres) of European forest may muster ten or a dozen species of trees, a hectare of tropical rainforest can include 200 species and more, with a similar ratio of flowering plants and other groups. South-east Asian forests alone include about one tenth of the world's total flora in less than one hundredth of its area.

Animals too show astonishing diversity. The forests of Malaya, Borneo, Java and Sumatra are together one quarter the size of western Europe, but between them possess at least twice as many species of birds and land mammals, and vastly more species of moths, butterflies, ants, wasps, beetles and spiders. Much the same comparison could be made with any similar area of rainforest in Africa or America: in diversity and wealth of species there is little to choose between them.

But each block of rainforest has a *different* flora and fauna from the others, distinctive enough for a competent biologist, landing in the forest by parachute, to know within minutes which continent he was on. Asia has its teaks, tigers and orang-utans, Africa its sapele and gorillas, South America its balsa trees, sloths and toucans. There are rhinos in both African and Asian forests, but they are different species of rhinos. There are cats and monkeys in all the forests, but again distinctive African, Asian or American species; the differences extend from the smallest mosses and insects to the largest trees and mammals, with only a tiny minority in common. Small wonder that together the rainforests provide the home of almost one half of all the plant and animal species in the world – including, as a special case, possibly three-quarters of all the species of insects.

Scientists have many good reasons for wanting to save the rainforests of the world. Their beauty and diversity are two important factors, with diversity valued not just for its own sake, but because of its possible implications for man. Already tropical rainforests have yielded dozens of useful products. Bananas, avocados, coffee, Brazil nuts, cocoa, cloves, cinnamon, nutmeg and rubber are all rainforest crops; there are many more recognized, and who knows how many still unrecognized, in the depths of the forest. Some of the many chemicals produced by tropical forest plants, often in self-defence against insects, are also being exploited by man; derris, strychnine, reserpine, quinine, and curare have long been in use, and pharmocognocists are finding new products – catching up with the witch doctors – every day. To destroy this bounty of actual and potential benefits is an act of lunacy that, in the long term, we and our descendants will certainly come to regret.

But the most pressing demand on the rainforest at present is a short-term one involving its devastation. The demand is for timber, to be used both for construction and as raw material for various processing industries, mostly for the benefit of the developed countries of the world. In this lies the danger, not only to the forest, but to the whole menagerie of rainforest animals – the colourful birds and insects, the rhinos, tapirs, sloths, tigers, apes and monkeys, and the thousands of other species, less colourful and less well known, that make up the fauna. Their home – the one for which they are superbly adapted, and the only one they can live in – is being cut down and carried away to

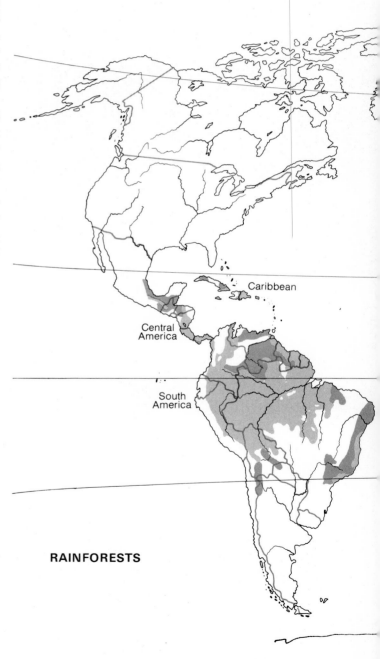

Caribbean

Central
America

South
America

RAINFORESTS

Japan, America and Europe at a staggering rate.

Tropical rainforest grows where temperatures are high and rainfall, spread evenly through the year, exceeds an annual 2,000 mm. Roughly twelve per cent of the earth's surface meets this requirement, all of it lying between the tropics of Capricorn and Cancer. Only about half of that area is currently covered with tropical rainforest, because a lot has already been cleared during the past millenium for agriculture. Much of the world's food is produced – most of its plantations of rice, coffee, bananas, cocoa, rubber and tropical timber grow – where once there was virgin rainforest. Forest has been lost also in towns and villages, roads, quarries, railways and man-made lakes, especially during the past half-century of human population

Above Devastated rainforest in Sumatra. Clear felling completely destroys the habitat, displacing the animals and exposing the soil to erosion under the heavy rainfall.

TROPIC OF CANCER

South Asia

Continental South-east Asia

Central Asia

Insular South-east Asia

EQUATOR

East Africa

Central Africa

Oceania

TROPIC OF CAPRICORN

Tropical lowland and montane rainforest

Tropical semi-evergreen and monsoon forest

Previous pages Vine snakes climb high in the forest and lie in wait, well camouflaged by their colouring among the branches. Lizards, birds and small mammals are their prey.

expansion and ever-increasing industrial development.

Now recent decades have seen a sharp increase in the rate of felling, which IUCN scientists currently estimate at about 110,000 km^2 per year – roughly five square miles every hour, day and night. Felled at this rate, the six per cent of the earth's surface now covered with forest could be halved within a decade. By the end of the century virtually all of the easily accessible lowland forest will have disappeared; if extraction technology improves, as it most certainly will, much of the less accessible mountain forest will have followed it.

Cutting down the rainforest shows neither vandalism nor waywardness on the part of its Third World owners. Timber is one of their few assets: its sale brings them capital for investment, that could allow them to industrialize and lift themselves, even marginally, above the poverty line. Unfortunately they are selling in a buyers' market; they do not get much for their timber, but have not yet found the political strength to form cartels and raise its price to realistic levels. They are obliged to keep working costs low, and the method of extraction that keeps costs lowest – large-scale clear felling – is also the most devastating. Much of the mineral resources of the forest accumulates in the timber during its growth, and is exported with it. Only impoverished soil remains, and that may quickly be leached and even washed away by the constant rain once the forest cover is removed. All that grows in place of rainforest is a meagre secondary scrub, with none of the majesty or variety of the original, and only a fraction of its productivity.

If current trends continue, as they probably will, much of this singularly beautiful and fragile forest is destined to be lost fairly soon: what then can be saved? IUCN and the World Wildlife Fund have for many years been involved in the problems that accompany rainforest destruction. While much of their early work was short-term, over the years their project ecologists have built up a body of knowledge and management expertise which is currently being applied to the rainforest problem in several areas. They cannot stop the felling of the forests, but they can advise on ways of minimizing the damage, and help in developing management programmes that avoid wasteful exploitation as much as possible.

A keystone in their policy has been the establishment and maintenance of reserves – huge areas of virgin forest set aside in perpetuity as permanent reservoirs of flora and fauna. The first rainforest reserves were established long before IUCN and World Wildlife Fund came on the scene, even before the turn of the century in the former

The small insectivorous tree shrew lives entirely in the trees; the long, sensitive nose and sensory bristles help in its constant hunt for insects.

Belgian Congo (now Zaïre), and before the Second World War in south-eastern Asia. But the concept of static reserves, dedicated simply to being themselves without protection or working policy, has not stood the test of time. People starved of land and protein tend to see reserves as wastelands waiting to be farmed, and protected animals as meat on the hoof; reserves work best when they bring tangible benefits to the local community, as well as to scientists and philanthropists in distant countries.

The World Wildlife Fund has supported many projects to save rainforest species and gained considerable experience in managing rainforest reserves. On a small scale it continues to support studies of threatened species, tying them in with reserve development. A three-year study of the Philippines eagle should, for example, promote the setting up of reserves which will help to save the remnants of rainforest on the Philippine Islands, and incidentally provide refuges for several other species including the endemic tamarau, or wild buffalo. On a larger scale WWF has helped to develop whole National Parks, complete with management plans.

One success in this field was Manu National Park, a vast area of forest, mountain and swamp on the eastern flanks of the Peruvian Andes. Manu covers 15,000 km² (almost 6,000 square miles), and is virtually undisturbed by man, except for small groups of forest Indians who live and hunt within it. WWF began its assistance in 1967 when the idea of the Park was first mooted, and its support has continued through the years of development.

Manu has spectacular wildlife, particularly in the lowland rainforest region. Along the rivers jaguars sun themselves on the beaches and spectacled and black caiman rest on the shore with river turtles. Giant and Amazon otters are common in the river meanders and ox-bow lakes (chapter 10). Though the fauna has not yet been thoroughly surveyed at least nine species of primates are known from the Park, including the rare emperor tamarin, Goeldi's monkey and the weird, bald-headed red uakari. Two species of peccary (distant relatives of the pigs) and capybara, the world's largest rodents, root about on the forested river banks by day: there are shy tapirs with their striped infants, and brilliantly dappled ocelots, now all too rare in other forests of South America. Over 400 species of birds have so far been recorded in Manu, including brilliantly plumaged parrots and humming-birds.

WWF helped to fund an initial study that surveyed the physiography, climate, geology, vegetation, wildlife, legal status and administration of the Park, including existing plans for mineral and timber exploitation, and colonization. From this study objectives of Park management were defined, and a master-plan was put forward covering the long-term development of the Park. There were recommendations for administration, organization, duties and training of staff, establishment of guard systems, and other details including the role of Indians within the Park, and plans for the development of tourism and wildlife observation programmes. This master-plan was accepted by the Peruvian government, which increased the budget of the Park six-fold and gradually put the development scheme into effect.

WWF gave further help toward running costs, including grants for the purchase of vehicles, outboard motors, radio transmitters and receivers and camping equipment, and an encouraging salary boost for the staff. Manu, the first national park in the Amazon region, has provided a model on which other parks and reserves in the Latin American region can base themselves. WWF's policy is to encourage other countries to designate reserves, and to offer help in preparing management plans and putting them into operation, so that they may be as effective as possible both in conserving rainforest, and in developing the interests of the local population.

In 1975 World Wildlife Fund launched its major international appeal on behalf of the world's threatened tropical rainforests. Under the slogan 'Save the jungle – save the world' it raised over US $2 million in support of rainforest management campaigns, carrying them to other parts of the world where the threat to rainforest was severest. Indonesia received considerable help under this banner, most of its funding coming from the Netherlands National Organization of WWF, which has for many years supported work in south-eastern Asia.

Indonesia's special interest lies in its extensive rainforests that straddle 'Wallace's Line' – where Asian wildlife (deer, large cats, monkeys, elephants, rhinos and bears, for example) meets the quite different fauna of Australasia (tree kangaroos, birds of paradise, cassowaries, bandicoots and cockatoos). Its problems are endemic poverty and one of the fastest-growing human populations in the world – despite which its government has consistently supported IUCN and WWF in their efforts to save its threatened flora and fauna, offering the best cooperation it could afford. Under the 'Save the jungle' campaign Indonesia has committed itself to a conservation programme that includes the setting up of a further 100,000 km² (40,000 square miles) of tropical forest reserves by 1984, and WWF is weighing in with its experts to help in surveying potential reserves and setting up management programmes.

A small but important facet of the 'Save the jungle' campaigns has been the provision of mobile education units – panda-marked vans that, with slide projectors and leaflets, take the conservation message to the villages and small towns in rainforest areas of Africa and Asia. Through them many thousands of adults and children have heard, possibly for the first time, why their forest and its animals are important to them and to the rest of the world, and what the world is doing to help them save at least part of their rainforest heritage for the generations to come.

SAVING THE TIGER

FIFTY THOUSAND years ago, when the ice sheets of the last glacial period spread far across eastern Siberia, many different kinds of animals retreated southward into the lush, forested zones of the subtropics. By the time the ice sheets were dispersing, the descendants of these invaders from the north were fully adapted to their southern habitats; scattered far and wide, many were already dividing into separate populations and developing into distinctive races. Among the new settlers were the tigers, the great striped cats of Asian forests and savannas.

Tigers spread from Manchuria to south China, down into Malaya, Sumatra and Java, and westward to India, Afghanistan, Turkestan, northern Iran, and the mountains of Armenia. Nowhere are they plentiful, for tigers tend to be unsociable, solitary creatures that spread themselves thinly, even at the best of times. They formed scattered, disjunct populations, which zoologists now group into anything from five to eight subspecies or races.

The tigers (*Panthera tigris*) of Asia and the lions (*Panthera leo*) of both Africa and Asia are together the greatest of the great cats. Though easily distinguishable on sight and generally thought of as separate species, under the skin they are remarkably similar; it is hard to tell their skeletons or skulls apart, and they interbreed freely in captivity.

Attractive as zoo animals, widely acclaimed in literature for their fierceness and burning beauty – yet tigers have never achieved even a quarter of the lions' popularity: lions are voted King of Beasts, while tigers rate only a grudging lordship. The tigers' bad press dates far back to the eighteenth century and beyond. The French naturalist Buffon, whose early classification of the carnivores was widely read and popularized, formed his opinions of animals mainly on travellers' tales from Roman times onward. Summarizing the qualities of the large carnivores, Buffon placed lions first in his order for their

Siberian tigers enjoying a swim.

'magnanimity and mercy'. Tigers came a poor second for their 'low ferocity, excluding all pity'.

Fashions change: naturalists who know them both today favour tigers as lively, exciting animals that live by their wits and work hard for their living; lions in comparison (especially male lions) are dull oafs that lounge in the sun and hardly work at all. But the Buffon image, reinforced by generations of writers who copied from him, stuck in the public imagination. Lions remained King of Beasts; tigers were the big cats that skulked in the undergrowth, waiting for a chance to become man-eaters. It was never a fair comparison or a realistic one, but the image may well have helped over the years to put tigers in the very precarious position that they occupied in the early 1970s, when WWF came to their rescue.

Tigers are large, colourful mammals that seldom live easily in company with man. Generally bigger than lions, they vary in size according to race. In maturity males are larger and heavier than females. Largest of all are the shaggy, pale golden and chestnut tigers of Siberia and Manchuria, with nose-to-tail length of $3\frac{1}{2}$ to 4 metres (12 ft) or more and weighing over 300 kg (700 lb). Typical large tigers of the Indian race measure 3 metres ($9\frac{1}{2}$ ft) or more in length, stand almost a metre (3 ft) tall at the shoulder and weigh 170 to 200 kg (400 to 500 lb). 'Viceroys' tigers' – those shot by viceregal parties – were always slightly bigger than the rest, measured (rumour has it) by specially shrunken tapes with short feet. The southern tigers of Java and Bali tend to be smaller, with vividly marked coats that were much in demand by furriers when they were available.

Wherever they live tigers are secretive animals that keep to cover and often hunt in the half-light of evening or at night. Jungle forest is their favourite habitat, with dense savanna grassland a close second. Too heavy to be agile climbers, tigers seldom use trees in their hunting. Instead they patrol their territories or lie in wait for prey along forest paths, making use of sloping ground that gives them a good vantage point and a quick take-off. Their pattern of bars and stripes, so lurid in the open, blends magically with the dappling of light and shade in the forest and among tall savanna grasses. By day or night tigers simply disappear into their background like oversized Cheshire Cats – to the discomfort of their prey, and of scientists and game

Tiger hunting in the 1880s. As agriculture spread across the plains of India, enormous numbers of tigers were displaced: a few became man-eaters, and many were hunted for their skins.

wardens whose job is to watch them and estimate their numbers.

Though heavy animals, they are surprisingly light on their feet. They run fast over short distances, knocking down heavy prey, crushing or strangling them, biting the nape or throat and breaking their necks. Tigers are a match for deer, antelope, pigs, cattle and other large mammals, but agile enough to grab smaller creatures – even birds – that come their way. They like water and are strong swimmers, sometimes catching fish, turtles or semi-drowned animals in the floods that follow the monsoon rains. Males and females keep separate but overlapping territories, seeking each other out only when the females are on heat; they part company again after a brief courtship and repeated mating, and the females bring up their two or three cubs alone.

Tigers were probably hunted by Stone Age man; they certainly fell victim to the snares and traps of primitive hunters in south-eastern Asia and probably throughout the whole of their range. As cattle-killers and occasional man-eaters they would certainly have been unpopular and subject to persecution near human settlements. With the coming of European colonizers to India and South-east Asia the persecution doubled and redoubled, for more

forest was cleared, more farms were developed, and the settlers introduced both the gun and the concept of trophy-hunting as a sport.

It can never have been difficult to justify a tiger hunt – giving tigers a bad name made it all the easier to shoot them. Established as dangerous vermin, their skins and heads became coveted prizes. In consequence enormous numbers were killed, especially in India during the time of British rule, both for sport and for the protection of settlements. At the same time their natural habitat was under attack as forests were cut by roads and railways or converted to rice-paddies, and grassland was turned over to cereal production for the growing human populations.

The World Wildlife Fund's first major involvement with tigers began in 1972 with the launching of 'Operation Tiger', up to that time its largest and most extensive campaign. The story began in 1965, when the Survival Service Commission of IUCN drew attention to serious long-term declines in tiger populations in every part of their range; no fewer than seven of the eight races that its consultant scientists distinguished qualified for inclusion in the Red Data Book of endangered species, with only India's Bengal tiger considered safe at that date. By 1969, when the General Assembly of IUCN met in Delhi, the

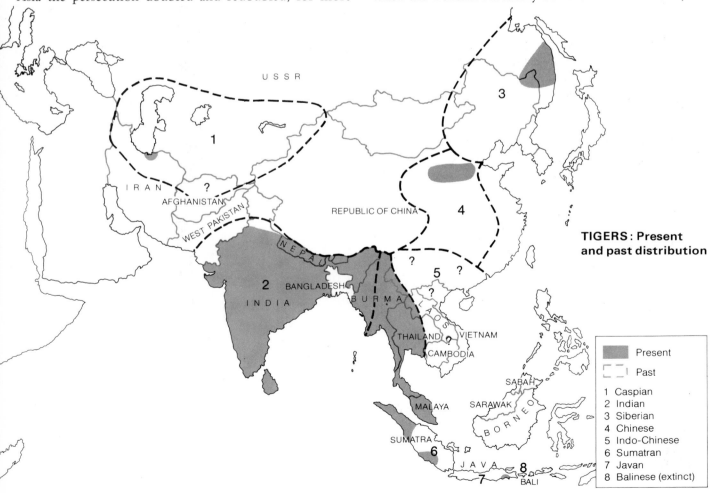

TIGERS: Present and past distribution

Present
Past

1 Caspian
2 Indian
3 Siberian
4 Chinese
5 Indo-Chinese
6 Sumatran
7 Javan
8 Balinese (extinct)

Bengal tiger too was declared an endangered species. Formerly by far the most plentiful, its stocks were currently estimated at no more than 2,500, and it was clearly liable to extinction within a very few years if nothing was done to save it.

The desperate situation of tigers was summed up in 1969 by Guy Mountfort, the British naturalist who eight years before had helped to found WWF. An international trustee, he was making tigers his special concern. He saw as the main cause of their decline the progressive destruction of habitat by encroaching man – the rededication of jungle, swamplands, savanna and grasslands to crop-raising, new towns, airfields, roads and railways, and hydro-electric developments. Coupled with loss of habitat was loss of prey. Axis and swamp-deer, blackbuck, gaur (wild oxen) and many other species on which tigers formerly relied for food had been wiped out by hunters over huge areas of India, Nepal and Bangladesh; only wild boar and domestic cattle remained, and tigers that attacked cattle were – understandably enough – destroyed out of hand by irate villagers.

A third factor in their decline was the relentless persecution by trophy hunters that still persisted even when tigers were known to be scarce. The advent of air travel brought wealthy hunters in from all directions to bag their tigers before the supply ran out; this in turn stimulated a boom in mounted skins, heads and furs, placing even more pressure on the declining stocks. A fourth point was the spread of poisons. Both defoliation of jungle during the Vietnam war and the release of defoliants for agriculture under aid programmes put tigers at risk from cumulative effects of poisons. Rodenticides and other toxins could also be used more directly, sprinkled on bait, to kill tigers and other cats for their furs.

In later reports Guy Mountfort summarized the losses that tiger populations had suffered. There had never been accurate counts, but rough estimates for the whole of Asia were 100,000 in 1920, 60,000 in 1940, about 30,000 in 1960 and only 5,000 by 1972. Every race was now known to have been reduced severely, by forces that still remained and were if anything intensifying. Of the Bali tiger, restricted to the one small island immediately east of Java, only a single specimen had recently been seen; this was perhaps good news, not bad, for it was generally supposed that the Bali race had been wiped out in 1937. On neighbouring Java there was growing evidence that hardly any of the beautifully marked Javanese tigers survived; on Sumatra a few hundred of the local race were thought to be living, most of them in dense forest at the northern end of the island, and suffering persecution wherever they were encountered.

Of the magnificent Siberian tigers, once very numerous across the whole of north-eastern Asia, fewer than 150 were likely to be surviving in the eastern USSR, north-eastern China and Korea. Only a few scattered survivors of the southern Chinese race could be expected, living precariously under a regime that (quoting the Red Data Book of the period) 'encourages its destruction, as it is regarded as a menace to human life and a hindrance to agricultural and pastoral progress.' The same source added ominously that almost every part of the tiger is highly esteemed by the Chinese for its alleged medicinal properties. Of the Indo-Chinese race, thinly scattered in the forests of Vietnam, Laos, Kampuchea, eastern Burma, Thailand and Malaya, larger numbers – perhaps 2,000 to 3,000 – were thought to be still in existence despite the continuing wars. Only about 2,000 of the Indian race could be accounted for in the whole of the subcontinent from the southern tip of Madras to the Himalaya. And of the Caspian race, that in former times extended from the eastern Black Sea coast to the Tien-Shan and beyond, only about fifteen individuals were thought to be left in the mountains of northern Iran.

There were nature reserves in several of the countries where the last remaining tigers lived, and legislation existed to protect the animals from indiscriminate hunting. But tigers were still at risk. Reserves were often ineffectual, ill-manned and poorly equipped, with inadequate resources for defending their animals against poachers – or even knowing how many were there to be defended. The law too was often ineffective. Where tigers were raiding farmland and a tiger-skin was worth a year's pay, then tigers would undoubtedly be shot despite all the government regulations that aimed to protect them. With skins openly on sale in the bazaars and tourist shops, and regularly exported to foreign markets, there was need for urgent action to safeguard the small remaining stocks. 'Time', concluded Guy Mountfort, 'is not on the side of the tiger.' But he himself was, and his travels on behalf of tigers had shown him what could be done about them.

At a joint meeting of IUCN and WWF at the Morges headquarters in late September 1969 Mountfort called for an all-out effort to provide properly equipped and well maintained sanctuaries for tigers, in areas that offered the best chances for their long-term survival – mostly in India, Bangladesh, Bhutan and Nepal. The first need was for a comprehensive long-term management plan for the Bengal or Indian tiger, preferably one devised by and operating through existing organizations – government bodies and accredited wildlife societies – already on the spot. The second need was money – a large pump-priming fund that would help the governments concerned (all of them poor and sorely pressed by human needs) and encourage their cooperation. A management plan and money – and Guy Mountfort's 'Operation Tiger', mounted in 1972, provided handsomely for both.

First the ground was carefully prepared. In response to an IUCN resolution at the 1969 Delhi meeting, the government of India had already taken steps to ban hunting in all the states, and set up a Tiger Task Force, directly responsible to the Prime Minister (Mrs Indira Gandhi), to begin ecological surveys and prepare a management plan. Soon Project Tiger, a six-year programme drawn up by the Task Force, was ready to be put into effect, with a substantial dowry from the government (equivalent to about US $4½ million) promised during the next four years. Similarly the governments of Nepal, Bhutan and Bangladesh, alerted to the need for action, prepared plans that could be adopted by Operation Tiger and given financial support.

In essence the governments were asked to show willing and do what they could with the limited means at their disposal. Operation Tiger would then provide additional funding (in doubly valuable foreign currencies) to buy the expensive equipment needed to man the reserves, and provide salaries for overseas specialists who would come in to advise and to train local people in research and management techniques. Both the equipment and the trained wardens would be used in making effective and strengthening reserves already in existence, establishing new ones on a sound footing, and developing ecological

Narcotized by a hypodermic dart, a tiger is fitted with a radio transmitter collar that will allow it to be tracked in dense jungle.

surveys that would help everyone to understand how tigers live.

Operation Tiger was launched formally in October 1972 by Prince Bernhard of the Netherlands, with the full support and backing of the World Wildlife Fund. For WWF it was a milestone – the 1,000th project and largest campaign to date, involving simultaneous fund-raising efforts by all of the National Appeals then in existence. As a cause for popular support, Operation Tiger had everything in its favour, including the magic of simplicity. There was a large, well-known and attractive animal to be saved, through a simple plan of action that everyone could understand. There was a comprehensible prime target of US $1 million, to which anyone could contribute. And every contributor to the Operation Tiger fund, through its WWF sponsorship, was made to feel part of a global bid for unity, important at a time of international tension. Though divided on a hundred political issues, the world was uniting on one issue – the fight to Save the Tiger.

Launched in a well organized flurry of publicity (Guy

51

Mountfort's experience in advertising was put to good use), Operation Tiger got away with a bounce. During 1973, its first full year, the world was made tiger conscious. Tigers appeared everywhere; majestic tigers stared from posters, funny tigers advertised all kinds of products from tea to petrol; playful, thoughtful or sleeping tigers displaced politicians and blondes from magazine covers, and tiger toys for all ages filled the toy-shop shelves. It was an extraordinarily successful campaign, raising half the total target by the end of the first year and going on to raise a total of US $1,700,000 – well over the target – in eighteen months. With the money rolling in from all its National Appeals, WWF was able to give generously toward the work in the field, which was by now well under way.

Project Tiger, the Indian master-plan, provided for nine national parks or former reserves to be designated tiger reserves and allocated additional guards, rangers and equipment to increase their effectiveness. These areas represented a wide range of habitats from the Sunderbans (mangrove swamps of the Ganges and Brahmaputra river deltas) to dense teak and bamboo forests. While the life of local villages and farming communities continued in parts of the reserves, inner areas were declared sanctuaries where tigers could be left to live their own lives, safe from the attentions of poachers and with as little human interference as possible. WWF money from Operation Tiger was used mainly to buy the equipment needed to protect the reserves – four-wheel-drive vehicles to give guards and rangers mobility, jet-boats for patrolling the rivers and swamps of the Sunderbans, mobile radio, fire-fighting and hydrological equipment, binoculars, laboratory stocks, typewriters and other office equipment, and books – all helping to encourage the staff responsible for the management programmes to increase their efficiency in the field.

In the neighbouring state of Bhutan the Manas Reserve, an area of Himalayan forest adjoining an even bigger Indian reserve and likely to contain about fifty tigers, was given new protection. The government of newly-independent Bangladesh, still recovering from war, adopted the tiger as its national symbol and undertook to develop its own area of the Sunderbans into a national park and tiger reserve as soon as possible. The government of Nepal designated three extensive reserves for tigers and in one of them, Chitwan National Park south-west of Katmandu, WWF helped to fund the first full-scale programme of ecological research on tigers.

Previously discouraged by tigers' reticence and possibly

Tigers' brilliant stripes provide excellent camouflage in the depths of the forest, helping them to stalk their prey undetected.

Young tigers lazing in the Chitwan National Park, Nepal.

by their reputation for ferocity, and daunted too by the difficulties and expense of working in dense jungle, biologists had shied away from detailed ecological studies of them on their home ground. Now a full research campaign was mounted by the Smithsonian Institution, involving American and Nepalese field workers who examined the vegetation and animal life where the tigers were living. Their studies included tracking tigers, using radio transmitter collars and mobile telemetering stations – research that told them how far tigers travel, how much space they occupy, how they divide an area and its food between them with the minimum of conflict. Food species and their ecological needs were studied too – all essential information toward the development of sensible management programmes.

While the main thrust of Operation Tiger was directed toward Indian tigers, the fortunes of other races were not forgotten. Surveys supported by Operation Tiger funds confirmed that, while the Bali tiger was almost certainly extinct, hope remained for the indigenous race of Javan tigers. Once widely dispersed through the almost continuous forests that formerly covered Java, these tigers had met the full force of the human population explosion in south-eastern Asia. Their forests were fragmented into pockets and patches too small to support tigers and their prey species; only from one remote mountain wilderness in the south-eastern corner of Java were there persistent rumours of tigers, and surveys in 1971 confirmed the presence of a tiny remnant population – probably under a dozen.

By 1973 the Indonesian government had linked several blocks of forest in the area to form the Meru-Betiri Reserve, and a substantial grant from WWF, under

Indo-Chinese race, providing vehicles and ranger stations in Khao Yai National Park and other reserves to step up the battle against poachers. A search for Caspian tigers in Turkey and northern Iran, also supported by WWF, indicated that they were almost certainly extinct, at least in those areas.

Has Operation Tiger worked? If the predictions of the late 1960s and early 70s were correct (and there is no reason to suppose with hindsight that they were not), then the continuing presence of several races of these splendid animals in the world testifies that it has worked indeed. The Balinese and Caspian races had probably gone before Operation Tiger began, and the Javan race was too far along the road to extinction to be saved. Chinese and Siberian stocks are probably no worse off than before, and may indeed be in better health because of enquiries made on their behalf by WWF. Guy Mountfort reports a probable total of 400 to 450 Siberian tigers in Russian reserves, where they are breeding successfully, and the discovery of a further 150 in north-eastern China and 50 in North Korea. China is now cooperating as never before with IUCN and WWF, and reports probably fewer than 100 of its own indigenous race in existence.

About 600 to 800 Sumatran tigers are now thought to be alive in the island's forest reserves, surviving despite continuing poaching and the steady reduction of natural forest. Trade in their skins through Hong Kong and Singapore has been halted, and their future looks promising so long as adequate forest reserves are left for them. The Indo-Chinese race, now thought to number about 2,000, is holding its own, with an increasing interest in its welfare spreading through peninsular Malaya, Thailand and possibly southern China, where new reserves are planned.

And the Indian tiger is saved. The leader of Project Tiger was certain, as early as 1976, that the headlong decline of the species had been halted. Numbers are now increasing: Guy Mountfort reports a total of about 3,300 in India, Bangladesh, Nepal, Bhutan, Sikkim and west Burma, with breeding successful in most of the Operation Tiger reserves.

The work of Operation Tiger is by no means over, but its main objectives are reasonably assured. There will still be tigers, and with good fortune several races of tigers, in the world at the end of the twentieth century.

Operation Tiger, funded field studies and other research toward the development of a management plan for the area. The plan was completed in 1980, but the latest reports indicate that it has not succeeded. Meru-Betiri was not ideal tiger country. Much of the lowland forest that would formerly have held deer and other prey in plenty was already given over to rubber and teak production, and the highland forests were relatively poor in prey species. By 1981 the remnant tiger population was no more than one or two animals, competing with leopards and wild dogs for a dwindling food supply, and very unlikely to survive.

Sumatran tigers have fared better; though still subject to poaching there are a few hundred of them remaining in their island forests, and WWF has helped in funding surveys to find the best potential reserves. Substantial funding under Operation Tiger also helped the government of Thailand to improve protection measures for the

RHINOS AT RISK

SOUR CRITICS who claim that the World Wildlife Fund exerts itself only for woolly, cuddly-toy animals with appealing eyes would do well to contemplate the rhinoceroses. Angular, hidebound, like battered cabin-trunks on stumpy legs, hairless or nearly so, with piggy eyes and rancid temperaments, it is difficult to imagine animals less woolly, cuddly or appealing than any of the five living species of rhinoceroses. Baby rhinoceroses have the bumbling charm that is every small mammal's defence against the wickedness of the adult world; good friends might call them engagingly ugly. But they lose it faster than most; as yearlings they are just as creased and cross-grained as their parents – cuddly as a Chieftain tank, and rather less predictable.

Yet rhinoceroses of all kinds – white and black, Asian and African – have benefited from WWF involvement in their affairs. White rhinos of East Africa were one of the first species of all to receive attention and support in the very early days of the Fund. Since then every other species has been surveyed and assessed, and Rhino Project, a combined IUCN/WWF campaign launched in 1979, is a coordinated effort to save the world's rhinoceroses from the danger of extinction that still looms over them.

In evolutionary terms the rhinos of today are relics, five species surviving from an earlier age when rhinos flourished all over the world, in far greater numbers and variety than they muster today. The mid-to-late Tertiary period – the last thirty million years up to the start of the Ice Age – was their time of greatness, and their variety was truly remarkable.

There were rhinos as small as sheep, and rhinos far bigger than any land mammal alive today, *Indricotherium*, the largest terrestrial mammal that ever lived,

White rhinos – also known as broad-lipped rhinos – close-cropping the grass. Formerly widespread in southern Africa, they are now restricted mainly to reserves.

was just one of several species of giant rhinoceros, standing half as tall again as a modern African elephant. There were rhinos with horns on their forehead, or twin horns growing side by side on their nose; there were long-legged and short-legged forms, and nightmare rhinos with elephantine tusks. In the mid-to-late Pleistocene less than a quarter of a million years ago there were at least two species of twin-horned rhinos in the forests and grasslands of south-eastern England, similar to the black and the white rhinos of central Africa today. Even later throughout northern Europe and Siberia there were woolly rhinos, closely akin and indeed closely similar to the modern rhinos of Malaya and Sumatra. And like the modern rhinos, they were helped on their way to extinction by man – the meddlesome little ape that began in East Africa and spread across the world during the Ice Age.

The closest living kin of rhinoceroses today are the tapirs – smaller hornless mammals of Malaysian and South American forests. Next closest are the horses. The three groups together make up the small Order Artiodactyla, the 'odd-toed ungulates' with one, three or vestiges of five hooves to each foot. These are all herbivorous mammals – grazers and browsers with huge appetites for forage of relatively low energy content. White rhinos of the African savanna are grazers, with broad lips adapted for cropping

grasses and herbs. Black rhinos of African bushlands and the forest rhinos of Asia are mainly browsers, with long, mobile upper lips for grasping twigs and leaves. They are without front teeth and do not ruminate, but have a formidable row of grinding molars on either side and a complex gut to deal with their unpromising forage.

All living rhinos are large and ponderous, with thick hides, creased and ridged, that seem tailored for animals half a size bigger. Despite its apparent toughness the skin is well supplied with blood vessels and often covered with ticks, which feed on blood and drop off when sated. The Sumatran rhino is the smallest, standing up to 1.5 metres (almost 5 ft) at the shoulder weighing up to 500 kg (1,100 lb). Largest of all are the great white rhinos which stand up to 2 metres (6½ ft) and weigh 3 tonnes (6,000 lb) or more. Most rhinos are almost hairless; some have tufts of hair on ears and tail. Only the Sumatran rhino has a thin, overall

RHINOS: present and past distribution

Indian
Past
■ ■ ■ Present

Javan
/ / / / Past
● ● ● Present

Sumatran
\ \ \ \ Past
▲ ▲ ▲ Present

African
Past
Present

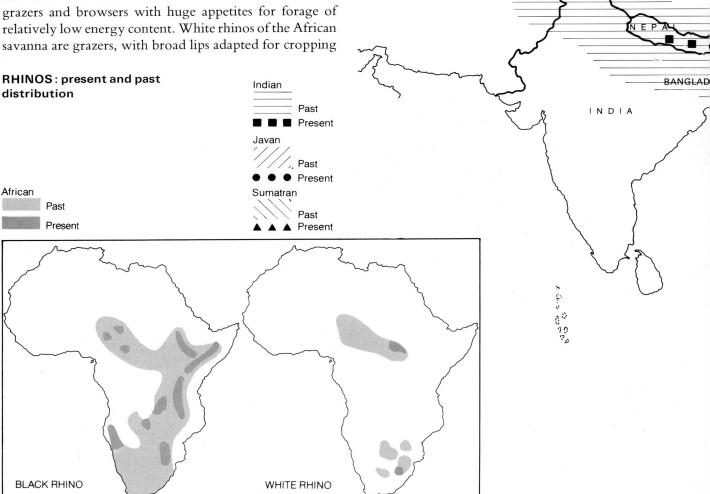

BLACK RHINO

WHITE RHINO

NEPAL

BANGLAD

INDIA

covering of hair, a faint reminder of the more generous insulation that covered woolly rhinoceroses, their northern forebears.

A rhino's crowning glory, and all too often the direct cause of its death, is its horn – or twin array of horns – worn jauntily along the bridge of the nose. The two African species have two sharp horns; Sumatran rhinos also have two, a sharp one in front and a lower, blunter one behind. The remaining Asian rhinos have just one horn. Horns grow from the skin; made of keratin (the substance of hooves, hair and fingernails) they continue to grow very slowly throughout life, changing shape gradually as they wear. The front horn, always the larger, may grow to 1.5 metres (4½ ft) or more. Horns can be knocked off in battle or through injudicious butting: a young rhino that loses its horn grows another one quickly; older rhinos take longer and may produce only a bump.

Rhinos use their horns in several ways. Walking with head held low, the horns lead the way and clear the path in front of them. They can be used for digging and scraping, breaking branches off trees, and thumping rivals and attackers. Large and prominent in profile, they may serve as signals of threat or indicators of dominance, but they are functional too: an angry rhino charges with lowered head at 10 to 11 metres per second (20 to 25 miles per hour) and the horns become the sharp end of a very formidable battering ram. Up-to-date rhinos use their horns to frighten tourists and ram their automobiles.

Travellers in African game parks often comment on the unpredictability of rhinos, which are – and it is an alarming combination – both short-sighted and short-tempered. In game parks they are normally peaceful, accepting the presence of tourists and vehicles with grace. Females have been known to flirt myopically with

Anaesthetized with a dart, this black rhino is being transported to the safety of a Kenyan reserve. Only about 2,000 remain in Kenya, under heavy hunting pressure from poachers.

REPUBLIC OF CHINA

BURMA

LAOS

THAILAND

CAMBODIA

MALAYA

SARAWAK

BORNEO

SUMATRA

JAVA

stationary cars, perhaps the only objects large enough to be mistaken, at a passing glance, for a potential mate. Occasionally a cow with calf, an injured animal, or one that has taken offence for less obvious reasons, charges and overturns a car, punching holes in the bodywork with a weapon that (as an American conservationist was heard to remark with glee) might just have been made for the job.

Whatever their danger to rivals and motor vehicles, a rhino's horns are regrettably dangerous to itself. For centuries they have been coveted by man and used by him for many purposes, both trivial and serious. They carve well: plates, cups, snuffboxes and other small objects were made from them in medieval times. There has recently been an enormous demand in the Yemen for carved rhinoceros horn dagger handles, a demand big enough (according to a WWF-sponsored survey by Dr E.B. Martin) to require the killing of 1,000 rhinos per year between 1969 and 1979. Powdered rhino horn is used in India as an aphrodisiac or sexual stimulant. Far more significant in terms of rhinos killed is its very wide use across the length and breadth of Asia as a medicine, generally to reduce fever and protect against a wide spectrum of ailments, from toothache to snake-bite.

Western observers, smug about Western medicine, tend to write off the medicinal properties of rhino horn as though they had no validity – a joke, perhaps, or an Oriental confidence trick on a vast scale. This misses the point. Whether satisfactory or not in a pharmacological sense, rhino horn is a medical remedy that has stood the test of time: millions believe in it. Other parts of the rhino, the blood, urine and skin, for example, also find their uses in Oriental medicine. But the horn has a special magic of its own. A few flakes taken in water bring comfort and hope of relief to sufferers from Arabia to Taiwan, to whom comfort and hope may well be strangers. Magic it may be, but it is a strong magic – strong enough to withstand an increase in the wholesale price of rhino horn from US $35 per kilo in 1975 to US $675 in September 1979, a rise of almost 2,000 per cent in four years.

The figures are Dr Martin's, and the implications are devastating beyond measure for rhinos the world over. 'The reliance on rhino horn as a medicine', writes Dr Martin, '... is probably the greatest long-term threat to the survival of rhinos.' While the magic lasts – until it is replaced by a better magic – a single horn is worth US $400 (several months' wages) to a poacher, three or four times as much to a dealer, and more than its weight in gold to an apothecary. While the magic lasts, no rhino in the world is safe.

IUCN and the World Wildlife Fund have had a long and in some ways frustrating involvement with rhinos, both directly in species-saving projects, and indirectly where rhinos have been helped through the development of parks and reserves. Not all of the projects have succeeded. Some have succeeded well, only to be overtaken by wars, revolutions, and civil disturbances that set back the clock for man and animals alike. 'Project Rhino', the most recent plan launched in 1979, is a concerted effort to save all five species from the otherwise certain extinction that awaits them at the hands of illegal hunters.

First to be aided by the Fund were the white rhinos of eastern Africa. The white rhinos' problems began in the early nineteenth century, when the species was first encountered by white settlers on the grassy plains of southern Africa, south of the Zambezi River and east of the Kalahari Desert. Most placid of all the rhinos, whites move like cattle in small family groups, lying up during the day, watering at the rivers and waterholes in the cool of the evening, and grazing through the night.

White rhinos are not white; they are grey or brown, and often covered with mud from their wallows. 'White' is said to be a corruption of a Cape-Dutch word meaning 'wide', and to refer to the broad-lipped grazing mouth. Whatever their colour, the meat, hides and huge trophy heads of white rhinos recommended them to the early settlers and sportsmen, who shot them by the thousand. By the end of the century they were almost exterminated, only a small population remaining in the Umfolozi Valley of Natal. This was spared by direct government intervention, and held under careful management and protection in one of southern Africa's earliest national parks. Today the descendants of that protected group form the main breeding stock of white rhinos, numbering several thousand in all. So successful is their management that surplus animals are farmed out to suitable reserves all over southern Africa, and also exported to zoos all over the world.

But this, it transpired, was the southern white rhino: some time after its discovery a completely separate population of white rhinos was found further north in Uganda and the southern Sudan. Northern white rhinos, identified by zoologists as a distinct race, were shot just as ruthlessly as southern ones over many years. Stocks in parks and reserves stayed relatively safe, but by the late 1950s the value of rhino horn was rising rapidly, poaching was rife, and the number of white rhinos both inside and outside the reserves was falling rapidly.

World Wildlife Fund's sixth project, effected from 1961 to 1963, was a grant toward the White Rhino Conservation Campaign of the East African Wildlife Society. In close liaison with the Uganda Game Department the Society had been monitoring the decline of white rhinos in

White rhinos drink deeply at the end of the day, then roll in the mud to rid themselves of biting flies.

Uganda, and supporting a policy of moving animals from some of the most heavily poached areas into the comparative safety of the Murchison Falls National Park (now the Kobalega National Park), where it was hoped that a breeding group would be established. The WWF grants provided specifically for ten additional Game Department guards to form anti-poaching teams, the purchase and maintenance of two Land Rovers, and the recruitment of a CID officer, with two Arabic-speaking assistant detectives, to investigate the local black market in rhino products and bring proceedings against those involved. There was provision also for a publicity campaign to convince the District Councils, chiefs and people of the value of wildlife and to enlist their active cooperation in conserving it.

The success of this far-sighted programme encouraged further support for Uganda's anti-poaching campaigns: between 1965 and 1969 WWF contributed toward the costs of light aircraft, Land Rovers, guards, radios and other equipment for use in the Queen Elizabeth National Park and other reserves where poachers were operating. Elephants, hippos, buffalo, crocodiles and several other species benefited equally from the protection of these units. However, the coup that in 1971 brought Idi Amin to power in Uganda proved disastrous to its wildlife. Despite the best efforts of devoted staff, the parks and reserves declined. Poaching again became rife, especially during and after the 1979 war, when gangs armed with automatic weapons foraged freely in the reserves for meat, skins, ivory and rhino horn.

A recent (1980) survey of wildlife in Uganda, sponsored by the New York Zoological Society and the World Wildlife Fund, concludes – among ample further evidence of devastation – that the white rhinoceros is almost certainly extinct in Uganda. Small stocks totalling about 1,000 remain, however, in the southern Sudan and Zaïre. As part of Project Rhino, and with the help of a very active African Rhino Group of the Species Survival Commission, WWF is currently finding ways of protecting these remaining stocks. One important development is the Sudan government's recent expansion of a small game reserve in the Nile Valley to form the 800 km² Shamba White Rhino National Park. In support of the park, WWF is financing an extensive two-year research project toward the development of a management programme which should ensure a safe future for at least several hundred of the remaining northern white rhinos.

Black rhinos, the second and slightly smaller African species, are still widespread in scattered populations through central, eastern and southern Africa, though mostly hunted out of the forests further west. Open rangeland and forest margins are their typical habitat. More solitary than white rhinos, they live alone or in loosely-knit groups of four or five, browsing in extensive overlapping ranges. Piles of dung mark their range boundaries; they snort irascibly on meeting others of their kind, but seem to live peacefully most of the time. Watering places are essential within their feeding grounds, both for drinking and for wallowing.

Black rhinos mate at any time of the year, giving birth after a gestation period of about fifteen months. Calves run with their mothers for two to five years. Becoming sexually mature at seven or eight years, they probably live to an age of thirty or more. Like all other rhinos they are short-sighted, relying on scent and sound to identify each other and find their way about their home ranges. Few predators but man can harm them, though lions or crocodiles are occasionally reported to drag down and kill small calves. The total population is currently estimated at 10,000 to 20,000, and up to a few years ago the species was regarded as reasonably safe. Now it is severely endangered by poachers, and WWF's Project Rhino is active in helping to support mobile anti-poaching units in National Parks in many countries.

Black rhinoceroses declined slowly during recent decades as their forests were taken over for agriculture and human settlements, but the species was still plentiful up to about ten years ago. Then the demand for rhino horn increased and the serious slaughter began. Despite protective legislation the rhino population of Kenya fell from 20,000 in 1970 to 2,000 or less in 1980. Other east African countries have also lost ninety per cent of their stocks and in the past five years similar losses have occurred throughout the continent. The total population for Africa as a whole, currently estimated at 10,000 to 20,000, is split into many small groups, some of which are probably too small to be viable. In response to the black rhino emergency WWF is funding urgent action through the African Rhino Group. Now a network of save-the-rhino working groups operates throughout Africa, surveying the numbers and status of local rhino populations and looking into ways of managing and protecting them. With WWF help, anti-poaching activity has been stepped up in Zambia and Kenya, and in other countries both protective measures in the field and control of the trade in rhino products are being strongly advocated.

Asian rhinoceroses too have suffered severe hunting pressures, and over many generations longer. Great Indian rhinos, once common in northern India, Nepal and Burma, are now mostly restricted to small populations in forest reserves. About 700 live in the Kaziranga National Park, on the floor of the Brahmaputra River valley in Assam. Five other reserves in the same area hold 100 to 150 Indian rhinos between them; 35 to 40 more live in two reserves in West Bengal, and Nepal's Royal Chitwan National Park holds a stock of about 300. They live mostly

in low-lying grasslands and valley swamps, a few ranging into drier upland areas where forests give way to farmland. Though officially protected, they still suffer poaching and competition for grazing from domestic stock, and an unnatural level of crowding. Periodic flooding of the river valleys, and reduction of natural forage by alien species of plants – less palatable 'weeds' that compete for space with their food species – are further dangers for the small remnant stocks.

World Wildlife Fund has supported research and management over many years to improve the efficiency of the Indian and Nepalese reserves, and to boost the morale of guards and wardens in their constant battles against poachers. In Kaziranga National Park the provision of roads, radio communications and well-equipped guards gave immediate relief from heavy poaching, allowing the stocks of rhinos to stabilize and start a slow recovery. In Royal Chitwan National Park WWF grants have helped

Asian rhino – a one-horned species once widespread in northern India and Nepal, now restricted almost entirely to reserves.

to establish boundaries, keep out domestic stock and provide additional guard posts, with promising results.

Smaller reserves have also been helped with equipment and guard posts, but WWF's most important contribution is to make everyone involved in reserve management, from senior administrator to the most junior guard, feel that the world outside the reserves is concerned in the fate of rhinos, and expressing its concern with money. The WWF panda logo on boats, Land Rovers, jeeps and signboards is a constant reminder of outside interest, at least as strong financially, and possibly more rewarding in the long run, than the fly-by-night interest of the poacher or logging contractor.

Javan rhinos have even more clearly been saved by

Above The Sumatran rhino is found widely scattered in upland forests throughout Indonesia. Only a few dozen remain in Sumatra, mostly in the Gunung Leuser Reserve.

Right The foul-smelling mud that coats wallowing rhinos later dries and brushes off as they walk, scent-marking their trails.

WWF. They formerly ranged through India and southern Asia from the Chinese border to Java and Sumatra, inhabiting lowland forest edges and clearings where conflict with man was inevitable. Their horn was unfortunately ascribed a special value in Eastern medicine, making them a certain target for hunters. By the early years of this century they were all but eliminated through their whole range; only on Udjong Kulon, a forested peninsula of Java, were they known to survive after the Second World War.

Udjong Kulon became a reserve (of about 40,000 hectares) in 1921, but by the 1960s standards of management had declined, and a survey of 1964, sponsored by WWF as part of its south-east Asia Project, could account for only about thirty Javan rhinos. So from 1966 onward WWF supported a long-term study of the species and its ecology, undertaken for the Indonesian government by two Swiss scientists, Drs Rudolf and Lotte Schenkel of the University of Basle.

The Schenkels' first surveys showed that rhinos were indeed few, but the presence of young animals indicated recent breeding. They disclosed many interesting points of ecology and behaviour – the importance of wallows, for example, in providing urine-scented mud that helped to scent-mark forest trails – and showed how, in feeding on saplings, the animals stimulated the plants into further growth. This pointed the need for an overall management programme to bring the habitat back to its former carrying capacity, as well as additional protection to keep domestic stock, farmers and poachers away from the critical rhino areas.

Under expert guidance the number of rhinos in the reserve doubled within a decade. Today Udjong Kulon is an important National Park and tourist attraction, and the rhino population, still slowly expanding, is starting to spread beyond its borders. Plans are afoot to move some of the surplus stock to other reserves where additional breeding groups can be established.

Sumatran rhinos, like Javan, are forest animals but their preference is for mountain habitats; by hiding away in upland forests that man has no use for, they have managed to survive in remote parts of Malaya, Thailand and

Kalimantan, as well as on Sumatra itself. Their populations are small, and mostly stable or declining due to deforestation and poaching. Those of Sumatra number between 50 and 100, and populations elsewhere are unlikely to be larger.

It is difficult indeed to count animals – even large ones – in rainforest where visibility on the ground is never more than a few metres. But over the years, studies of tracks show that most of the Sumatran rhinos are concentrated in Gunung Leuser Reserve, in the central mountain massif. Indeed one young female announced herself by walking into the investigators' camp; she was the only animal seen in several weeks of hard, slogging survey by one of the WWF-supported teams involved. Only in this reserve are Sumatran rhinos at present likely to survive, for forests elsewhere on the island are unlikely to be saved in large enough blocks to support further populations. Malayan and other stocks have also been assessed by WWF-sponsored surveys. Except in a few reserves where logging and poaching can be controlled, the outlook for them is unpromising.

However, for rhinoceroses as a whole the long years of decline are over. With specialist groups alerted, action plans in operation for every species, and – above all – strenuous efforts being made to devalue rhino horn and stop international trading before it is too late, there is every chance that rhinoceroses of all existing species will survive and possibly show increase by the end of the century.

MONKEY BUSINESS

EVERY DAY, in a hundred different forests of the world, wild apes and monkeys by the score are captured alive, packed into cages with food and water, and shipped off on long journeys into bondage. They travel by road, rail, river, sea and air, usually in mounting squalor, waiting patiently at frontiers while their captors shuffle papers. Those that survive live out their lives – often curtailed by disease or mishandling – in zoos, circuses or laboratories, or as pets in private homes.

This is no furtive, hole-in-corner racket; it is legal business on an enormous scale. In the 1950s medical research in the United States alone required the shipment of 200,000 rhesus monkeys from India; by the 1970s the demand had dropped, but tens of thousands of rhesus monkeys were still supplied for that one trade alone. Rhesus monkeys happen to be plentiful, but other, rarer species, for example marmosets and squirrel monkeys, are much in demand as pets and for sale to unscrupulous zoo dealers. Thousands still travel each year, far too many of them in filthy, overcrowded conditions that shock the civilized world – but only when some appalling case of neglect and animal suffering hits the headlines.

We are one of the few kinds of animals that take other animals prisoner – certainly the only one that takes captives to serve intellectual curiosity. We do it on a spectacular scale; some hundreds of thousands of animals of a wide range of species from parrots to tortoises, from dolphins to fruit-bats, are caught and transported every year. Many of our captives are monkeys and apes, our closest kin – fellow primates for whom our understanding and concern might reasonably be strongest of all.

Men have the highest motives for imprisoning animals.

A baby vervet monkey bites a vine experimentally while its mother keeps watch. Superbly adapted for life in the trees, monkeys have no other home when the forest is destroyed.

Zoos are educational and circuses entertaining, often giving people their only chance to see exotic animals. Laboratories are places of learning. Medical research, fully justified by its results in human lives extended and saved, would be severely hampered if the supply of monkeys and apes suddenly ceased. Many reject these arguments and want the traffic in live animals stopped; among those who justify the traffic are plenty who would see it more carefully controlled, with fewer species and animals involved, and better travelling conditions demanded for them. Whichever argument is right, time is taking a hand; several species are already unobtainable and the price of others is rocketing – a sure sign of scarcity.

There are two main reasons for the shortage. The first is that international legislation covering the capture and movement of animals, including apes and many species of monkeys, has recently been tightened – unscrupulous dealers are finding their activities increasingly curtailed. Both IUCN and WWF played their part in drawing up the new protective legislation (CITES, p. 32). The second reason is a grimmer one: whole areas that once supported monkey and ape populations are now denuded of them. Collectors all too often have concentrated on the most popular or most easily caught species, or those most likely to survive in captivity. Demand has exceeded supply; the dealers have come and gone, and the monkeys and apes have gone with them.

Time is a healer in forests, as elsewhere; given a chance the few animals that remain will restock the canopy with their descendants. But where the forest has gone too – sold down the river for timber and paper-making – all the indigenous animals are left without homes, and here there is less hope of recovery. The Red Data Book of endangered species lists over fifty different kinds of monkeys and apes currently at risk; deforestation is the main cause, with hunting – either for food or for trading – a close runner-up.

Monkeys, apes and men form one of the two suborders (Anthropoidea) of the Order Primates, distinguished from other primates by their bipedal walk and large fore-brain. Man stands in a family (Hominidae) on his own, and gibbons and other apes share a second (Pongidae); monkeys make up the remaining three – the New World monkeys and marmosets (Cebidae and Callithricidae) of Central and South America, and the Old World monkeys (Cercopithecidae) of Africa and Asia.

Monkeys and apes are mostly tropical forest animals. As jungle is easier to swing through at treetop level than on the ground, they spend most of their time in the trees. Only a few species, the patas monkeys and savanna baboons for example, share our own preference for living at ground level, though they climb with agility and often choose cliffs, ravines and steep mountainsides to live on.

Protein from the South American rainforest – monkey, armadillo and tapir trotters for sale on a Guyana market stall.

Tropical forest is many-layered, with a variety of foods and opportunities for species to diversify. So there are many kinds of monkeys. Those of the New World evolved quite separately from the Old World monkeys and apes, and the two groups never meet except in zoos. They tend to be similar because their forests are similar, but there is no overlap of species between them. Life in the trees has helped to make monkeys and apes among the most successful and intellectually advanced of all animals. It could prove their undoing: specialization for forest life can be a disadvantage when the forest is cut down and carried away.

New World monkeys have broad flat noses with nostrils on the side, and long furry tails. Marmosets and tamarins – there are about seventeen species – are small, very hairy monkeys (the smallest only slightly bigger than large mice) with long slender tails which they use for balancing but not for grasping branches. Some have splendid manes like miniature lions, some are bearded and moustached, others bare-faced, and many are strikingly coloured in gold, white or russet brown. Living in the lower canopy where vines and branches interlace, they feed mainly on insects which they dig from the bark with tiny clawed fingers; they also take lizards, birds and their eggs, and ripe fruit and nuts. Widespread throughout Central and South America, they are entirely creatures of the forest, with no alternative way of life.

The cebids are a varied group – about thirty-two species – of forest monkeys, mostly larger than marmosets and living lower in the trees. Specialized in different directions, several species can live side by side in the same forest with little competition between them. Douroucoulis for example are nocturnal, with owl-like eyes that help them to see and catch insects and small mammals in dim light. All the others are diurnal, feeding actively through the day and bedding down by sunset. Saki and uakari monkeys feed mostly on fruits; howler monkeys (intensely social creatures with resonant rallying calls) browse on shoots and leaves; spider and woolly monkeys feed on fruits, flowers and shoots, and squirrel monkeys and capuchins include insects and other animals in their diet. All the diurnal cebids are lively, active monkeys that run and leap among the branches: howler, woolly and spider monkeys swing by their arms, and have developed their tail as an additional grasping organ.

Old World monkeys and apes have narrow, pinched noses with forward-pointing nostrils; the human nose is an extreme example, the chimpanzee nose a more typical one. The monkeys have tails, used for balance but not for grasping; apes are tailless. Old World monkeys form a large and very diverse group of about seventy-six species. They take their family name (Cercopithecidae) from the largest genus *Cercopithecus* – the guenons or 'typical' monkeys of the African tropical forest, of which there are nineteen species. Guenons live everywhere in Africa wherever there is dense forest; colourful animals (some are distinctly green) with expressive bearded faces, they swoop through the forest in noisy chattering troups, living on fruit, leaves and insects.

Guenons are entirely African; so are the leaf-eating colobus monkeys, the savanna and forest baboons and colourful mangabeys, and several other smaller genera. Macaques are almost entirely Asian. An exception is the Barbary ape of North Africa and Gibraltar, that may have crossed the Mediterranean with man to gain its toehold in Europe. But most of the seventeen species of macaques live in India, China and south-east Asia. The rhesus monkey of India and Burma, perhaps the best-known macaque, is still widely used in medical research and the species most likely to be seen dying in overcrowded cages at airports. The leaf monkeys with their flat, leaf-like noses, the snub-nosed and proboscis monkeys are all Asian too, but difficult to keep in captivity and seldom seen away from their native forests.

The apes, including gibbons, are closely related to each other and closest of all primates to man. Gibbons have remained in the treetops, developing fully the wonderful art of brachiation or swinging by the arms from branch to branch. The great apes – chimpanzees, gorillas and orang-utans – are all heavier animals. Though capable of some brachiation, they are far more sedate than gibbons, and seldom swing so high or move so fast. Adult gorillas especially spend much of their time close to the ground. Gorillas are almost entirely vegetarian. Orang-utans, gibbons and chimpanzees too eat shoots, leaves, fruit and flowers, but also take insects, lizards and young birds. Chimpanzees seem especially fond of ants and termites.

IUCN and WWF have for long been concerned with the welfare of primates. In 1964 and 1965, following a report on the decimation of chimpanzee stocks in many West African countries, WWF made grants toward a chimpanzee reserve at Beni, in the Republic of Congo, and a photo-survey of chimpanzee habitat in East Africa. In 1967 a WWF-supported survey of vervet monkeys in Kenya revealed that the species was much reduced by trapping for export; as a result the Kenya government drew up new regulations that controlled the traffic, making it more humane and less wasteful. In Ghana WWF supported studies of colobus and Diana monkeys in the Bia National Park, and provided anti-poaching equipment to protect chimpanzees, monkeys and other forest game within the Park. In an area where primates are an important source of protein for man, local hunting activities were surveyed to see how they could be reconciled with conservation. Several WWF-funded surveys of endangered primates – for example golden lion marmosets – have been carried out in Central and South America, with a view to controlling the trade in live animals from Latin American centres.

Gorillas too have benefited from management and ecological studies that WWF has supported over the years. Largest of all the primates, gorillas may stand taller than a man and weigh considerably more; a large male can tip the scale at 300 kg (over 650 lb). Living exclusively in African lowland and mountain forests, they feed in small family groups on herbs, roots, and the pith of tree stems. Their only serious enemy is man, who competes for space, disturbs them with his agriculture and cattle, and until recently kidnapped their young for illegal trading with zoos. Despite an early reputation for ferocity, gorillas are gentle animals that live quietly in their forests and, left to themselves, give offence to no one.

Of the three races currently distinguished, eastern lowland gorillas of Zaïre are least at risk; a WWF survey of 1979 gave a population of up to 15,000, with about twenty per cent living in the relative safety of national parks. Western lowland gorillas, with a range extending from south-eastern Nigeria to the Central African Republic and Congo, are locally at risk but still plentiful; a WWF-supported project of 1976–7 gave details of their ecology in forests of the Cameroon, where reserves are planned for their safety. The third race, the mountain gorilla, is more certainly endangered. It lives in the damp upland forests of the Virunga volcanoes on the borders of Zaïre, Rwanda and Uganda, where it was studied by the American naturalist George Schaller in 1959. Mountain gorillas later became victims of the political struggles that affected the area in the early 1960s. A survey of 1972, sponsored by WWF, gave a gloomy picture of habitat destruction, encroachment by farming, and division of the forest into small blocks, with only a few mountain gorillas remaining.

In this out-of-the-way corner of Africa former game-park laws were virtually ignored, guards were de-moralized and turning to poaching, and population pressures were making nonsense of park boundaries. Farming on the lower ground was forcing elephants and buffalo up into the mountain forests, breaking them up and making them untenable for gorillas. From 1974 onward the World Wildlife Fund gave grants toward the improvement of conditions in the Volcanoes National Park, Rwanda, where most of the remaining mountain gorillas lived; smart uniforms and equipment boosted the morale of the Park guards, and an education programme improved the knowledge of both its wardens and the local population.

Over the years this plan has worked. The Park, an area of outstanding beauty, has become a tourist attraction, and now accommodates a Mountain Gorilla Programme (funded jointly by WWF and both US and British conservation groups) which has brought in ecologists and students of animal behaviour. The mountain gorillas, accustomed to the presence of benevolent human observers, can often be seen by tourists, providing an additional attraction in an already exciting Park. Clearing cattle and goats, and persuading poachers to keep away, are continuing tasks for which IUCN and WWF accept continuing responsibility; a new impetus was given to the Rwanda gorilla programme in 1979, with the provision of more anti-poaching units and further education pro-grammes for local people in the Park area.

Of the many other stocks of primates helped toward survival by WWF, those of Siberut, one of four forested islands off the west coast of Sumatra, are especially interesting. A deep-water channel separates Siberut from its neighbours, and it supports many endemic species, evolved during half a million years of isolation. Included in these are four primate species – the Kloss gibbon, Mentawi macaque, pig-tailed langur and Mentawi langur. For over 3,000 years man has hunted on Siberut, but only recently has his predation begun to take serious effect; forestry too is making inroads, and the primate population was found to be in rapid decline when the island was first surveyed during a WWF-sponsored study of 1976.

Now WWF is providing for a more thorough survey to find room for a large reserve for the threatened primates

Top Guy, a gentle male mountain gorilla, well known to thousands of tourists who visited his central African reserve. Killed by poachers, his hands were sold as souvenirs.

Above The scarlet face of a red uakari, a New World monkey of the Amazon rainforest.

Opposite A thoughtful chimpanzee in the forest of Gambia, West Africa.

and other species, and also for a study to promote the socio-economic development of the people of Siberut – one that will help them to continue in harmony with their environment. For this a WWF expert is helping the Indonesian conservation authorities in their work, and cooperating with a development project financed by Survival International, a London-based charity concerned with the welfare and survival of indigenous peoples in a changing world.

On Sumatra itself World Wildlife Fund has a long-term commitment to studies of rainforest (chapter 3), but an even longer-term link with another species of primate – the gentle orang-utan (the name means 'man-of-the-forest') of Indonesia. Orangs are curiously dignified apes that endear themselves to all who work with them: 'one of the most beautiful, serious and intelligent of the apes', wrote Tom Harrisson, a scientist who knew them well and

was their champion for many years. It was he who, as Chairman of IUCN's Survival Service Commission in the 1950s, first drew attention to the appalling traffic in orangs and the dangers they stood from deforestation, and it was his wife Barbara Harrisson who first saw the need for rehabilitating orangs that had been taken from the forest as babies, and could not be returned to it without a period in protective custody.

Orangs stand just over a metre (3 to 4 ft) tall and can weigh as much as a man; males grow larger and heavier than females in maturity and develop a wide moon-face. They are the only entirely arboreal great apes, living exclusively in the canopy of mature rainforest; solitary animals, they are seldom found in groups of more than two or three. Once they were widespread through southern China, Malaysia and the East Indies, but now they are restricted to the lowland rainforests of northern

Young orang-utans queuing for their milk at a Sumatran rehabilitation centre. When old enough, restored in health and self-confidence, they will be released in the forest.

Borneo and Sumatra. Widespread killing for food, sport and scientific specimens brought them to their present low numbers. World population is currently estimated at about 30,000, divided more or less equally between their two main island centres.

Orangs have always been popular in zoos and, throughout Indonesia, as pets; though reputable zoos have refused since 1959 to handle animals brought in from the wild, there has remained a market for orangs, especially young ones, that local collectors are always eager to exploit illegally. Adult orangs are too big to be caught, and too refractory to settle in captivity. The most easily caught and readily marketable orang is an infant just a few months old, taken from its mother's arms – usually after the mother has been shot.

The technique is to kill the mother with a lucky shot and hope that the infant will survive the fall. Young orangs secured in this way are already half-weaned, and can be caged and fed on bananas and other easily accessible fruit, and transported in small boxes to the dealers. Handled with care, though not always with skill or affection, they stand a chance of surviving for several years in captivity. However, for each infant caught, a mother orang lies dead on the forest floor; for each one reared successfully, several die from injuries sustained during capture, from disease, parasites or malnutrition, or simply from loss of interest in life due to close confinement in dull, monotonous captivity.

Encouraged by IUCN and WWF, the Indonesian government severely restricted the trade in orangs during the early 1960s, creating the problem of what should be done with young animals confiscated from poachers. Too small and inexperienced to be returned directly to the wild, they needed a period of rehabilitation equivalent at least to the extra year or more they would have spent with their mother in the forest. Barbara Harrisson set up the first orang rehabilitation centre in North Borneo in 1964, and others were established in Kalimantan and Sumatra during the early 1970s.

These stations, created or run with help from WWF, took in young orangs from captivity and, after veterinary treatment to clear them of parasites and disease, gave them a chance to get used to freedom gradually. The patients moved freely in the forest by day, gradually learning to feed and climb and regaining the self-confidence sapped by months or years of captivity. They returned at dusk for a meal and the safety of a locked cage overnight. After a few months of this treatment they were transported to another part of the forest, where the natural population of orangs was known to be low, and given their freedom. The stations worked well, handling several dozen orangs each year and releasing most of them with a good chance of survival.

The rehabilitation stations had another important function. They became focal points of conservation education, to which hundreds of local people flocked on holidays to see the orangs (possibly for the first time, for they are not easy to see in the wild), and to learn about them and about the rest of the rainforest wildlife.

Orang-utans are not yet safe in any part of their range, but the governments responsible for them are now well aware of their importance, and the reserves in which many of them survive are taken more seriously than at any time in the past. So there remains some hope for their survival, mostly in protected reserves where they are relatively safe from kidnapping, and from the chainsaw and bulldozer of the logging contractor.

IUCN sponsors a lively and well-funded group of primate biologists to coordinate conservation studies of all the non-human primates, and continues to give monkeys and apes high priority in its plans for further work on species and habitats at risk. WWF has committed substantial funds – almost one million dollars – for primate studies during the next three years. The welfare of many endangered species of monkeys and apes depends less on field research than on protection of their habitat and continuing vigilance all over the world against illegal trafficking, and here WWF's substantial financial support for law enforcement and reinforcement should prove particularly effective.

Coral sand and granite boulders at Mahé, Seychelle
Islands.

ISLANDS IN THE SUN

DARWIN'S ISLANDS

IN September 1835 HMS *Beagle*, a small survey ship of the Royal Navy, dropped anchor off the shore of Chatham Island, easternmost island of the Galapagos group. It was not an inviting shore: even after five weeks at sea, ploughing northward from Peru, nobody on board was impressed with what they saw of the land – dark slopes of black, twisted lava, a thin covering of skeletal shrubs, a lowering canopy of cloud. No humans but the crew of a whaler, ashore to kill animals for fresh meat. The *Beagle* crew took one look, then got down to the serious business of fishing over the deckrails. The captain, Robert Fitzroy, declared it 'a shore fit for pandemonium' and went below. Only the naturalist on board, Charles Darwin, found anything of interest in Chatham Island. He puzzled over the volcanic vents (like a row of derelict chimneys), the sulphurous smell, and the general appearance of desolation, which put him in mind of the iron foundries and spoil tips close to his home in industrial Shropshire.

During the next four weeks, spent cruising between the islands and exploring their rough lava plains, landing, observing and collecting wherever possible, Darwin found a great deal more to puzzle him. The plants were similar to those of mainland South America, but slightly different, as though seen in a distorting mirror. There were giant tortoises (the name Galapagos meant 'place of the tortoises'), much bigger than any on the mainland and different on every island. There were huge marine lizards that ate seaweed. There were finches, no doubt closely akin to each other and to South American forms, but again different, and varying from island to island. Some were seed eaters, with large or small seed-cracking bills like finches the world over. Others ate flowers or fruit, or were

Marine iguanas on Española (Hood Island) in the Galapagos group. Like many other Galapagos animals, they vary slightly in form from island to island.

Above Buccaneer Cove, a sheltered anchorage on San Salvador (James Island), Galapagos Islands. Volcanic islands that arose from the sea less than five million years ago, the Galapagos were colonized by species from the mainland which have since evolved independently on the different islands.

Right Blue-footed boobies on Española (Hood Island), southernmost of the Galapagos group. Many seabird colonies have been devastated by predators.

mainly insectivorous, with bills of quite different shapes: some hammered the trees like miniature woodpeckers, and one form had become a tool-user, digging insect grubs out of their holes with twigs and cactus spines. All the animals were strangely tame: Darwin easily caught birds under his hat.

Already awash with facts and data collected over four years of voyaging, the young Darwin could hardly absorb in four short weeks all that the Galapagos Islands and their strange plants and animals had to tell him. But reflecting on them later, he realized that these ugly, dark islands changed the whole of his thinking, and indeed the shape of his life. For they held the key to a huge biological and philosophical problem, 'that mystery of mysteries,' as he later wrote, 'the first appearance of new beings on this earth.' On the remote Galapagos Islands, among the tortoises, finches and marine iguanas, Charles Darwin discovered the great truth of evolution, key to the origin of species and the origin of man.

Today the Galapagos Islands are better known: though still remote from shipping lanes and relatively untouched by commerce or industry, they now have a permanent human population. Scientists of many nations visit them, still studying and poring over the curious plants and animals that so intrigued Darwin. Often the scientists use the facilities of a permanent research organization, the Charles Darwin Foundation for the Galapagos Islands, based at Academy Bay on Santa Cruz Island in the middle of the group. Many have been helped in their research by the World Wildlife Fund, which has supported the Foundation in all kinds of ways through twenty years of rewarding partnership.

The Galapagos Islands are a scattered group of sea mountains, standing in deep water 1,000 km (600 miles) off the west coast of South America. Entirely volcanic, with long, sweeping slopes and low summits, they are formed almost completely of consolidated ash and lava. Their peaks are volcanic cones, the tallest rising to 1,700 metres (5,600 ft) on the largest island, Isabela. There are sixteen big islands and dozens of smaller ones, with a total land area of 8,000 square km (3,000 square miles). Straddling the Equator, they are hot and arid at sea level, with thin soils, and a covering of dry desert scrub. The higher slopes are often hidden in cloud; cooler and moister, damped with dew and frequent rain showers, they carry a richer and more varied vegetation.

Discovered in 1535, the islands received their Spanish name and were noted on charts as a place where giant tortoises, seals and seabirds were found in plenty. Providing fresh meat and a little water, they became a stopping-off place for pirates, sealers and whalers; a handful of settlers farmed and traded, releasing domestic animals – mice, rats, cats, dogs, sheep, goats, cattle and pigs – that in their various ways wrought havoc on the indigenous plants and animals. At the time of Darwin's visit the islands had recently been claimed by Ecuador, the nearest neighbouring country on mainland South America. Still very sparsely inhabited, they remained relatively untouched by man. Hence the tameness of the birds and the general abundance of wildlife, though even then Darwin noted the hundreds of tortoise carapaces that littered the beaches, testifying to the popularity of their meat among visiting sailors.

The biological importance of the Galapagos Islands is based on their newness and isolation. Volcanoes that have sprung up from the sea and taken on their present form during the last five million years, they have never had direct contact with South America, their nearest continental neighbour, or with any other land mass. The plants and animals that live on them today are descendants

of colonists that have invaded and gained a foothold during the relatively short time since their eruption. Practically all of the invaders came from South America, drifting across in air and sea currents from the south and west; it is not difficult to see how birds and seeds of plants might make the journey, and even tortoises, lizards, insects and molluscs can travel long distances on floating tree trunks or rafts of matted vegetation.

But, as Darwin observed, the plants and animals on the Galapagos are *different* from those on the mainland; they have suffered sea-changes since their ancestors first set foot on the islands, and further changes in colonizing one island after another. It is as though the species had altered to meet the slightly different conditions they found on each island – had descended in fact from common ancestors and adapted according to different needs.

Nowadays we accept that adaptation can happen: the fact of biological adaptation is taught in schools and there is no intellectual or moral problem in accepting it. That plants and animals vary among themselves, that different environments can favour particular variants and reject others, that the characters selected can be passed on to future generations, and that accumulation of different characters add up to new forms, races and species – there is nothing in any of this to upset the most conservative thinker these days, even if the argument is extended to include the origins of man himself. Everything changes, everything grows from something else: why shouldn't animals have changed, and why shouldn't man have evolved from ancestors that were more like apes?

Today this is common sense, but in Darwin's day such ideas were free-thought amounting to heresy. Orthodoxy supported a static world, not a changing one, a world in which species were specially created, not evolving. Holy writ required men to believe in special creation, or so the priesthood interpreted it, and Darwin was a trained theologian with as yet little practice in original thinking. It took twenty years and more for him finally to shake off his old understandings, and accept the truths that the Galapagos Islands had disclosed to him during that eventful month in 1835.

Good for the Galapagos Islands and good for Darwin, but why worry about them now? The islands keep their value for many different reasons, historical, moral and aesthetic. Biologists value them highly because the lesson was unfinished when Darwin sailed away; we still have much to learn from them. That evolution is a working process is little in doubt. *How* it works is still worth intensive investigation, and islands – especially island groups like the Galapagos – are workshops where evolution can be seen in action. They repay every effort and every dollar spent in saving their flora and fauna from casual destruction, and in trying to understand the evolutionary processes happening among them.

After Darwin's visit, little research was done on the islands during the nineteenth or early twentieth centuries, though cruising ships occasionally dropped by to collect animals, alive or dead, for zoos and museums in America and elsewhere. Revival of interest began after the Second World War, when there were more opportunities for scientists to travel and work in out-of-the-way places. Disquieting reports began to appear – that the islands were suffering devastation from introduced species, that colonies of the indigenous seals, seabirds and reptiles were rapidly disappearing, that some of the unique forms (island stocks of tortoises, for example) had already been wiped out through hunting, predation and casual destruction of habitat.

It became clear that neither the Galapagos settlers nor the Ecuadorean government had resources to prevent the

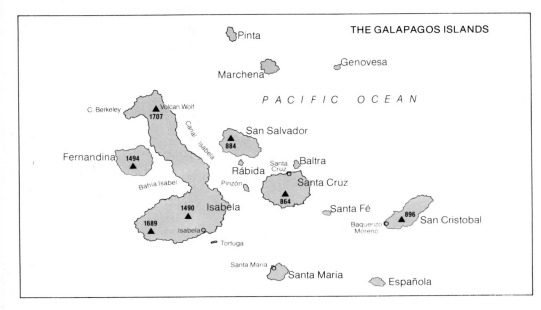

Opposite left Land iguanas of the Galapagos Islands have evolved in the absence of predators, but now face interference and predation from man and other intruding species.

Opposite right Giant tortoise of the Galapagos. These were formerly killed in large numbers by visiting seamen, who valued them for their fresh meat.

Above Giant tortoises mating. Many of the distinctive island stocks, reduced by predation, are being bred in captivity for repatriation to their home islands.

Left Galapagos sea lions. Much reduced by sealing during the nineteenth century, their stocks are now holding their own under protection.

gradual destruction of all that was most valuable on the islands. So in 1959, in response to international concern and a worldwide appeal for funds, the Charles Darwin Foundation for the Galapagos Islands was established under UNESCO patronage. Backed fully by the Ecuadorean government, and buoyed up by the goodwill and grants of British, American, Dutch, Swiss and German scientific societies, the Foundation in 1960 set up its research station alongside a small settlement on Santa Cruz (Indefatigable) Island, and began the programme of research which still continues over twenty years later.

Names have always been confusing on the Galapagos Islands. On some old charts they were called the Enchanted Islands – but so were many other groups scattered across the Seven Seas. The Royal Navy, responsible long ago for much of their original survey and charting, gave all the major islands English names, often with resounding naval or aristocratic connotations – Indefatigable, Albemarle, Narborough, Chatham, Hood. The Ecuadoreans, who have owned them since 1832, call the group as a whole Archipiélago de Colón and give the islands gentler Spanish names – Santa Cruz, Isabela,

Fernandina, San Cristóbal, Española. Today most people continue to call the group the Galapagos, but Spanish names are replacing English for the individual islands.

World Wildlife Fund's long involvement with the Galapagos began in 1961; in one of its very early projects – No. 5 – it contributed a nominal $1,000 toward the costs of building and equipping the new station at Academy Bay. Part of this grant was used in fencing off an enclosure for giant tortoises, where they could be kept under observation. This marked the start of a long and extensive programme of research and rehabilitation on the tortoise populations, which WWF has helped for many years.

Galapagos tortoises are generally regarded as belonging to one species. However, each of eleven main islands has (or used to have) its own distinctive race or subspecies; Isabela (Albemarle), the largest island, has no fewer than five races, centred in its five volcanic peaks which were originally isolated islands in their own right. The different stocks have all suffered at the hands of man, directly from his hunting or indirectly through competition or predation from his introduced domestic animals.

Most island tortoises were reduced in numbers, and three races may have been exterminated altogether by hunting parties from whalers and other passing ships: they were butchered on the spot or carried alive on deck to provide fresh steaks later in the voyage. Collectors too took surprisingly large numbers for sale to zoos throughout the world. Those that avoided capture (usually by living well away from the shore) found themselves harried by wild dogs, competing for grazing with goats, sheep, or donkeys, or sharing their meagre waterholes with thirsty mammals. Pigs dug up their nests and ate the eggs: the slow-moving and slow-growing young tortoises had little defence against foraging pigs, dogs, and other ground predators – a hazard they had never before met in their long history.

Checking stocks of tortoises on the different islands, especially in some of the less accessible corners, disclosed several that were thought to have been wiped out earlier, and steps have been taken to safeguard them. Under the leadership of Miguel Castro, a keen Ecuadorean conservation officer, and with the help of successive WWF grants, an egg hatchery has been set up at the Charles Darwin Research Station. Eggs of some of the rarer races have been brought in and hatched; the young have been reared in the safety of the hatchery compounds and ultimately returned to their islands of origin. Young and adult animals have been marked on several of the islands, to check the viability and longevity of known individuals, and reserves have been set aside on Santa Cruz, Isabela and some of the smaller islands to give the remnant stocks as much peace and freedom from competition as possible.

Island surveys on the Galapagos archipelago are more

difficult than they sound: the widely scattered islands present formidable logistic problems for anyone trying to work on them. Distances involved are enormous. While the closest islands stand in sight of each other, the outliers are up to 160 km (100 miles) away by sea from Academy Bay. Though the weather is usually fair, long swells and heavy surf often make landing difficult, and uncharted reefs are a further hazard along the mean, inhospitable shores. There are few roads or tracks, and walking over black fields of lava under a hot sun – surveying vegetation, looking for tortoises or counting seabird nests – is difficult and exhausting work.

Practically all of the work of the Charles Darwin Foundation is spread among the islands, and there has always been the need for a good, reliable survey ship. At first the Station had the use of hired craft, but in 1963 WWF provided half the cost of a more substantial boat, *Beagle II*, a stoutly built Cornish fishing ketch with auxiliary engine. By 1967 there was need for a larger, faster and more powerful boat to service the many research projects, and WWF contributed to the cost of a specially built, steel-hulled research vessel, with twin diesel engines and far more space for crew, scientists, cargo and equipment.

Beagle III justified her existence every day, not only in transporting scientists and their gear but also in anti-poaching patrols. There is still an illegal trade in tortoises and other rare Galapagos species for zoos and museums, prevented where possible by patrol boats of the Ecuadorean Navy. Now *Beagle IV* helps the other official boats in Galapagos waters to make poaching more difficult and perhaps less profitable.

From 1968 onward World Wildlife Fund has contributed generously to the costs of maintaining and running the research station at Academy Bay, and in 1971 helped to provide a museum and lecture hall. The Fund has also made possible extensive surveys of some of the islands' other endemic or rare species – the fur seals and sea lions, flightless cormorants, penguins, flamingos, hawks, owls, buzzards, and land and marine iguanas. Many of these species are already at risk; others may be hazarded as the human population of the islands increases. The Fund has also helped to pay small salaries for local wardens who look after the interests of the Foundation on some of the outlying islands, and to support an education programme for wardens of the National Parks Service. It has provided money for educational films and photographs that explain the work of the Foundation, and the scientific importance of the islands, to those who live there. In 1971 it also financed a survey to assess the impact of tourist visitors to the islands, and show how this growing industry – a significant source of revenue for the islanders – could be developed with the least possible harm to the islands.

The courtship dance of waved albatrosses, Galapagos Islands.

Perhaps the most extensive and important projects to earn WWF support are the campaigns to bring alien species under control. The targets are some of the many plants and animals that man has introduced to the islands and allowed to run wild. They range from rogue citrus trees to exotic grasses, from fire-ants to black rats, from cats and dogs to pigs and goats; and their effects are seen everywhere on all of the islands. Some species – black rats, mice and cats are regrettable examples – will never be eradicated by present methods, and others – many of the weed species – spread faster than any campaign to stamp them out. But goats, pigs and dogs have already been brought under control on some of the islands. Removal of goats has allowed spectacular regeneration of the natural vegetation, and hunting the hunters has vastly improved chances of survival for young tortoises, fur seals, iguanas and ground-nesting birds.

Control campaigns are costly and time-consuming. They require dozens of skilled men in the field to carry them out, and further visits and detailed studies to assess their effects. Not all the residents of the Galapagos Islands support them, for wild goats and pigs provide tasty fresh meat; islands have been known to acquire new populations mysteriously after successful shooting campaigns.

But the results of clearing unwanted species are often spectacular, and may ultimately be seen to bring benefits not only to the scientists and administrators, but to all who live on the Galapagos Islands.

Apart from support for scientific work on the archipelago, the World Wildlife Fund has cooperated with the Ecuadorean government in developing an overall strategy for conserving the unique Galapagos ecosystems. About ninety per cent of the total land area is now designated as a National Park, with a Park Service dedicated to carrying out effective research and management programmes under a well-thought-out Master-Plan. A Marine Extension Plan covers and protects a zone of two nautical miles around each island with some additional areas between the islands. There is now every indication that the Galapagos Islands are – if not yet safe – far safer from casual destruction than they have ever been since the time of their discovery, and WWF's continuing involvement is a guarantee of their future.

MADAGASCAR AND OTHER ISLANDS

To NATURALISTS, islands are places of magic, full of strange plants and animals spawned in isolation from the rest of the world. Not all have the remoteness and fascination of the Galapagos group, but almost every island, large or small, has a character of its own that distinguishes it from the mainland and from its neighbours: no two islands are quite alike. They share, however, a common quality of vulnerability. Always their populations of plants and animals are small, and small stocks are easily destroyed. Few islands are now untouched by man, and many have been devastated partly or completely by our heavy-footed invasions. But there are islands all over the world that still have things of interest to tell us, and some have kept their natural magic despite centuries of human occupation.

One such island is Madagascar, a landmass of high mountains, uplands and narrow plains roughly twice the area of Britain, standing alone off the east coast of southern Africa. About 1,600 km long and over 500 km wide (1,000 by 350 miles), it was presumably joined to Africa in the past, and shared a common heritage of flora and fauna. But the Mozambique Channel has formed a barrier for fifty million years and more, and Madagascar's wildlife has gone its own way. Evolving in isolation it has produced a herbarium of exotic plants, a menagerie of strange and unique animals.

The degree of difference is astonishing and in some ways hard to account for. Up to about 1,500 years ago, when man first arrived, Madagascar was heavily carpeted with a rich tropical flora. Of its 7,400 species of plants no fewer than eighty per cent were endemic – peculiar to Madagascar and found nowhere else. They included 96 species of ebony, 128 different kinds of palms, and 9 species

Fairy terns on Bird Island, Seychelles. These delicate white terns lay and incubate their eggs on bare branches, without the protection of a nest.

of baobab trees (Africa has only one). Many of these plants retain archaic ancestral characteristics that must long ago have been lost from the plants of the mainland. The Madagascan flora shows kinship with Australian and South American floras, harking back to the time – less than a hundred million years ago – when all the southern landmasses were joined in a single supercontinent. These are all features that the botanists would be glad to explore, and to protect, not just for the sake of the plants themselves, or their history, but for the rich resource that may lie in their genetic diversity.

But the botanists will have to hurry and may indeed be too late, for already ninety per cent of Madagascar's magnificent forests have been felled. Only scattered patches remain, and with the human population of the island increasing by three per cent each year, they may not remain long. The unique endemic thorn forest at the dry southern end of the island is equally rapidly being knocked down by zebu cattle and gobbled up by goats, and soil erosion is severe in many parts where the forest has gone. Madagascar's strange and beautiful flora is sadly depleted, with only a dozen scattered forest reserves and three national parks to give an indication of its splendid past.

A high proportion of Madagascar's animals too are endemic, including four families (thirty-six genera) of birds and at least forty genera of reptiles. Madagascar has some forty species (about half the world's total) of chameleons – slow-moving, pop-eyed reptiles that crawl in the bushes and throw out a sticky tongue to catch insects. There are tortoises, boa-constrictors and iguanas too, some showing puzzling affinities with the South American rather than the African fauna. Several of Madagascar's birds and reptiles qualify for the Red Data Books of endangered species.

Above Artist's impression of an aye-aye, the rare Madagascan lemurid, now reduced to a single population on a small, forested island.

Left Mahé, one of the Seychelles Islands in the Indian Ocean. Their granitic structure (rare in oceanic islands) and unique fauna make them especially interesting to conservationists.

The island's mammals are indeed unique, including five families and thirty-four genera of its own. Among them are the 'lemurids' – the lemurs, sifakas, indris and aye-ayes, included in three distinct families of primates of the Sub-order Prosimii, whose nearest kin live in Africa and south-east Asia. Small mammals up to the size of big domestic cats, lemurids originate from the same stock as monkeys and apes but have evolved along their own prosimian lines. There are currently about nineteen lemurid species, most of them tree-living and nocturnal; no fewer than nine of them are listed as endangered animals in IUCN's Red Data Book. Over a dozen more lemurid species, larger, slower-moving and probably diurnal, are known only as sub-fossils. Ground-living species, they were almost certainly hunted to extinction by man. Lemurids were once widespread about Madagascar, but are now restricted mainly to vanishing strips of coastal forest.

Also included among Madagascar's strange mammals are the tenrecs – a family of tree-living insectivores whose closest living relatives are the solenodons of Cuba, and several species of cat-like viverrids including civets, fossas and mongooses. There are no native cats, dogs, wolves or bears, no deer, sheep or cattle (except those recently introduced by man), no monkeys or apes, and man himself is a relatively recent arrival on the island.

World Wildlife Fund's first involvement with Madagascar was over the aye-aye, a lemurid once widespread in coastal forests about the island. Aye-ayes are strange-looking animals with cat-like body, squirrel tail, rodent teeth, mouse-like ears, huge forward-looking eyes, and the hands and feet of a monkey – with an especially long middle finger on either hand. Fruit, leaves and insects are their main diet. Nocturnal animals with strange chinking calls, ayes-ayes were regarded with fear by Malagasy villagers, whose amiable tradition it was to kill them on sight. Combined with the steady destruction of their rainforest for agriculture, this reduced their stocks to danger point and beyond, and by the 1930s it seemed likely that aye-ayes had disappeared altogether.

However, Dr Jean-Jacques Petter, of the Muséum National d'Histoire Naturelle in Paris, discovered a small population of aye-ayes one night in 1956, while studying other species of lemurs in the east coastal rainforest. We owe the continuing existence of this species to Dr Petter and his colleagues, for in cooperation with the Malagasy government and IUCN, and with WWF support, he arranged for the transfer of eleven aye-ayes to the safety of Nossi Mangabe, a forested offshore island reserve where they can survive in peace. Several other species of lemurids share the island sanctuary, as part of a wider conservation scheme for these strange and sadly endangered primates.

Dr Petter was among the first to draw attention to the threats facing Madagascan flora and fauna in the years following the Second World War, when the new Malagasy nation had just achieved its independence. From the late 1950s onward he was one of a few scientists fully aware of ecological changes taking place on Madagascar, and spoke up constantly for the forests and other endangered habitats. In this he had the backing of IUCN, but conservation was not the highest priority of a new nation faced with a host of other pressing problems, and the forests continued to fall.

In October 1970 the World Wildlife Fund, along with other conservation organizations, helped to promote an important International Conference on the Rational Use and Conservation of Nature of Madagascar, in the University of Tananarive. Convened by the Malagasy government, this proved a turning point in the island's conservation history, though not as quickly as everyone present might have expected and hoped. Some 200 delegates from seventeen nations converged on Madagascar to discuss every aspect of the environment, guided by a draft conservation plan that IUCN ecologists had prepared for the occasion. The Conference pinpointed the major ecological threats to the island (foremost among them the rapid expansion of an impoverished human population) and recommended priorities for action. Following this the Malagasy government, helped by a small IUCN task force, sat down to work out a comprehensive long-term programme of conservation for the island, and WWF's continuing interest and assistance was virtually assured.

However, there ensued a spell of political unrest that plagued Madagascar through much of the 1970s, and conservation, as always, was among the first casualties. Only in 1977 did it again become possible to pick up the scattered threads; in that year, following a visit by Dr Petter and Dr Luc Hoffman of WWF, a new World Wildlife Fund office was opened in Tananarive, the island's capital, with a Malagasy biologist, Barthélémi Vaohita, in charge. With the full support of the government, with help and advice from IUCN, and with some US$100,000 of WWF money already pledged, the scene is now set once again for a major programme of conservation to develop on the island.

Above A chameleon – lizard-like reptile of the Madagascan forest. Slow and deliberate in their movements, they shoot out a sticky tongue, almost as long as themselves, to catch insects for food.

Left A green lizard stalks insects on a palm leaf on Mauritius, isolated island of the southern Indian Ocean.

Above Sooty terns descend on the islands every year, nesting in large noisy colonies and laying eggs by the thousand. Only a small proportion of the chicks are reared to maturity.

Right Collecting tern eggs on Ile Desneuf, Seychelles group. Fresh eggs, taken from nests on the sand, provide welcome additional protein for the islanders.

The new approach to Madagascar, though based mainly on programmes drawn up after the 1970 Conference, forms part of IUCN/WWF's Conservation Programme for Sustainable Development 1980–82, which projects the joint plans of the two organizations for conservation activities in a rolling three-year programme. The philosophy behind the programme is that of the World Conservation Strategy (p. 217), prepared by IUCN, with the help of WWF and the United Nations Environmental Programme (UNEP). World Conservation Strategy (WCS) stresses the importance of linking conservation and human needs; developments that carry its mark take full account of man's environmental aspirations, as well as the needs of the plants, animals and habitats.

Madagascar's forest remnants, for example, may be the habitat of rare lemurs, but they are also living resources that, rightly or wrongly, provide building materials, herbs for cooking and medicine, even meat and vegetables for the local people – who have no other sources of supply. Fencing them off, setting guards over them, and employing clever expatriates to turn the forest remnants into reserves may well save the trees and lemurs for a time, but will not save the situation. Both government and people need convincing that there are advantages for them in the protection of the forest and lemurs – advantages that

Above Long isolated from contact with Africa, Madagascar has a distinctive fauna of its own. This grey mouse lemur is one of many species of lemur peculiar to the island.

Left A ring-tailed lemur, one of several species of lemur found in the remnants of Madagascar's rainforests.

will, for a start, outweigh the immediate disadvantage of lost building materials, herbs and food. Conservation aims in Madagascar are based on these premises; the government is at least part-convinced, and education and information campaigns are helping to spread the word among the people – that it is in their own interest to protect what remains of their island heritage.

So the work of IUCN and WWF in Madagascar is essentially catalytic, with education high among the conservation priorities. WWF's shopping list is headed by educational equipment – cameras and mobile projector facilities, for example – to encourage conservation teaching throughout the island. This is needed especially in colleges of education where Madagascar's future teachers are in training, and in villages close to the conservation areas. The forest remnants too are receiving their protection, for example the Antkarafantsika forest, where at least seven species of lemurids are known to live, and the Ambohitantely forest high on the mountain plateau. Some forest reserves will have buildings, equipment and staff to make them centres of conservation education, and management plans for their future are an important aspect of the conservation programme.

WWF also plans to support surveys of Madagascan moths and butterflies, conservation research on its rare tortoises and even rarer serpent eagles, and studies of threatened species of plants. Nossi Mangabe, the lemurid island refuge, is being surveyed again to see how the aye-ayes and other guests have prospered since their rescue programme began over a decade ago. Breeding studies of Madagascan animals are starting at Tananarive's Tsimbazaza Zoo, where a programme of education for conservation is also being developed.

Madagascar is perhaps the largest and most exciting of WWF's island projects, but many other islands and island species have been helped through periods of difficulty or danger by WWF grants. During the early 1960s WWF supported ecological surveys of neighbouring islands in the western Indian Ocean, including Aldabra Atoll and Cousin, Mahé and Praslin in the Seychelles group. With its help (and largely through funds raised by the Birmingham and Eastbourne Groups of WWF), Cousin Island became a reserve, where its unique flora and fauna – especially its vast population of seabirds – could be both protected and studied by visiting scientists. Cousin's birds – delicate fairy terns, fodies, noddies, turtle doves, kestrels, brush warblers, tropic birds and brilliant cardinals – proved attractive also to visiting tourists and local parties of schoolchildren and students. On the Seychelles too WWF helps with the planning of marine national parks, designed to attract visitors to areas where they can see and appreciate the beauty of the islands' underwater life with as little environmental disruption as possible.

In the 1970s conservation studies spread to species and habitats of other Indian Ocean islands, including Mauritius, Round Island and Rodriguez. When first occupied by man in the sixteenth century, Mauritius was heavily forested and bore a unique fauna, including endemic reptiles, birds and mammals; its most famous inhabitant was the dodo, a giant pigeon-like ground-living bird that was hunted to extinction by settlers and visiting mariners. Now with a large and still expanding human population, Mauritius has lost much of its forest cover, and many of its endemic species are seriously endangered.

Mauritius parakeets, kestrels and pink pigeons, rated as three of the world's most critically endangered species of birds, are being studied in WWF-sponsored programmes. They live in patches of native forest in the Black River Gorge and other areas, and aviaries have been established for captive breeding experiments. About thirty of the pigeons now nest in the wild and the species breeds well in captivity. Locally-bred birds, and others reared in Britain's Jersey Zoo, have been returned to the forests to swell the wild population. The kestrels, which feed on insects, lizards and small birds, were reduced to six adults

in 1973 – two wild pairs and one captive. They have proved difficult to maintain in captivity, and the wild birds are bedevilled by monkeys that raid their nests for eggs. The population, currently about fifteen birds, is still far from safe. Mauritius parakeets now number about twenty, all in the wild. They too have monkey trouble, and monkey-proof nest boxes have been provided for them. A cyclone that recently destroyed the fruit crop did not increase their chances of success. Rare Rodriguez fodies and fruit-bats are also being studied and reared in the Black River Gorge aviaries, for ultimate release on their home island.

In its early days WWF was helpful in saving two endangered species of Hawaiian birds. First to call for aid was the néné or Hawaiian goose, a species known for some years to be close to extinction on its northern Pacific home islands. World population in 1950 was estimated at less than fifty birds, about half of them in the wild and the rest captive in zoos and wildlife collections. A programme of breeding, based mainly on a small stock at the Wildlife Trust, Slimbridge, succeeded in raising several hundred birds over the years, and WWF helped to fly successive groups first to captivity and then to freedom on suitable islands in the Hawaiian chain.

Another Hawaiian candidate for help was the koloa or Hawaiian duck, once widespread among the islands but discovered in 1962 to be rare and seriously endangered. Life history and ecology studies were undertaken by the local Division of Fish and Game, financed largely by WWF. Surviving stocks were surveyed, and small breeding groups were distributed among selected zoos and game parks of the world, just in case the island birds disappeared altogether. These measures succeeded; koloa have bred well in captivity and stocks have been released in likely-looking habitats throughout the islands.

In the southern Pacific Ocean, WWF supported a survey of endangered birds and their habitats on several small islands in 1969, and in 1970 helped to fund an initial ecological survey of Papua New Guinea – pump-priming for a wider programme of conservation in the future. Several Pacific projects have been concerned with the protection of coral reefs (p. 197) or turtles (p. 205), and most recently with the establishment and running of national parks and reserves by newly independent island communities – for example Western Samoa.

Atlantic islands too have had their share of WWF attention. Among the first to benefit were the Falkland Islands in the south-western Atlantic, where a status survey of endangered species was undertaken by a dedicated local naturalist, Ian Strange. That was in 1964; four years later a longer conservation study was also given support. Two large and many small islands make up the Falklands group; all are grass covered and heavily grazed

Black-browed albatrosses nest among tussock grass on windswept cliffs of the Falkland Islands.

by sheep, which support the human population of about 1,800. Only on a few of the islands can some semblance of the original flora and fauna be found, including banks of tussock grasses over 2 metres (6½ ft) tall. Some of these have been freed from the ravaging sheep and dedicated as reserves, mainly thanks to Ian Strange's efforts, and the interest of the outside world demonstrated by WWF support. There are large colonies of fur seals, sea lions and many kinds of seabirds, among them albatrosses, smaller petrels and five breeding species of penguins.

WWF has also supported conservation work on Tristan da Cunha in the southern Atlantic, Little Swan, Jamaica, Dominica and several other islands in the Caribbean, and the northern Atlantic Selvagen and Canary Islands. It helped British ornithologists to buy the Orkney island of Copinsay as a memorial to James Fisher, a distinguished and popular ornithologist, and is currently supporting conservation work among the islands that will make up a new national park in south-western Finland.

A mangrove swamp on Mahé, in the Seychelles.
Mangroves grow from rich, muddy water on tropical
coasts.

THE WETLANDS

WATCH ON
THE WETLANDS

ETLANDS have a magic of their own. They need it, to get over the more immediate disadvantages that so forcefully put people off them. The name itself is a public relations disaster: what on earth could be attractive about a habitat that has 'wet' as its main feature? And the wetlands themselves – bleak, unsheltered, soggy under-foot, icy and windswept in winter, damp and mosquito-ridden in summer – you need webbed feet and feathers to appreciate wetlands properly. There's not enough water to sail in, and it's too smelly and muddy for swimming. Wetlands are marshes, bogs, slobs – there are dozens of unattractive names to show we dislike them, and have very little use for them as they stand.

So what do you do with wetlands? If you can, you buy them cheap and drain them for agriculture. If you can't do that you buy them even cheaper and lease for tipping: the local council will probably be interested and promise to help. Once you have got good, solid ground you sell it in building lots, or carve it into a marina for weekend sailing. That way you turn wastelands (no, wetlands) into something useful and everyone gets to enjoy them. Except the birds. But there is plenty more down the coast for the birds and birdwatchers to pick over, so we needn't worry too much about them.

This philosophy, all too understandable, destroys huge areas of wetland every year. Ecologists and conservation-ists who wring their hands over the destruction have only themselves to blame. To the man in the street or the planner at his board, the natural value of wetlands – like the magic claimed for them by wetland enthusiasts – is nowhere near so apparent as the value to everyone of a developed coastline. 'Wetlands are wonderful' may be true indeed, but it needs a continuous hard sell to get the message across.

Siberian cranes, long-distance migrants that winter in the wetlands of southern Europe.

The magic of wetlands is there right enough. Peter Scott caught its essence in his paintings of marshland Britain: as their popularity has shown, there is something in wetlands – far more than a cold in the head – for just about everyone. There is the magic of colour and rippled reflections, of remoteness and tranquillity, of ducks, geese and waders going about their business without human fuss or interference: many sample it comfortably through the window of a painting, and devoted naturalists are just as glad to enjoy it – perhaps more acutely – in the damp, cold reality of the marshes.

More readily shared, and by far more people, is the magic of tropical and subtropical wetlands – the massed flamingos of Lake Nakuru, harsh morning light on the Spanish Marismas, or the dim, green, watery corridors of Florida's Everglades. Wherever they occur, wetlands have a special interst for ecologists, for they are often the most lively and varied habitats for miles around, with the richest spectrum of species and a surprisingly high turnover of life and activity. Peter Scott's ducks, rising from the marsh in early morning, know just what they are about; they have a busy day ahead of them in a rich and rewarding wetland environment.

The main ecological secret of wetlands is mineral accumulation. Usually in drainage basins, they accept mineral-rich water from the surrounding region and, by evaporation and rapid plant growth, contrive to keep the minerals in store. Their still or slowly-moving waters grow rich from the rivers and streams flowing into them, and their mud, often brought in by seasonal floods, stores all kinds of wealth for the future. Run-off from wetlands is always a rich brew, fertilizing the sea or lake system that receives it. Warming under the spring sun, wetlands support rapid growth of algae (phytoplankton) and the tiny floating animals (zooplankton) that feed on them, as well as floating weeds and emergent vegetation; fish, snails, insects, worms and other small fry flourish too, providing a rich venue for larger animals, especially birds.

With plentiful rations, cover close at hand, islands and tussocks enough for safe nesting and a clear horizon, wetlands provide ideal habitat for waterbirds and waders – ducks, geese, swans, herons, grebes, divers, rails, gulls, terns and a host of other familiar species in temperate regions, and their exotic equivalents in the tropics. Semi-aquatic reptiles and mammals too find them welcoming habitats, from beavers, otters and mink in the cooler waters to crocodiles, turtles, water snakes and hippopotamuses in warmer wetlands. Though difficult for man to get about on (it is hard even to find good vantage points), they are usually lively environments with an abundance of species and plenty of action. Hence the naturalists' dismay when they are drained or filled in – or, much worse, used mindlessly as dumps for civilization's toxic rubbish.

World Wildlife Fund turned early to supporting wetland conservation. Each year it has provided income for the International Waterfowl (previously Wildlife) Research Bureau, which works with IUCN and other organizations to promote and monitor wetlands conservation on a world scale. But WWF has also funded many wetlands programmes directly; saving a corner of the Guadalquivir Marismas, for example, was one of its first dozen projects (p. 22). The Marismas are a vast area of impenetrable marshland close to the estuary of the Guadalquivir River, between Seville and the Gulf of Cadiz in south-western Spain. They form an eastern boundary to the more famous Coto Doñana, a former hunting reserve of Spanish noblemen and until recently, through isolation, an almost completely undeveloped area of semi-arid wilderness. The Marismas and Coto together form a fabulous region of natural beauty, with an unparalleled flora and fauna: half the breeding birds of Europe can be seen there as residents or migrants, with such colourful semi-exotics as hoopoes, bee-eaters and flamingos.

The area was known to Guy Mountfort, then an International Trustee, from three expeditions of the 1950s. Largely through his influence and interest, World Wildlife Fund contributed substantially to buying sections of both the Coto and the Marismas. These were presented to the Spanish government for the creation of a large nature reserve, ultimately to become a national park, with the promise of further help toward the development of management plans and programmes of research. Today the Doñana National Park forms one of Europe's finest and most spectacular wildlife sanctuaries, relatively though as yet not entirely safe from commercial development. Apart from its splendid waterbirds, the Park is probably the last stronghold of both the Spanish lynx and the magnificent Spanish imperial eagle.

French wetlands play an important role as staging posts for migratory birds, and over the years WWF has made significant contributions to several. In the Rhône valley of eastern France, close to Lyon, a small grant helped to link the Bois de la Bogue, a wood containing an extensive heronry, with the much larger wetland and lake reserve of La Dombes, to the enrichment of both. Previously pestered by nest robbers, the heronry prospered under the new arrangement, increasing its holding of little egrets and acquiring stocks of both squacco and night herons.

Further south WWF contributed substantially to funds for extending the Camargue, the huge reserve of marshes, lakes and lagoons in the delta of the Rhône. A complex of saline and freshwater wetlands, part-cultivated and even

Draining wetlands – converting them to agriculture or building lots – involves the loss of many species of birds: bitterns, once common in Europe, are now relatively rare.

Above left Semi-wild cattle on the Camargue, a huge wetlands reserve on the delta of the Rhône, southern France.

Above right Black-tailed godwits, like many other migrant waders, rely on wetlands in temperate regions to provide them with their winter food.

part-industrialized, the Camargue still contains enormous areas of relatively unspoiled lakes, laced with solid ground. Famous for its wild white horses and black bulls, it is also a breeding area for thousands of waterbirds (including a colony of flamingos) and Mediterranean landbirds. WWF has also supported research on pollution and other problems in the Camargue, helping to keep a safe environment for its main tenants, the wildlife, as well as an attractive one for visitors.

In central and eastern Europe WWF helped to protect the Seewinkel, the western extremity of a large area of shallow lakes and marshes extending across eastern Austria and Hungary. Agricultural and other development pressures were eroding the 'Hutweider', a stretch of natural grassland that had never been ploughed, and altering the character of the nearby lakes. Leasing land and hunting rights protected these key areas of the Seewinkel, which have proved a focus of great interest for thousands of visitors, and ensured a continuing welcome for migrant and breeding wetland birds. Morchauen Nature Reserve, a smaller area of riverine forest on the eastern border of Austria is part-owned and maintained by WWF. The Fund has also been involved in establishing wetland reserves in the Reuss River Valley of Aargau Canton, Switzerland, and a chain of coastal and upland marsh sites in Italy. In the Netherlands, Germany and Denmark WWF has helped conservation groups in many ways to secure the future of the Waddensee, Europe's largest extent of coastal wetland, which has for long been threatened with land reclamation and development schemes. WWF aims to help in coordinating efforts to develop a good management policy for the whole area.

In Britain WWF contributed to the purchase of the Ouse Washes and Welney Wildfowl Reserve, areas of seasonally flooded ground in the fenlands of East Anglia. In winter these bleak areas attract hordes of migrant waterbirds, including Britain's largest concentrations of Bewick swans and pintails, and in summer are breeding grounds for crested grebes, waders, and at least ten species of ducks, geese and swans. In association with the Wildfowl Trust, Welney has since been developed as an important wildfowl observatory and research centre, and further wildfowl reserves have been acquired at Martin Mere, Lancashire, and Caerlaverock in south-western Scotland. In Ireland WWF helped the Irish Wildfowl Conservancy to buy and establish reserves on Wexford Slobs, grasslands and mudflats north and south of Wexford Harbour, where large populations of migrant geese winter every year. Ultimately the Conservancy was able to set up an observatory and research centre, and pursue research on the over-wintering wildfowl.

One of WWF's largest wetland projects, funded

Wetlands support a variety of species: while the flamingos feed in the shallows, the white pelicans prepare to fish in deeper waters offshore.

entirely by the US National Organization, was the establishment of a 4,000 hectare (10,000 acre) reserve on the low-lying coast of New Jersey. Most of the area was tidal saltmarsh, lying inside protective barrier beaches. Access to the sea made them important as nursery grounds for flounders, menhaden and other fish of commercial importance, enriching local fisheries. They were also breeding grounds for thousands of herons, egrets and ibises, wintering areas for geese, ducks and waders, and staging-posts on the flyways for over 200 species of migratory birds. In summer too, they were recreation areas for thousands of tourists from the heavily populated conurbations inland. Ripe for draining, dredging and development, they were bought piecemeal by WWF (US), and maintained instead as an important reserve and wetland research centre.

WWF has contributed in this way to the establishment and maintenance of wetland reserves all over the world, including India, several African countries, and both North and South America. Perhaps its remotest job of maintenance is taking place at Lake Atitlan, high in the Andes of Guatemala, where giant pied-billed grebes, a species unique to the lake, are in trouble of an unusual kind. Earthquakes have opened their lake floor and let out some of the water, and the dense reedbeds surrounding the lake are left high and dry. So are the giant pied-billed grebes, that rely on the reeds for nesting cover. Never numerous, and already stressed by man-induced ecological changes in the lake, their numbers have recently been down to as few

as eighty. A WWF grant has helped the Guatemalan government to buy a motorboat, which will allow the resident warden and his teams to plant the new lake edge quickly with reeds and other vegetation, so the grebes can nest once again in seclusion. Within the same project is an education programme for local villagers to show how pollution and habitat destruction threaten their livelihood.

Lake Nakuru in Kenya's Rift Valley is wetland with a difference – a large tropical saline lake with an unusually rich flora and fauna. Algae abound, insect larvae and crustaceans swarm, and the lake is the home of thousands of spectacular waterbirds including flamingos, pelicans, spoonbills, ibises and storks. About 400 species are estimated to use the lake and its surroundings, and there is a corresponding wealth of game – hippopotamuses, waterbuck, reedbuck, impala, eland, gazelles, buffalo, leopards, and many other species. Declared a National Park in 1968, Lake Nakuru gradually became the centre of a farming and urban community that encroached on the shores and threatened the lake with severe pollution. To meet the problem, WWF in 1973 launched a special campaign in which the children of Europe raised money – over US$500,000 – to buy up the land surrounding the lake and have it included in the national park.

The park area was more than trebled, and sponsors

treated some of the children concerned in the campaign to a blissful fortnight in Kenya to see where the money had gone. Since then WWF has raised additional funds for fencing, pollution studies, and a comprehensive development and management survey designed to meet Lake Nakuru's needs for the foreseeable future.

Less publicized but no less important was the development of a marine wetland national park at Banc d'Arguin, a strange semi-desert area of islands, shallows and muddy shore on the coast of Mauritania, West Africa. The land is arid, but banks of marine grasses and rich mudflats support huge numbers of aquatic birds, both European and African, including several million over-wintering waders. Flamingos, spoonbills, pelicans and terns jostle for position to feed as the tides advance and retreat, and cormorants, herons and many other birds breed on the desolate islands. The area is also an offshore gathering ground for whales and dolphins, and rare monk seals breed in caves along the shore. For long isolated and left inviolate by an incurious local population, Banc d'Arguin is now subject to disturbance by parties of tourists and fishermen. WWF has provided patrol boats, radios and other aids, encouraging the Mauritanian government to uphold its Park status and try to ensure the protection of its wildlife.

An important advance in wetlands promotion and conservation occurred in 1971, when after much effort from

Above A breeding flock of greater flamingos in East Africa. Flamingos feed in shallow water, with head upside down and bent bill acting as a plunger to collect algae.

Opposite A roseate spoonbill, shallow-water feeder of southern US and South American wetlands.

the International Waterfowl Research Bureau and other bodies, the Convention on Wetlands of International Importance was finally agreed. Known as the Ramsar Convention (from the Iranian town where the final meeting was held) this is an international convention committing all countries in agreement to identify specific wetland areas within their borders, and maintain them as reserves under conditions as natural as possible. As the number of signatories grows, more and more countries are pledged to recognize at least some wetlands as worth saving.

WWF from time to time helps in creating and managing reserves – for example seven important wetland areas recently defined in Tunisia – in support of the Convention. The Ramsar Convention for the first time provides official international recognition – and perhaps an element of respectability – for wetlands, encouraging member governments to take them seriously, and strengthening the hands of conservationists who try to save them from development, as rich, interesting and valuable habitats in their own right.

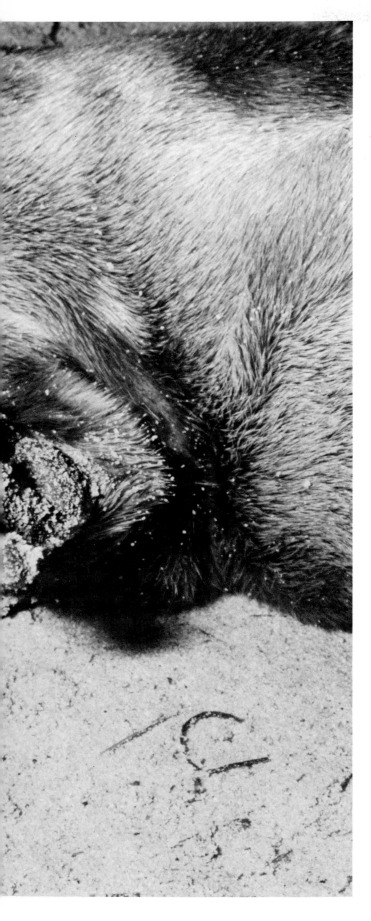

OTTERS

THE Carnivora, or meat-eating mammals, come in a variety of forms and sizes. There are different kinds of live prey, and different ways of catching and chopping them up; the seven families of living carnivores represent seven basic patterns of predator that, over millions of years, have been tested and found successful. Many are familiar animals. The cats form one distinctive family, the dogs, wolves and foxes another, the bears a third and the hyaenas a fourth. Close to the hyaenas are the lesser-known viverrids, including the genets, civet-cats and mongooses; close to the bears are the procyonids, including the raccoons and ring-tailed cats. And central to the whole order of Carnivora are the family Mustelidae, including the weasels, stoats, ferrets, badgers and otters.

Mustelids are central to the rest of the carnivores in that they seem to follow most directly from an ancestral group, the miacids, that appeared at the start of the Tertiary some seventy million years ago. Miacids were weasel-like animals with long sinuous bodies and short limbs, clearly carnivorous, with blade-like cutting teeth and strong jaw muscles; they lived in forests, no doubt preying on the birds and the small mammals – insectivores and rodents – that were starting to proliferate at that time. From miacid stocks the carnivores began to diversify fifty to sixty million years ago. Dog-like, cat-like, bear-like and other recognizable forms all appeared in the fossil record during the same period, as the different groups took up options on particular prey and particular methods of hunting, and adapted accordingly.

The mustelids remained close to their ancestral miacid form, keeping the long, slinky weasel-like body, and developing the characteristic short, powerful jaws with shearing teeth, and the long skull to house an inquisitive, active brain. This combination of characters has proved immensely successful: there are now about seventy

A smooth-coated otter of south-eastern Asia

Above The African clawless otter is one of several species listed as endangered. All species of otter are hunted for their smooth, dense fur, and endangered by the spread of man.

Right Short-clawed otters of Malaya and south-eastern Asia have adapted to life in rice-paddies and canals.

different species of mustelids alive in the world today (almost as many as dogs, wolves, foxes and cats together) in a wide range of niches on every habitable continent.

While most of the other kinds of carnivores tended to grow bigger, taking advantage of larger prey, the mustelids on the whole remained small, continuing to specialize in hunting birds and small mammals, and making up in fierceness for their lack of size. Those that did grow larger were mainly ground-living forms – the wolverine, for example, big enough to attack deer and sheep, and the badgers, with their mixed diet of small mammals, insects, earthworms, shoots, berries and carrion. One group among the larger ground-living mustelids took to fishing in rivers, lakes, streams and seas, possibly twenty million or more years ago. Their widely-scattered descendants, now living in Asia, Africa and both North and South America, are grouped by zoologists into the sub-family Lutrinae, and the English-speaking world calls them otters.

Otters are oddly distinctive animals, with the slender lines and quizzical alertness of their mustelid cousins the stoats and ferrets, but larger and more graceful in their

movements. Common or European otters of Europe and Asia measure up to $1\frac{1}{2}$ metres ($4\frac{1}{2}$ ft) from nose to tip of muscular tail and weigh 10 to 15 kg (22 to 30 lb). Mature males are always noticeably larger than females. Canadian otters, still a common species in lakes and waterways all over North America, are on average slightly larger than European otters; largest of all are the giant otters of South America, that measure two metres ($6\frac{1}{2}$ ft) and weigh up to 30 kg (65 lb).

With their short face, pug nose, widely spaced eyes and bristling, vibrant whiskers, otters have a look of constant awareness that exactly reflects their character. The small ears, set far back and almost lost in the fur, show the relatively enormous length and breadth of the skull: otters look intelligent, and indeed seem to be far more intellectual and perceptive than most other mammals of their size. Completely at home on land, they walk like weasels with long body slightly arched and tail trailing: an otter's track is quite distinctive, with marks of five splayed, slightly webbed toes in the footprint on either side and the sinuous trail of a broad, slithering tail between. Equally at home in water, otters swim slowly with webbed feet pedalling, or quickly with body low in the water and tail vibrating rapidly from side to side. Usually only the head and hump of the back appear at the surface, with little rippling or other disturbance in the water around them.

Mammals that spend much of their time in water, especially cool water at temperatures well below that of their blood, need better-than-average insulation. Without it they waste precious energy in maintaining body temperature, and may well die of cold and exhaustion. For small animals that live in shallows and dodge in and out of the water continuously there is no insulation better than a double layer of fur – a dense, velvety underfur lying close to the skin like a waterproof undervest, and a coarse outer fur of protective guard hairs, that keep both wind and water out and shed surplus water readily on shaking. This is the kind of fur that otters, fur seals, coypu (nutria) and other semi-aquatic mammals possess. Its texture, especially that of the dense underlayer, gives it a considerable value in the fur trade. Otters have long been hunted for the dark, lustrous beauty of their pelts. Recently every species of otter has suffered severe hunting pressure, some to the point of extinction, to satisfy commercial demand.

The first species of otter to suffer near-extinction for the value of its skin was the sea otter of the North Pacific Ocean. Larger and heavier than Canadian otters, weighing up to 40 kg, sea otters have an especially rich, dark fur, that keeps them warm in chilly ocean waters. Entirely marine, they live on sheltered stretches of coast from California to Alaska in the eastern Pacific and from the Bering Sea to the Kurile Islands in the west. Shortly after Europeans explored these coasts in the eighteenth

Above Sea otters, ranging from Alaska to California, were reduced almost to extinction in the nineteenth century. Stocks are now recovering under rigorous protection.

Right The Canadian otter is still widespread in Canada and the United States. The elegant whiskers are probably sensory, helping the animal to hunt for fish and other living prey in the water.

century, Russian, British and American ships swept in to capitalize on the wealth of furs that the explorers had reported. Fur seals were the main prey, but sea otters too were taken in enormous numbers. By the early twentieth century only a tiny fraction of the original population – perhaps a few hundred animals – remained.

The sequel to this story is encouraging for conservationists, for it demonstrates the successful recovery of a species left to its own devices under a regime of rigorous protection. In 1911 an international agreement was drawn up between Canada, the United States, Russia and Japan to protect the remaining stocks of sea otters. Recovery was slow at first, but then speeded up and has increased rapidly in recent decades. Under strict supervision of the Alaskan state authority stocks have been transferred from areas of plenty to areas of scarcity, and the total population in Alaskan waters is now estimated at well over 100,000 – and still expanding. Local fishermen are complaining about unfair competition from sea otters, and steps are being taken to monitor and if necessary control populations that are thought to have reached the limits of their food supply.

Southern stocks of sea otters in Californian waters have been less successful: there is probably more competition for food, and certainly more disturbance from humans in this more heavily populated area. But there is hope that southern sea otters will re-establish themselves too, so that more people have a chance to enjoy the company of these intriguing little animals in the wild. They have for long been known to bring up clams and sea urchins from the sea bed and break them open at the surface, using a stone as a hammer and their chest as an anvil. Skin-divers who have studied them hunting off California now report that in searching the sea bed for food they pay particular attention to abandoned beer cans, which small squid – one of their favourite food species – often use as a temporary shelter.

River otters the world over have adopted a simple way of life based on a constant search for food, most of which comes from the water or close to its edge. Several species live near the sea and readily hunt along the shore or in the inter-tidal zone. They travel long distances overland from one river or arm of the sea to another, climbing steep slopes and crossing moorlands and fells. They move along traditional trails impregnated with the scent of their droppings and musky glandular secretions – trails that they and probably their ancestors have used many times before. Travelling over mud or snow they pick up their feet and slide, skidding happily on sleek belly fur; sometimes they return for the fun of a second go, for otters are playful animals, especially when young. Adults live solitary lives, occupying large overlapping ranges marked out by their droppings. They roam constantly, meeting and exchanging grunts, hisses and whistles with neighbours, but usually hunting alone. In most species males and females consort briefly for mating, then go their separate ways; only the females are involved in rearing the young. Giant otters of South America and tropical Asian species are exceptional in forming stable family groups.

Otter cubs are born in holts – natural cavities or holes dug in stream banks and lake shores – in litters of two to five. Like the young of most carnivores they are blind and helpless for some weeks after birth. Once mobile, they travel with their mother on hunting trips, following her in line astern along the trails and through the water, learning by example and practice the skills of being an otter. In most species, perhaps all, the young remain with the mother for several months, dispersing to live on their own when she comes on heat and mates again.

Otters are quiet, elusive creatures that usually lie up during the day and hunt or wander mostly at night. You seldom see or hear them unless you know where to look; otter watchers need time and a special kind of patience that relatively few possess. In comparison therefore with deer, antelopes and other more prominent mammals, otters remain relatively unstudied and unknown, and there are only a handful of naturalists in the world competent to champion their cause. When anglers accuse otters of wasteful predation on fish, or commercial fishermen blame them for damage to expensive nets, otters find few friends in court. When they seem to be getting scarcer in their usual haunts, for any of a variety of possible causes, it is hard to find anyone with real knowledge of the species who can pin the blame firmly where it belongs and set about halting the decline.

One notable defender of otters, well known in Britain, was the late Gavin Maxwell, a naturalist and writer whose pet European otters featured in his books and television films. Through *Ring of Bright Water* and other writings Maxwell alerted a whole generation to the wit and beauty of this species, and formed a trust, the Edal Fund (named after his best-known otter), to help otter species in danger of extinction. From this imaginative action developed a World Wildlife Fund interest in otters, for the British National Organization, under its Chairman Sir Peter Scott, gave financial support to the Edal Fund. Sir Peter, who in 1961 had helped to found WWF (p. 20), drew attention in the 1968 Yearbook to the sad plight of otters in many parts of the world, and reported on steps that WWF had taken and was planning on behalf of some of the species at risk. Though the word 'otter' has not often appeared in lists of projects funded by WWF since then, the Fund has in fact contributed considerably to their welfare in many ways.

The British Council for Nature and Faunal Preservation Society combined with WWF to support the Mammal Society in the first-ever major study of a riverine otter – an enquiry into the status of European otters in Britain. European otters are attractive animals, fawn or tan with silvery-white underparts. They range across Europe and Asia from Britain to Japan, and south into northern Africa, India and Sri Lanka. Living in lakes, streams and rivers they show a strong preference for clear water, in quiet neighbourhoods where fish are plentiful and there is dense cover nearby; woodland, shrubs, reeds or long grass serve equally well. Many live on estuaries or close to the coast, foraging happily along the shore and in shallows beyond the low-tide mark. They catch fish, frogs, mice, freshwater crayfish, mussels, sea urchins, and a host of other small foods, taking whatever happens to be plentiful at the time. This may include salmon, trout and other fish that anglers and commercial fishermen prefer to catch themselves. They also take eels and pike, which are predators of young salmon and trout, but otters are never welcome along a stretch of river where fishing interests are strong. In a fish farm or hatchery they can be as devastating as foxes in a henhouse. On shore otters take game birds and their eggs; gamekeepers often regard them as vermin, and trap them or shoot them on sight.

Hunted fairly consistently for their predations, for sport or for pelts, wherever they come into contact with man, European otters still manage to maintain low populations over much of their original range. The Mammal Society survey of the late 1960s and early 70s showed that otters were still fairly plentiful in Britain. Organized hunting does not materially affect their numbers (the hunting interest may indeed help to protect them from less predictable and more dangerous forms of violence). However, their numbers have decreased in recent decades, mainly because of a dramatic extension of river pollution, and reduction of woodlands, copses and other suitable cover. Any further decline could prove disastrous.

The biology of otters came under review again in late March 1977, when WWF gave financial backing for an IUCN gathering of otter specialists in Surinam, South America. Reports on other populations of European otters in Sweden, Spain and elsewhere suggested a general decline, due to much the same problems as in Britain; some stocks – those of Italy, for example – were indeed on the point of extinction and could be saved only by immediate action. No anxiety was expressed over Canadian otters, the equivalent and closely-related species of North America. Formerly hunted intensely for their fur and still under considerable local pressure, they are reduced in numbers but still present throughout most of the continent, from the tundra of northern Canada and Alaska to the bayous and forested valleys of the southern United States.

But the Surinam meeting disclosed serious problems for otters in other parts of the world. While European and Canadian otters as species were relatively safe, no fewer than four out of nine kinds of South American otters were seriously in decline, and the status of several others in Asia and Africa was found to need immediate investigation.

The species deemed most seriously to be at risk in South America was the giant otter, a magnificent animal formerly widespread throughout the riverine forests of the Orinoco and Amazon basins. Surveys supported by WWF and other organizations showed that giant otters differ from most other species in ways that work strongly to their disadvantage when hunting parties are out to get them. Not only are they the largest of all otters; they are also the noisiest, most gregarious and most conspicuous. They live in small family groups, marking out 'camp-sites' on the stream banks to which they return frequently; most active during the day, they are easily spotted and shot. Their furs are large and very valuable. It is not surprising, therefore, that the species has been cleared from most of the accessible parts of its range, and now survives only in the depths of the forests where dealers have so far been unable to penetrate and organize their collection.

Two forms of river otter closely akin to Canadian otters

In the Sunderbans of Bangladesh otters are trained to catch fish in the muddy waters.

were also found to be at risk – La Plata otters of Argentina and neighbouring countries in the basin of La Plata river, and southern river otters of Patagonia and southern Chile. The fourth endangered species was the marine otter or chungungo, a little-known but beautiful animal of Chilean and Peruvian coastal waters. All these species were reported to be under severe hunting pressure: even in areas where they were legally protected there was little chance of their survival, for their skins were valuable and could readily be disposed of in the black market.

The Surinam meeting heard good news of two species of otters on the Malay peninsula; the large Indian smooth-coated and the smaller short-clawed otter both seemed to be surviving well. While smooth-coated otters remained in their coastal mangrove swamps and forest rivers, short-clawed otters had adapted to agriculture and were flourishing in rice paddies and irrigation canals. South African otters too were reported to be plentiful at low densities in Natal, and did not appear to be endangered there. However, the otter specialist group concluded that the ecology of neither Asian nor African species was well enough known, and that further studies were needed in case their numbers began falling to critically low levels.

It was the business of the specialists to recommend courses of action to the Survival Service Commission of IUCN – action that could be taken by IUCN and the World Wildlife Fund to ensure the protection of endangered otter species. This they did; recognizing that most of the danger to the threatened species lay in illegal hunting for furs, which could be controlled only with difficulty on the spot, they placed emphasis on stricter control of the trade in furs, mostly through the enforcement of existing legislation Their recommendations were incorporated into the Survival Service Commission's Outline Action Programme 1976/79, to be put into effect as soon as possible.

In order of priority SSC listed first the three most endangered species of Latin America – the giant otter, southern river otter and marine otter – recommending that all governments in whose territories these species remained should be urged to enforce existing protective legislation, including bans on the export of skins, and to support field projects and surveys and the establishment, where possible, of new reserves. The Commission mentioned especially the Peruvian Manu National Park, where WWF grants were already helping to provide sanctuary for giant and river otters, and the Chiloe Island Survey, also assisted by WWF, involving southern river and marine otters.

Much the same measures were recommended for La Plata otters, with an additional note on the need for control of river pollution where it was known to affect this species. There was a stong recommendation that more pressure be brought to bear on all countries to adhere to the terms of CITES – the Convention on International Trade in Endangered Species of Wild Fauna and Flora (see chapter 20) – which lists marine, giant, La Plata and southern river otters, together with European, southern sea and Cameroon clawless otters, in its Appendix I ('species which are threatened with extinction and are or may be by trade' and therefore authorized for trading only in exceptional circumstances).

The Survival Service Commission's Action Programme also urged, at a lower level of priority, protective measures for European otters including a precautionary ban on all hunting and trapping, and further surveys into their status. Finally, taxonomic studies and surveys were recommended for the African clawless otter, the status of which remained uncertain over much of its range.

Through its contacts with IUCN the World Wildlife Fund has already contributed substantially to the welfare of otters, and many of its current projects in South America and elsewhere, designed to provide safe habitats for a range of indigenous animals, include otters incidentally among the species that benefit. But no less important and effective is WWF's continuing support for IUCN in its fight, through CITES, to destroy the illicit trade in the skins of threatened species, a fight which is ultimately to the benefit of every species of otter.

While fairly plentiful in parts of Britain and Europe, European common otters are declining in numbers. Interference and harassment from man, river pollution and loss of cover are among their main problems.

CROCODILES AND ALLIGATORS

C ROCODILES AND ALLIGATORS are by no means everybody's idea of animals worth saving. Like snakes and lizards they are reptiles – hard-skinned, hard-eyed, cold-blooded animals that many people find repellent on sight. They are ferocious reptiles, making no secret of their formidable teeth and rat-trap jaws. Some are big and powerful – much bigger than a man, and quite strong enough to pull a pony or young buffalo under water and drown it. As man-killers and cattle thieves they have a proven record. We would be horrified – we'd call out the police, the fire brigade, the army – anything to get rid of them if they took up residence in the Thames or Lake Geneva. So who wants crocodiles and alligators? Why should we bother to protect them?

It is a curious fact that despite their personal un-popularity, millions of people want crocodiles, for many different reasons. Zoologists and animal enthusiasts favour them just because they are animals – interesting, venerable creatures with a long fossil history going back to the dinosaurs and beyond. Conservationists want them because they are threatened, and any species lost to the world can never be recovered. Many people want them simply because they are there – rather *there* than *here* perhaps, but part of a world heritage that should be handed on, and not lost casually through our greed, negligence, or lack of wit to save them. And in a sombre world any animal with a cheerful grin – even a crocodile grin – should surely be encouraged.

But it is quite clear also that many people want to save crocodiles and alligators most of all for their skins, which can be tanned into leather, polished, and made into shoes, handbags, and a host of other fashion goods. To judge by the trade statistics – by the numbers of skins that pass

American crocodiles. In crocodiles, the large teeth fourth from the front on either side fit into a notch on the upper jaw, and can be seen when the jaws are closed.

Stuffed caimans in a souvenir shop in Guadeloupe.
Hunted for their meat and skins, and sold to tourists as
souvenirs, the small crocodiles of South America suffer
severe predation from man.

legally from one country to another, and the enormous
additional numbers known to be smuggled, and the
rapidly escalating value of skins – there are hundreds of
thousands, perhaps millions, of people who would find the
world a poorer place if crocodiles and alligators
disappeared.

Armies of legal hunters and perhaps as many poachers
would be out of a job. Traders, tanners, carriers and
factory workers would need to find alternatives, and the
thousands who buy crocodile leather articles would be
disappointed. All of this could happen fairly soon, for the
demand for crocodile leather far exceeds the amount that
crocodiles caught in the wild can supply. As recent
IUCN-sponsored surveys have shown, every accessible
species is at risk, most are endangered, and several may
already be lost. In almost every case, hunting for skins is
the prime cause.

Zoologically the crocodiles and their kin form the
Order Crocodylia, one of the four orders of living reptiles.

An ancient group, their history goes back at least 190
million years; there were recognizable crocodiles in the
Upper Cretaceous, and the order was far more widespread
and varied in late Mesozoic and early Tertiary times than it
is at present. They shared ancestors with the dinosaurs, and
lived through the long period of evolutionary history
when these and other great reptiles ruled the world.
Crocodiles survived then, and through the turmoils that
swept away the ruling reptiles at the end of the Mesozoic,
by taking early to the unique life-style that they adopt
today. They live half-immersed in lakes, rivers and
estuaries, coming ashore to bask in the sun and lay their
eggs, returning to the water to cool off and feed. Protected
by tough leather and bony armour-plating they live
quietly, seldom exerting themselves, and in every way
keeping the lowest of low profiles.

The Order Crocodylia is divided into three families, all
loosely known as crocodiles but with other common
names that help to differentiate them. The Alligatoridae
include the two species of alligators (American and
Chinese) and five species of caimans, all of South and
Central America. The Crocodylidae or true crocodiles are
similar in size and shape to alligators, but distinguished by
having prominent lower teeth (the fourth from the front

on either side) visible when the mouth is closed. True crocodiles are more cosmopolitan than alligators. There are eleven species of the genus *Crocodylus*, distributed in North, Central and South America, Africa, India and Australasia, and two further genera, each of a single species, in Africa and south-eastern Asia. The third family, Gavialidae, has only one species, the long-snouted gavial of the Ganges, Brahmaputra and other great rivers of the Indian subcontinent.

Crocodiles live largely on fish and waterfowl, and big ones take mammals from the shore. Lying in the shallows like derelict logs, with only eyes and nostrils above water, they are well positioned to catch animals coming down to drink. A snap of the jaws or a whisk of the powerful tail secures their prey, which they drag into the water and drown. Crocodiles lack the complex facial muscles of a mammal and cannot chew. But they can hold their prey in a dogged grip and tear away chunks by twisting their whole body. In this way they deal with carcasses of buffalo and other large animals. An antelope drowned at the river's edge may be held for days in an underwater larder, and returned to at intervals as it softens and rots. Lesser crocodiles take fish, frogs, turtles and other small prey. Long-snouted gavials feed almost entirely on fish, which

Alligators and crocodiles feed mainly on live prey, mostly fish and amphibians caught in the water. Only the largest can tackle big mammals, including man.

Overleaf Hatching crocodiles.

their needle-sharp teeth are well adapted to catch and hold.

Crocodiles are normally quiet animals, but some – Nile crocodiles for example – roar and bellow at mating time. They mate in the water, and the females climb well up the beaches to lay their eggs, often in traditional areas where nesting has been successful before. Some lay in sand pits, others in nests of vegetation, where the eggs can remain warm and at a reasonably constant temperature. Nile crocodile mothers keep watch over their eggs, driving off potential predators for the three to four months of incubation. Nest thieves include mongooses, monitors and man, for fresh crocodile eggs make good eating and are a useful source of protein and fat for hungry villagers. Mothers that protect their eggs successfully through the hazards of incubation have the privilege of taking their twenty to thirty hatchlings down to water and swimming with them, with all the maternal fervour of a mother duck or swan. This is their period of greatest danger, for small

crocodiles are practically defenceless; the threat of being eaten, especially by other crocodiles, decreases rapidly as they grow.

Compared with lizards or turtles, modern crocodiles are advanced reptiles, with several mammal-like features that increase their efficiency – for example a four-chambered heart, and a hard bony palate that allows them to breathe as they feed. Many have behaviour patterns that effectively keep their body temperature high and relatively constant like a mammal's, yet use little fuel – far less than a mammal of equivalent weight – and need to eat only at intervals of several days.

By living in wetlands and swamps, often in countries where malaria, bilharzia and other tropical diseases were rife, crocodiles managed largely to escape the main impact of the human population explosion – we had no particular use for their land, and dispossessed them only where they interfered with our own welfare or that of our cattle. This has not stopped us crowding them in other ways, for example by building dams, diverting rivers, draining land, developing agriculture and polluting the water they live in. Hundreds are killed each year for folk medicine (the gall bladder is particularly valued) and for meat; egg stealing accounts for thousands more, and there is even a brisk trade in baby crocodiles between South and North America – they make cute pets, though only for a few months until they grow big and start biting.

However, in the view of the IUCN study group who advise on crocodiles, the continuing demand for skins is the one factor most likely to decide their fate; successful crocodile conservation depends mainly on wise control and management of the skin trade. Knowing more of their biology will also help; surprisingly little research has so far been done, least of all on the endangered species. WWF has been helping to support crocodile study projects in South America and elsewhere, and basic knowledge about these strange, ancient animals is slowly building up.

Until recently, for example, little was known about the black caiman, except that it could be found throughout the whole Amazon river basin and that, measuring $4\frac{1}{2}$ metres (15 ft), it is the longest caiman species of all. Now it is known to be seriously endangered. A few years ago biologists found that possibly the last undisturbed population of black caimans lived within the Manu National Park of Peru (chapter 3), and it was here that WWF supported a study of the species. The black caiman's optimal habitat was found to be low-lying grassy savannas that are periodically inundated during the rains. These are fertile lands, optimal for cattle-raising too, and the species has suffered from the extension of cattle ranging over much of its normal habitat. So today, it is more likely to be found in marsh-bordered ox-bow lakes, well away from ranching and human habitation.

Caimans use the rivers too, but mating, egg-laying and the development of young are more or less confined to the small lakes where there are no strong currents, and flash floods pose little threat. Black caimans have a menu of twenty-three species of fish. Although these were their major foods, caimans living near villages sometimes made themselves unpopular by grabbing domestic animals coming down to the water to drink.

The WWF-sponsored research group managed to capture, mark and release the entire caiman population of a single lake, and over three years monitored the development and growth of the animals. Wider surveys showed very few black caiman left elsewhere in the region, emphasizing the importance of the Manu National Park population and its future protection

The report from this study advocated a moratorium on caiman exploitation for at least eight years. It suggested that all skins in the process of tanning or export be registered, and that after the moratorium, stricter controls were needed on hunting, for example annually renewable licences, restrictions on size of animals taken, registration of all skins, and severe punishments for offenders. The report concluded that the greatest benefit to the black caiman would come from a programme of conservation education, drawing everyone's attention to its plight.

Less hopeful was a report on two smaller species of caiman under heavy hunting pressure on the eastern plains. Paraguay and broad-nosed caimans, once plentiful throughout temperate South America, are now restricted to small, patchy populations in areas well away from human settlements. One such area is the northern Argentine inland province of Corrientes, a huge area of rolling grassland and swamp. There in 1979 World Wildlife Fund contributed to a survey of the density and distribution of the two species, in cooperation with the US Fish and Wildlife Service and the New York Zoological Society.

Surveying caimans is not easy, especially in cool weather, when they tend to stay in the relatively warm water of the marshes. Only on sunny days would they haul out to be counted. The surveyors travelled the difficult country on foot or on horseback, and occasionally by canoe; interviewing hunters and hide-buyers they became aware of the huge network of industry dedicated to killing caimans – about 20,000 per year was their estimate – and sending the skins to Buenos Aires for the international market. They concluded, sadly but realistically, that broad-nosed caimans (the more popular species in the trade) were very seriously reduced and Paraguay caimans were diminishing fast. Further, the industry would continue despite conservation laws, and the final refuge of the caimans, deep in the heart of featureless swamp, would ultimately be invaded by the poachers.

They fixed their only hope on a programme of education in local schools that might ultimately turn a tide of public opinion against the slaughter.

The importance of thorough ecological study was demonstrated by a WWF-supported project on the Orinoco crocodile. This species, formerly widespread in the Amazon and Orinoco river systems, is now confined to a few parts of Colombia (where it is all but extinct) and restricted areas of Venezuela. Large-scale commercial hunting of the Orinoco crocodile began in the early 1930s, but by 1950 had virtually ceased because there were too few left to support the hunters.

Orinoco crocodiles do not fit readily into refuges, for their behaviour changes with the seasons and with age: more is needed than just a length of likely-looking river. Juveniles live in slow-moving water where they can swim without too much effort against the current and hide from

Armour-plated, low-slung, well camouflaged and equipped with formidable teeth, crocodiles are survivors from the Age of Reptiles.

Overleaf Siamese crocodiles breed well in this Thailand reptile farm: young ones can be raised for release into the wild, for sale to zoos, or for the skin market.

predators among the abundant aquatic vegetation; for small crocodiles, 'predators' always include their own kin. Adults inhabit the large rivers between the rainy seasons, but when the floods come both they and their fish prey retreat to the slower waters. When the rivers are down during the dry season they aestivate – the summer equivalent of hibernation – in small caves below the river banks: there are usually plenty of these, formed by the strong currents of the previous season's floods.

Areas set aside to protect a population of Orinoco

In the Everglades, Florida, an alligator attacks a baby egret.

crocodiles must provide for all these eventualities. For this species, however, reserves may come too late. A WWF survey in Colombia showed only a few hundred Orinoco crocodiles remaining – a density of barely one every 900 km². They may well have reached a stage where adults are so widely scattered that they stand little chance of meeting each other for breeding. Unfortunately there is little indication that their numbers will increase. Although legally protected, large crocodiles are sought and killed as a precaution to save domestic animals, and their skins command very high prices on the black market. The one remaining hope for the Orinoco crocodile is captive breeding (see below). But rearing crocodiles and releasing them at present would be a waste of time. Before such a scheme can be really successful, far more protected areas will be needed, guardianship assured, and the trade in skins eradicated or at least brought under control.

Many other species of crocodiles and alligators throughout the world have been surveyed during the past decade and found to be suffering severely from over-hunting. Australian saltwater and freshwater crocodiles, muggers or marsh crocodiles of India, gavials of northern India, American alligators, Cuban crocodiles, Morelet's crocodile of Mexico – with fifteen species listed in CITES Appendix I (threatened with extinction and possibly by trade) and all others in Appendix II (threatened by uncontrolled trading), every known species is seriously at risk now or heading rapidly into danger as the demand for skins persists. Only rarely is it possible for a government to take effective action in the field. Is there no hope for their survival?

Crocodiles are in fact great survivors, as their long history in a turbulent world testifies. They outlived the dinosaurs, and given half a chance they may well outlive the tiresome ape that has been troubling them throughout the twentieth century. Fecund animals with efficient reproduction, they have the capacity to replenish numbers quickly if they and their environment are left alone: an effective five-to-ten year ban on hunting is often enough to secure the recovery of a threatened stock. But they cannot recover while hunting pressures are intense, and their habitat requirements are simple but absolute: drain their wetlands, and you destroy the crocodiles as surely as by shooting them.

But given some environmental protection and periodic relief from hunters, crocodiles stand a good chance of recovery – a chance that can be improved by artificial rearing. With care and attention practically all crocodiles seem amenable to breeding in captivity. In the right circumstances eggs can be incubated and young crocodiles

reared to adulthood without undue difficulty. Animals raised in this way can be grown to a safe size and released into the wild, to replenish stocks where the hunters have been over-zealous. Re-stocking has for long been practised in South Africa by the conservation-conscious Natal Parks Board, and in Zimbabwe, where considerable numbers of Nile crocodiles are reared from eggs and released each year.

Or the young animal can be reared to economic size and slaughtered. Crocodile farming for meat and skins is a well-established industry in parts of south-east Asia, and farming may well provide an increasing proportion of the crocodile skins that enter world markets in the future.

Estuarine crocodiles, wearing perhaps the most valuable of all crocodile skins, are hunted to destruction in India, Sri Lanka and elsewhere in their extensive range. But in Papua New Guinea, estuarine and other species of crocodiles are farmed in village-based rearing programmes. Hatchlings are collected from the wild and kept in pens where they grow rapidly until large enough to be released into the wild: many can then be slaughtered and sold later for their hides and meat. This programme saves baby crocodiles that would otherwise certainly be lost to predators, increasing the overall population, and incidentally encourages villagers to protect their local stocks of adults, which provide the supply of hatchlings.

Schemes like this have not gained universal approval because of the difficulty in distinguishing legitimate skins on the market from illegally poached ones, and any measures from which poachers may benefit, even marginally, may in the end do more harm than good. The Crocodile Specialist Group of IUCN, helped by WWF funding, is keeping an eye on this and other possible developments, in its constant fight to save these ugly, engaging beasts for future generations to shudder at.

An Asian tusker in the grasslands of Assam.

SAVANNA AND DESERT

SAVANNA RESCUE

AT THE HEART OF every habitable continent lies a grassland. The Eurasian steppes, North American prairies, Australian outback, African savanna, and the pampas, punas and campos of South America are all grasslands, dominated by grasses, herbs and shrubs, and kept in trim by millions of grazing animals. Antelope, gazelle, bison, buffalo, zebras, horses, kangaroos, elephants, and several kinds of deer, rhino and wild sheep are grassland grazers, with grinding teeth and complex guts especially adapted for digesting cellulose in bulk. The grazing herds in turn support predators – lions, tigers, wolves, dogs, hyaenas, eagles and vultures. Grasslands are never so rich in species as rainforests, but they are far more accessible. There have been few animal communities so spectacular – or so readily destroyed – as those that wandered the great grasslands of the world during the early nineteenth century.

Accessibility was their undoing. Primitive man lived easily with the game herds, taking part of his living from them. Industrial man saw no immediate use for the herds except as ready sources of food and game, and he wanted their land to grow crops more directly useful to him than grass. Easily cleared by burning, simple to till and improve, the temperate grasslands have been taken over wholesale for cereal growing and as rangelands for cattle; there is little left today of natural pampas, prairies or steppes. The tropical grasslands too have been modified, the damper areas for crops, the drier areas for cattle-raising, and remaining regions of savanna are under constant threat of conversion to farmland as human populations spill on to them. In little more than a century most of the huge game herds have disappeared. But the tropical grasslands and the grazing animals that are left are still spectacular and productive, and all the more precious for their scarcity.

Burchell's zebras drinking at a savanna waterhole, Namibia.

Grasslands grow where there is enough rainfall to support small, rapidly maturing vegetation but not enough to grow forest. Their quality depends on soils, seasons and a host of other factors. They grow at any altitude from sea level to the mountain tops; 'alps' are high mountain grasslands where cattle may graze in summer. Some are treeless, others parklands with scattered stands of trees – often drought-resistant species like the acacias and baobabs of Africa, mesquite of North America and salt-bush, wattles and gums of Australia. The grazing herds help to keep the grass growing, keeping the minerals circulating with a constant top dressing of manure.

Grasses have one simple but important property: they grow from the base, rather than from the tips of their shoots. Lawn-mowing would be lethal if they did not; so would the constant cropping of grazing animals, and the flash-fires started by lightning that often sweep across savanna and steppe. So grass thrives on being eaten and trampled. Its root systems, often extensive and deep, protect the soil from wind and run-off, and its seeds, wind-fertilized and tough, lie dormant through long dry seasons to shoot in response to rain. There are many forms and species of grass. In rich dark soils grow the tall perennial grasses, higher than a man; on poorer, drier soils grow the short annuals and perennials that feed the hungry hordes of grazers.

Grass and the grazing animals evolved together. The earliest known bunch-grasses appeared in Miocene times some twenty-five million years ago. And small ancestral horses were beginning to develop the high-crowned teeth and elongate middle toes that were to make their descendants – the later horses, asses and zebras – successful grassland animals. Ancestral cattle, antelopes, sheep and goats, with complex, self-sharpening grinding molars and ruminant stomachs appeared a little later. These were all long-legged creatures, poised on the tips of their toes for fast travel over long distances. The marsupial mammals of Australasia evolved a rather different, down-under version of grassland grazers – the plains kangaroos, ecologically counterparts of the deer and antelope. Flightless birds too evolved long legs and complex digestions for life on the grasslands: so developed the ostriches, emus and rheas that are still with us today, and the moas that colonized New Zealand until their destruction by man.

Grazers and browsers that inhabit the grasslands feed together in separate or mixed herds. Often half a dozen species or more can be seen cropping the vegetation side by side, with no two species feeding in quite the same way.

Springbok, grazing antelopes of the dry African grasslands. Feeding well on poor pastures, springbok and other game animals are more efficient than cattle under semi-drought conditions.

On the tropical grasslands giraffes browse loftily in the treetops, eland and gerenuk reach high up the sides of the savanna trees and shrubs, dik-diks browse leaves from the lowest branches. Buffaloes and elephants take long, coarse grasses, impala the fine savanna woodland grasses, zebra and wildebeeste the mixed pasture grasses of the open plains. Each species selects carefully; what one leaves another takes, so between them they make highly effective use of the vegetation available. Warthogs eat anything left over, gouging out the roots when all else has gone.

This division of interests ensures that wild animals make excellent use of the savanna, more efficient use on the whole than man with his agriculture and stock-raising. Only about one ton of domestic cattle replace three to four tons of wild herbivores on a good stretch of savanna grassland. Domestic stock tends to overgraze, particularly when held for too long in a limited area, and many hectares of marginal grassland have been degraded to desert by the over-cropping of cattle, sheep and goats (chapter 14).

Grasslands may have to accommodate several months of drought each year, and the drying-off of vegetation forces the large herbivores into mass migration. The huge-scale annual movements of millions of American bison or South African springbok are no more, but the Serengeti, the large savanna reserve of northern Tanzania, can still provide the spectacle of thousands of wildebeeste and zebras on the move during the dry season.

The fortunes of these great African herds and the World Wildlife Fund are curiously linked. It was concern for East African wildlife that precipitated the formation of WWF (chapter 1), and the interest of Prime Minister Julius Nyerere of Tanganyika (later President Nyerere of Tanzania), at a critical stage in its development, that ensured the continuing integrity of the Serengeti as an African wildlife sanctuary. The Serengeti has always been a special interest of WWF, attracting financial and other support that, over the years, has helped it to develop as a major centre of wildlife management and research. So we have come to know more of grassland ecology in Africa than in any other continent.

When the boundaries of the Serengeti National Park were first drawn up, little was known of the great annual migrations or their significance in the lives of the grassland animals, and important sections of the traditional migration route were left out. This gave hunters, who were forbidden the Park, a chance to catch the animals along the route: in the Ikoma area north of the western corridor, and the Lamai 'wedge' linking the Serengeti with Kenya's Mara reserve, the poachers built huts and settled in, taking a heavy toll as the animals came past. WWF helped to provide a planning expert to demarcate the areas needing protection. The settlers were

moved, Lamai was brought within the boundary of the Park, and WWF provided additional funds for new staff quarters, field radios and a vehicle.

In 1962 the Serengeti Research Institute was established as a centre for scientists from all over the world to work on tropical grassland ecology. Recognizing the basic importance of the grasses and other vegetation, World Wildlife Fund supported an aerial photo-ecological study, using survey photographs to monitor short- and long-term changes in plant distribution – the kind of information on which good management plans could be established.

This study quickly yielded results, showing, for example that elephants crowding into northern areas of the Park (possibly because of human pressures outside) were inflicting permanent damage: high density and inability to move on caused them to over-browse and seriously degrade the vegetation, ultimately to their own detriment. A rather similar problem was identified in Tsavo National Park, where overcrowded elephants were destroying both their habitat and their own chances of

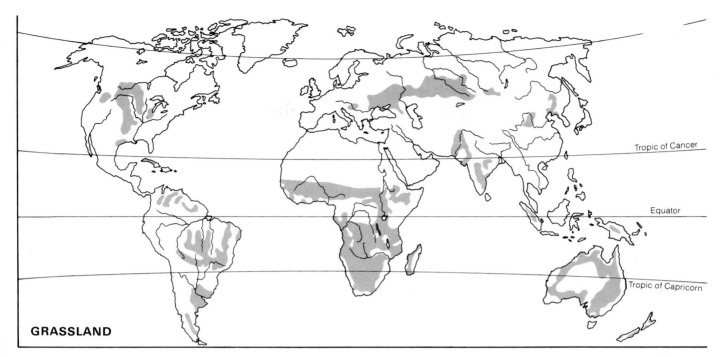

GRASSLAND

Tropic of Cancer

Equator

Tropic of Capricorn

Migrating gnus in their
thousands converge in
columns across the vast
plains of the Serengeti.

Above An antelope throttled by a wire snare. Poaching is a constant threat to the herds of grassland mammals.

Right A small herd of vicuna in the Pampa Galeras Reserve. Formerly hunted severely for their rich fleece, these animals are now increasing.

survival. While management plans were being adjusted to meet this threat, poaching for ivory intensified: the elephant problem was solved, though not in a way that the Park authorities appreciated.

Poaching, the perennial problem in all the grassland parks and reserves, is a constant challenge to the authorities and a drain on resources. Animals are killed mostly for meat, for which there is always a ready market in nearby towns: steaks command as high a price in African restaurants as anywhere else. Skins, and such special commodities as elephant ivory (p. 146) and rhino horn (p. 60) also attract the poachers, who work in formidable, well-armed gangs. Their methods cut across any plans for organized culling that the Park authorities may have; involving snares and traps, they are often inhumane and wasteful. WWF has always given priority to assisting Park authorities in their fight to reduce poaching: many grants have been given to provide extra guards, uniforms, aircraft, radios, vehicles, boats and other anti-poaching facilities. A little help can be highly effective: the Director of Tanzania's National Parks reported that, in 1975, over 400 poachers were arrested in the Serengeti, and more than 3,000 snares confiscated, with the aid of two vehicles provided by WWF.

Lions, leopards and cheetahs are the big cats of the African savannas, and the major predators of the game herds. Elegant in their spotted skins, leopards and cheetahs have become prime targets for poachers throughout

Africa (chapter 17): there is a world market for their furs, and enough are taken annually from African grasslands to make their future uncertain. In 1971–3 WWF supported a survey on the status of leopards, cheetahs and other species known or thought to be depleted, with funding primed by the International Fur Trade Federation. Dr Norman Myers, an ecologist working in Kenya, travelled throughout East and southern Africa in pursuit of evidence. He concluded that, despite hunting pressures, leopards were widespread and maintaining their numbers well, while cheetahs were seriously at risk, with loss of habitat and poaching their main sources of danger.

Secretive, adaptable, and seldom seen by day, leopards were not an easy target for poachers, though their habits of scavenging and storing food made them relatively easy to

trap or poison. Some stocks were locally depleted, but on the whole leopards were keeping up their numbers, often in continuing close contact with man. Complementary to this survey, WWF in 1973–4 helped to finance an ecological study of leopards in Kruger National Park, South Africa, when some of the secrets of their solitary lives were revealed.

In contrast to leopards, cheetahs were found to be diurnal hunters of the open plains, skilled in the chase but far less adaptable to environmental changes. Needing space and living at low densities, only a few could ever be protected in parks and reserves, and human disturbance, agriculture and hunting would take their toll of the rest. Dr Myers indicated a fifty per cent decrease in cheetah numbers since 1960, and expected the population to be halved again in a further decade. Poaching pressures on this species for the world fur trade are still high. In 1978 Hong Kong customs officers seized 336 cheetah skins, probably of African origin, consigned by a Swiss company despite the species' endangered status and its protection by international agreement.

Because the African grasslands can support more wild livestock than domestic animals, attempts have been made to encourage game ranching – for meat, hides and other products, and also to provide facilities for tourism, sport, hunting and fishing, game-watching and photography. Experiments have been tried in Zimbabwe, South Africa and Kenya, and in 1974 WWF supported an assessment of game ranching by Dr Archie Mossman, one of its pioneers, and Sue Lee-Mossman.

An African lioness – who probably made the kill – looks on while her mate feeds in the Kalahari, southern Africa.

Their report indicated that the full potential of this kind of management had nowhere been realized. While the 'safari' side of game ranching was often developed, for example, the meat production side was not – this despite high productivity in the animals and a dearth of protein in local communities. 'The potential of game ranching to provide food for protein-hungry people on a sustained basis has hardly been tested as yet in southern Africa', wrote the Mossmans. 'It is largely through the appeal to the common man's stomach that multiple species wildlife utilization will fulfil its two greatest values, the feeding and welfare of people and the conservation of wildlife and its habitats.'

Asia's tropical grasslands are mostly Indian and mostly man-made, following the cutting of the forest and centuries of grazing and cultivation. Indian antelope or blackbuck lived in great herds on the plains as little as half a century ago, but now only a few thousand survive. Chinkora or Indian gazelle, which formerly lived in semi-desert, have also taken to the grasslands: these too are severely depleted and threatened. Most of India's grazing species now survive in reserves, often on land set aside under 'Operation Tiger' (chapter 4). In one of the best tiger reserves, Kanha National Park of central India, WWF was able to snatch a unique subspecies of barasingha ('12 pointer') or swamp deer from almost certain extinction (p. 169).

There is little enough left of the Eurasian grasslands or their fauna, but one species, the saiga antelope, is a success story for conservation. During the Ice Age, saiga, woolly rhinoceroses and mammoths shared the steppes, and saiga were still abundant in huge migratory herds during the nineteenth century. By the end of the First World War there were barely 1,000 left, mostly in Russia, and their extinction seemed inevitable. However, the new Soviet government banned all hunting of saiga and, under the direction of Dr Andrei Bannikov, management plans for the species were gradually evolved. Despite hard winters when wolves and extreme cold exacted their toll, the saiga increased in number. Now there are probably two million of them in the grasslands of the Soviet Union, yielding a harvest of up to 300,000 skins and carcasses each year. Dr Bannikov has been awarded the WWF Gold Medal for his conservation work.

North American grasslands too are practically obliterated, their place taken by crops of cereals, stock ranches and burgeoning prairie cities. A few thousand bison and pronghorn antelopes, mostly confined to reserves, are all that remain of the once great herds. Similarly, there is little left of the rich grassland wildlife of South America. The pampas or temperate grasslands of Argentina had a unique fauna including deer, tunnelling rodents, maned wolves, armadillos and ostrich-like rheas: most of the large animals have been destroyed and nearly all of the pampas themselves have been ploughed up or turned into rangelands for cattle and sheep.

Early explorers reported huge herds of pampas deer, but commercial hunting and disease destroyed them long ago. In the single decade 1860–70 over two million skins of this species were traded, and livestock diseases imported with the cattle destroyed many thousands of animals. All three subspecies of pampas deer were listed as endangered in IUCN's Red Data Book, and in 1976 WWF took urgent action to save the southernmost subspecies, which was reduced almost to extinction. Dr John Jackson, a British biologist, worked with the Argentine Wildlife Foundation to set up a number of reserves and encourage the interest of the local people: though still numbering only a few hundred, the southern pampas deer has probably been saved.

Another rare species of grassland is the maned wolf, a dog-like animal that ranges from southern Brazil to northern Argentina. Studying it in Brazil's Serra da Canastra National Park, in a WWF-assisted project, Dr James Dietz has captured and fitted radio collars to several animals. Though branded as killers of livestock, maned wolves feed mostly on wild guinea pigs and other small mammals and birds. Many are killed by local farmers and hunters, and Dr Dietz sees little future for the species unless public attitudes toward it can be changed.

The world's highest savannas are the treeless punas of the central Andes, found at 4,000 metres (13,000 ft) and above in Chile, Peru, Argentina and Bolivia. Cold, windy

and wet, these are the home of the vicuna, a small graceful relation of the camel that lives in wild flocks high on the upland pastures. Vicuna fleece is the finest, warmest wool in the world. To the ancient Incas, who caught and sheared vicunas, it was the Royal Fleece. Modern Europeans and Americans prize it almost as highly: its popularity shortly after the Second World War led to the poaching and slaughter of some 400,000 vicunas for their fleeces. By the mid 1960s only about 15,000 were left in the wild, just over half of them in Peru, and the species appeared to be doomed.

The Peruvian government banned all further export of vicuna wool, and Britain and the US ceased to import it. Help with conservation measures came to Peru from the Federal Republic of Germany and IUCN/WWF, and the other Andean countries joined in an overall effort to save

Zebras, giraffes and warthogs gain some of their water from vegetation, but travel long distances each day to drink at waterholes among the semi-desert scrub.

vicunas. Now the species is again on its feet: there are probably well over 70,000 in the high Andes, with over 60,000 in the Peruvian Pampa Galeras National Reserve alone, where in 1964 there were fewer than 1,000. The Peruvian government is hoping to manage vicuna stocks for their wool and meat, with more of the profits accruing to the poor mountain communities that live in vicuna country.

ELEPHANT STORY

A HERD OF ELEPHANTS, swinging across the plains of Africa against a backdrop of snow-capped Kilimanjaro – this is the picture of African wildlife that every photographer, amateur or professional, wants for his own collection. There can be few sights so majestic and timeless; we share the awe that early man must have felt when he was part of the same scene a hundred thousand years ago.

In real life it is a motion picture. The herd – usually cows and juveniles under a matriarch leader – push slowly forward along a well-trodden path with ears flapping and trunks swinging, their little ones trotting among the moving forest of legs. It is late afternoon and time for a drink at the waterhole. Approaching through the bushes they pause with trunks raised to sniff for danger, then amble down to the water's edge. The young ones, hot and thirsty, push forward and sink almost to eye level, splashing and cavorting. For adults the serious business of drinking comes first: they suck up huge draughts of water, and only then spray themselves and each other as the edge of the pool becomes murky.

Finally they back out, blowing great clouds of dust over their flanks as they move away across the plain. Herds of zebra and gazelle part company to clear their path. Rhinos move aside; lions, leopards and hyaenas watch from the shade, but keep well out of the way. The elephant may not be King of Beasts, but he commands respect that kings would envy.

African elephants and their smaller Asiatic cousins are the last survivors of a much wider variety of trunked animals that roamed the late Tertiary world. Most of the earlier forms, the mastodons, gomphotheres and several kinds of mammoths, were already extinct before man appeared, but others persisted into the Stone Age. Woolly

Asian elephants, distinguishable from African by their smaller ears and tusks.

mammoths, with their thick, double-layered coat, towering skull and massive tusks, inspired cave artists in Europe and Asia; their carcasses have been dug, perfectly preserved, from the deep-frozen soils of northern Siberia and Alaska. Cro-Magnon man's cave paintings showed the mammoth being hunted; he more than anything else was probably responsible for its final extinction some twenty thousand years ago.

The two surviving forms of elephant are similar, with just a few small important points of difference. African elephants are larger, weighing up to $7\frac{1}{2}$ tonnes and standing 3 to 4 metres (9 to 13 ft) at the shoulder: they have large, flapping ears, a sloping or sagging back, and two sensitive 'fingers' on the tip of the trunk. Asiatic elephants are more compact, weighing up to 5 tonnes and standing no more than 3 metres. Their ears are small, they have a domed back and only a single trunk-finger. In African elephants both sexes have large tusks: in Asiatic elephants some males have small tusks, others only rudimentary ones like their females. And by a curious dispensation for which generations of zoology students

have been thankful, the huge molars of an Asiatic (Indian) elephant are identified with an 'I' on the grinding surface, those of African elephants with two rows of 'A's' joined at the base.

Elephants use their trunk – a muscular nose and upper lip combined – mainly for feeding, but it is also an all-purpose appendage, as sensitive and useful as a hand and arm. It can grasp large branches, pick up logs, tear bark and pull stalks of grass: it can also pull one tiny, ripe fruit from a bunch, or pick a single palatable leaf from the ground. It is an adjustable sniffer for sensing the atmosphere, a pneumatic hose that sucks and blows liquids and dust, a delicate hand for caressing, and a trumpet for sounding elephantine fanfares.

The tusks are vastly overgrown incisor teeth. Up to 3 metres long, they are virtually solid for two thirds of their length, and can weigh well over 50 kg each. Their substance is ivory, hard and resilient, and elephants use them in conjunction with the trunk for holding, tearing, digging, and sometimes for fighting. Man too has uses for ivory, which, like gold, is weighty, long-lasting, and

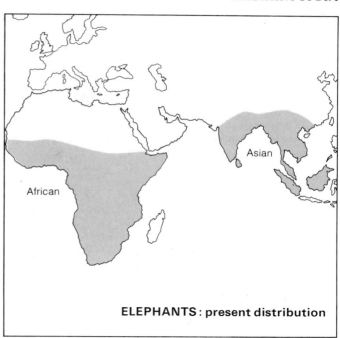

ELEPHANTS: present distribution

Left A parade of African elephants, ears flapping and trunks swinging, makes slow and majestic progress across the savanna. Herds are usually extended family groups of mothers and offspring, led by a dominant female.

capable of taking fine workmanship. As a hedge against inflation it is much in demand, and the fate of elephants – African elephants especially – is closely linked with its value from time to time in world markets.

Asiatic elephants once lived throughout Asia from Mesopotamia in the west to the Yangtse river valley in the east. Until quite recently they could be found anywhere in the forests that extended unbroken from western India to Indonesia. Those forests are now fragmented; there are still wild herds left over much of the range, though their numbers decrease as the forests disappear. Regarded in IUCN as an endangered species, there are probably some 30,000 to 40,000 of them altogether, living and wandering in small groups of five or six together. Though mainly found in the forests, grass seems to be their favourite food; they like the forest edge and clearings, and are particularly attracted to land cleared for agriculture with growing crops.

African elephants are animals of both forest and plain. They bathe in Atlantic surf on the shores of Gabon, and seem equally at home in the inland rainforests of Zaïre.

Best known are the herds that browse across the open savannas of eastern and central Africa; most remarkable are the semi-desert elephants of Mali, on the southern fringes of the Sahara near Timbuktu, which migrate long distances to satisfy their huge appetites for food and water. Listed as vulnerable in IUCN's Red Data Book of endangered species, African elephants are still quite plentiful; there are an estimated 1.3 million of them in the world, though this is probably nowhere near the number that existed even half a century ago. Cows and youngsters are sociable, wandering in small herds of three or four to about twenty under the leadership of one or two older cows. Bulls lead more solitary lives, joining the herds only when one of the females comes on heat and leaving as soon as the excitement is over. Gestation takes almost two years, and the young live a further eight to twelve years or more with their mothers and adoptive aunts before reaching maturity. Cows produce young at intervals of four to six years, and live – if permitted – to ages of fifty to seventy years. Grass, leaves, shoots, bark, and the soft, damp heartwood of savanna trees are their main foods.

Greed for ivory led to the extinction of elephants in North Africa by medieval times, and their severe depletion elsewhere in Africa by the early twentieth century. The last few elephants of Somalia were killed for their tusks as recently as the mid-1950s, and elephants have also been exterminated by hunting from Guinea-Bissau,

Ivory poachers caught by game wardens in a Kenyan national park. Large elephant tusks may provide over 100kg (220lb) of good quality ivory.

Gambia and possibly other African countries. Asiatic elephants have suffered mainly from the acute land hunger and need to grow food of the expanding human populations throughout their range for well over a century. A world without elephants would be unthinkable, and World Wildlife Fund has been deeply involved in helping to save both species.

During the 1960s and 1970s stocks of African elephants fluctuated considerably. Those in protected game parks and reserves increased dramatically in numbers to the point where they were seriously damaging their environment, then collapsed when droughts destroyed their forage. No sooner had stocks recovered than a wave of poaching swept over the reserves, triggered by a sudden demand for ivory. This dated from 1972, when the US dollar lost its links with gold and world finances wobbled. Political instability in Africa fuelled the fire: the price of a kilo of ivory rose from US$7.5 in the late 1960s to US$100 five years later, falling back to US$74 in 1979. The 1970s were accordingly a decade of massacre of elephants throughout Africa. The number killed is unknown, but the weight of ivory coming on to the market indicated that some 50,000 to 100,000 were being slaughtered every year, most of them illegally, and the evidence of their killing was all too plain in every African reserve.

How serious this might be for stocks as a whole could hardly be estimated, for nobody knew how many elephants there were, or how they were distributed about the continent. This was the situation in 1976 when the World Wildlife Fund, IUCN and the New York Zoological Society joined forces in an Africa-wide survey, to establish the status of the species and provide a scientific basis for elephant conservation.

Iain Douglas-Hamilton, a naturalist who had already studied elephants for several years in Tanzania, took charge of the survey. He, his wife Oria and their two small children were already well known, from their life in Lake Manyara National Park, as 'the family that lives with elephants', and his experience proved invaluable in setting up and running the survey. Leaving his forest and day-to-day contact with the elephants he knew so well, Douglas-Hamilton set up an office in Nairobi and established a network of contacts to establish elephant numbers throughout Africa.

An African mudpack: wallowing in damp mud helps an elephant to keep cool.

His work, extending over three years, was enlivened by aerial and ground surveys in which he was helped by a small team of field scientists. One of his young assistants, Dr Kes Hillman, while counting elephants became alarmed at the dramatic decline in the number of rhinos that shared their habitat. Using similar survey techniques, she now leads the Rhino Conservation programme that is currently estimating rhinoceros numbers throughout Africa (chapter 5).

Douglas-Hamilton's report showed a total population of over 1.3 million African elephants, spread over 7.3 million km² (almost 3 million square miles) of savanna and forest south of the Sahara, with stocks extending into thirty-five countries. Most of the elephants were concentrated in four countries: Zaïre and Tanzania each had over 300,000, Zambia and Sudan over 100,000. Three other countries, Kenya, Central Africa Republic and Mozambique, each held over 50,000, and numbers in the rest ranged from 30,000 in Zimbabwe to 80 in Togo. Dr Douglas-Hamilton did not consider the African elephant universally endangered, but was concerned that most countries reported declining numbers and feared that it would disappear shortly from many of its current haunts if present trends continued.

Surveys in some key countries disclosed the terrible toll taken by ivory poachers during the 1970s, the decade of elephant destruction. Of 30,000 living in Uganda in 1970, only about 2,000 remained in 1980: the rest were casualties of poaching during the Amin regime and the war that followed, and the killing was still continuing when the survey team arrived. In Kabalega Falls National Park, Uganda, where the Victoria Nile tumbles through a cleft in the rock only 6 metres wide, just over 1,000 elephants were seen north of the river, little more than one third of the 1971 population; south of the river only 172 remained of a previously estimated 10,000. In the same period neighbouring Kenya, a relatively peaceful and law-abiding country, lost over half of its elephants to poachers. Uganda's Ruwenzori National Park, bordering on Zaïre, could muster only 153 of a population estimated at 2,400 ten years before. Forested countries found it more difficult to count their elephants and estimate losses, but the trade records of importing and exporting countries give a good indication of ivory flow. Central African Republic alone exported 200 tonnes of it in 1976, a figure representing the death of 10,000 to 20,000 elephants, mostly in Zaïre and Sudan.

Ivory poaching is undoubtedly the most immediate threat to elephants, but a more insidious long-term danger is loss of living space, due mainly to deforestation and the spread of farming across their former rangelands. In many African countries human population growth rates are among the highest in the world and the demand for land is insatiable. In Uganda land suitable for elephants to range has been reduced from seventy per cent at the turn of the century to seventeen per cent today. In neighbouring Rwanda, the last non-forest-living elephants were eliminated by government order in 1975: there was simply no room for them within the borders of one of Africa's most densely populated countries. If erosion of their living space continues, the future of African elephants lies mainly in protected conservation areas. Of these there are currently about ninety, sheltering some twenty per cent of the elephant population.

Elephants can thrive well in suitable reserves where food, water and protection are adequate, sometimes reproducing fast and outgrowing their resources. A WWF-sponsored study of elephants in the Luangwa Valley of Zambia showed that, although female elephants mature at about fourteen years and produce young at long intervals, well-fed ones calve more frequently – about every fourth year – than those of poorer country: hence their ability to build up their populations quickly after a decline.

Based on the results of the African elephant survey, WWF and IUCN have now prepared a conservation strategy for presentation to all the countries that support elephant populations. With it go assurances of financial and technical assistance, to make sure it can be carried out. The strategy tackles the two main problems that beset elephant populations – ivory poaching and loss of habitat. Trading in ivory will never die, but it can be regulated by international cooperation between exporting and importing countries to ensure that stocks of elephants are not over-exploited, and that countries rather than poachers are the main beneficiaries of the trade.

With their relatively tiny tusks, Asiatic elephants have less to fear from ivory poachers. Their problem is the dense and still rapidly expanding human population that shares their Asian habitat and is gradually edging them out. Elephants have been displaced altogether from the great flood plains and fertile valleys that were once their birthright. They now live mainly in hill forests that, like the rest of the rainforest, are gradually being eroded for their timber. Scientists who have tried to estimate the remaining wild stocks in IUCN/WWF surveys report a total population of not more than 35,000, including 15,000 in India, 5,000 to 7,000 in Burma, about 2,000 in Sri

Above An African elephant using trunk and tusks to strip bark from a tree. Elephant herds can be extremely destructive, especially in overcrowded conditions on a reserve.

Opposite Nose and upper lip combined, this flexible trunk helps an elephant to reach a wide range of foods, from grass to high branches.

Lanka, and 2,500 to 4,500 in Thailand. Only 300 survive wild in the whole of Indonesia, 250 in Bangladesh, and fewer than 40 in Nepal. Domesticated elephants still play an important role in forestry and ceremonial parades: recent photographs from China show a caravan of elephants taking supplies to the battle zone of Kampuchea.

The problems of Asiatic elephants are typified in Sri Lanka, the beautiful island that for generations has used the elephant as its symbol. There human populations have risen from six million in 1950 to over fourteen today. Haphazard agricultural development, aiming to grow more food as quickly as possible, trapped wild elephants in small pockets of jungle from which, understandably enough, they broke out at night to feed on the new ricefields. Chivvied by angry farmers, and shot with muzzle-loaders, some became rogues and attacked their persecutors. During the 1960s the World Wildlife Fund and Smithsonian Institution sponsored Dr Fred Kurt, a Swiss biologist, to study the elephant populations of Sri Lanka and find out what was needed to allow their continuing coexistence with humans.

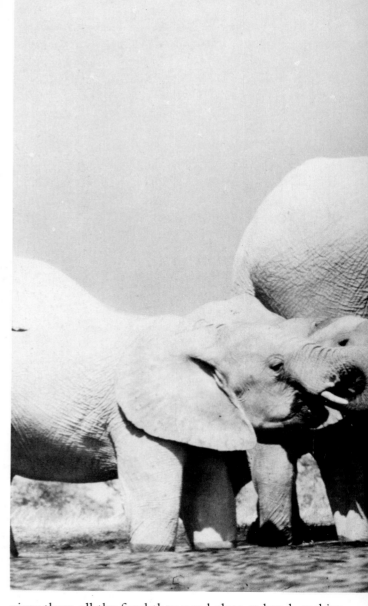

Above Calmed by tranquillizers from a dart-syringe, this Asian elephant wears a radio transmitter collar that transmits its position in dense jungle.

Right A breeding herd of African elephants at a Namibian water hole. Water drawn up the trunk is sprayed to the back of the throat.

In one of Sri Lanka's major development projects, the basin of the Mahoweli, its longest river, is being cleared of forests and converted to agriculture, and the river itself is being dammed to provide irrigation water. To minimize soil erosion the hills surrounding are now carefully maintained as national parks, with their forests dedicated as elephant sanctuaries. Forest corridors are maintained between them and existing sanctuaries, so that the elephants can continue their seasonal migrations unhindered. WWF is helping to determine satisfactory boundaries and solve problems with neighbouring farmers, and has given grants for equipment needed to manage and safeguard the parks.

Where forest clearance is essential the loggers work in harmony with conservation teams. Organized drives move the elephants from areas scheduled for felling along prearranged corridors into the reserves, then cut the forests behind them to keep them there. However, elephants are usually reluctant to stay in old forest when there is felled forest or agricultural land nearby. Dr Robert Olivier, now working in Sri Lanka, formerly studied the movements of elephants in Malaysia. In a WWF-sponsored programme he tranquillized wild elephants, fitted them with radio transmitter collars, and followed their movements from a light aircraft. He found that they cover less ground in the thick secondary forest that develops where the original rainforest has been felled; presumably the new growth

gives them all the food they need close at hand, making longer travel unnecessary.

This could help to account for a problem common to elephant conservationists in both Asia and Africa. Creating reserves for elephant herds may not be easy; but keeping them in bounds is certain to be difficult, for whatever is growing outside the boundaries, whether secondary forest or agricultural produce, will almost certainly mean better pickings for the herds. Elephants are sapient animals, but their approach to the everyday problem of stuffing themselves with food is a direct one. They know nothing of conservation problems and have little use for national park by-laws; healthy elephants see park boundary fences as no more than agreeable challenges to their strength and ingenuity, standing between them and the best food. They make interesting

but unendearing neighbours in Sri Lanka and elsewhere, and the problem of coexisting with them is far from solved.

Throughout both Asia and Africa it is becoming more and more difficult to designate large areas as reserves in which elephants can be confined. Arising from experience in Sri Lanka, Malaysia and Africa, WWF is now helping to develop a concept of 'elephant ranges' centred on national parks or reserves and dedicated to elephant conservation: the reserves provide undisturbed sanctuary, but controlled human activity – forestry, for example – is possible and indeed encouraged in a surrounding buffer zone. These can of course become sanctuaries for many species of animals. With their huge requirement of space, elephants are pre-eminent among species whose conservation serves the interests of other animals. A forest and grassland reserve for elephants, including the range of habitat they require to see them through the year, can also accommodate populations of rhinos, hippos, giraffes, antelopes, lions and leopards and cheetahs in Africa, or the equivalent species including tigers, tapirs, rhinos, deer and wild oxen in Asia. Carefully chosen, for example in critical upland areas, these reserves can be of additional service to man in protecting water supplies and soils, and have a great potential as recreational areas for the growing human population.

THE DESERT MAMMALS

Life in the arid zones of the world from time to time makes news, when a long-term drought in the Sahel, a huge area of Africa south and west of the Sahara Desert, results in the death of man and animals from thirst and starvation. 'Sahel' in Arabic implies 'flat': the Sahel is a plain of sands, stones and bedrock with a sparse covering of soil and patchy vegetation. Its mean annual rainfall ranges from 100 mm in the north, where it borders on the Sahara, to 600 mm in the south where it gives way to scrub, savanna and forest. By definition much of it is desert – land with rainfall of less than 400 mm per year.

If the Sahel remained desert all the time there would be no problem, for humans and their livestock, and all but a few desert animals, would regard it as an extension of the Sahara itself and keep away. But the Sahel is semi-desert, with margins that shift in both space and time. The problem comes not so much with the dearth of rainfall, as with its irregularity. 'Annual rainfall of 400 mm' may mean as much as that falling reliably every year: if so it is enough to promote farming and stock-raising, especially if most of it falls in the cool season when evaporation losses are low. But it can also mean 800 mm one year and nothing the next, or a run of several years with rainfall more than adequate for stock-rearing, followed by two, three or more years with virtually no rain at all. That is what it has recently meant in the Sahel, with devastating consequences for man and animals alike.

Desert and semi-desert – areas of low and irregular rainfall – are by no means devoid of plants and animals. They present challenges for which all kinds of organisms have adapted well, and there are no deserts anywhere in the world, other than the permanent icefields of Greenland and Antarctica, that are entirely without life. Desert shrubs and grasses have root systems that spread far and wide under the soil; dry and stick-like for much of the

Impala, antelopes of the desert edge.

153

time, they are ready to absorb water when it comes and burst into leaf, flower and seed in quick succession after a storm. Desert annuals may wait several years as seeds, ready to germinate on the stimulus of one or two good showers and flower after a few days' growth – hence the sudden 'blooming' of the desert after rain. All the long-standing plants absorb moisture from the atmosphere, especially at night, when cooling raises the relative humidity even to dew point. Browsing desert animals that feed at night benefit from this water, as well as keeping cooler and avoiding predators.

Desert creatures include many insects that browse and graze on the vegetation, and reptiles, small birds, rodents and insectivorous mammals that feed according to taste on insects and seeds. These plant and animal elements form the bases of simple food webs that are fundamentally similar for all the world's deserts, but differ in species from one desert to another. Many of the small mammals are burrowers or live among rocks, avoiding extremes of heat and aridity in deep, cool hideaways during the day and emerging to feed about sunset. They can be surprisingly numerous: the Saudi Arabian desert has at least fifty-three species of small mammals, including jerboas, hares, gerbils, several kinds of small cats, a hedgehog, two species of foxes, fennecs and hamadryad baboons.

Large mammals are fewer and less diverse, but still present in surprising numbers. The Sahel supports several species of large grazers and browsers including dorcas, dama and other gazelles, scimitar-horned oryx and addax – rather rarer long-horned antelopes. These form the prey of a wide range of carnivores, including leopards, caracal, hyaenas and wolves. Neighbouring mountain deserts of Africa and Arabia have a selection of long-horned sheep and goats as their main browsing mammals – the Barbary sheep of North Africa, for example, and the ibex of Arabia. Goat-like Arabian tahr are rare mountain animals now found only in the highlands of Oman and possibly the United Arab Emirate: WWF specialist Dr Paul Munton is perhaps only the third European ever to have seen them in the field. About 2,000 remain in existence, now rigorously protected by the government of Oman.

Small desert mammals live virtually without water; gerbils of the Sahara find all they need in seeds and leaves, and may never drink at all once they are weaned. Large mammals, less capable of avoiding heat, usually need some water at least. Dromedary camels, once wild animals of the desert but now entirely domesticated, have a battery of water-conservation mechanisms. They can allow their body temperature to rise 3°C – 4°C above normal before even starting to sweat (we cannot and would in any case be in raging fever long before reaching that point): they take the rise in temperature philosophically, shedding the surplus heat by radiation and returning to normal during the night. They produce a highly concentrated urine, and can recirculate some of their nitrogenous wastes through the stomach, so avoiding the need to lose water by urination. Finally, they can go days or even weeks without drinking, losing over twenty-five per cent of their body water and making it up in two or three huge draughts when they reach a water supply. Most other mammals, including man and his domestic stock, need a daily intake of water: they can lose only ten to twelve per cent of body weight, and would die of water intoxication if they tried to make it up immediately once water became available again.

We know less of the physiology of other desert mammals, but the fact that they live – and have lived for centuries – in desert and semi-desert conditions argues a high degree of specialization. Arabian oryx can go without drinking for several weeks, living on the water they pick up in their browsing. Perhaps just as useful to them is the capacity they have developed to detect rainfall or its consequence, a new growth of vegetation, many miles off and make their way toward it unerringly. This is

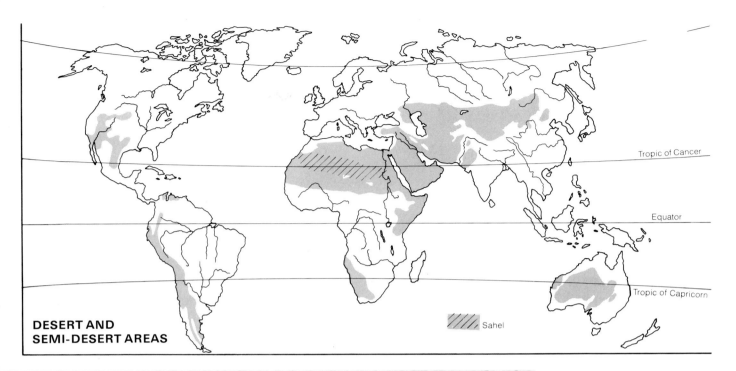

**DESERT AND
SEMI-DESERT AREAS**

Tropic of Cancer

Equator

Tropic of Capricorn

Sahel

An oryx at full speed in the Namibian desert. Even this desolate waste contains enough vegetation to feed herds of nomadic oryx.

an essential gift in an environment where acacia scrub, perennial grasses and other meagre vegetation may be present everywhere, but new growth occurs only patchily where rain has recently fallen, and soon dries out and disappears after the last shower.

The bitter poverty of Sahel nomads is based partly on their numbers, but also on the unsuitability of cattle for desert or semi-desert life. Neither cattle nor deer occur naturally in these areas: both are forest and grassland animals, selected by nature to live where the forage is richer and water more plentiful. Yet the nomad pastoralists of Africa base their livelihood on cattle. Like simple farmers the world over, they tend to stick to what they know best, and thin native cattle have served their forebears well for hundreds of generations on the richer and more reliable grazing grounds of the savannas. Now when population pressures and increased holdings of livestock tempt them into the Sahel, they are on much less certain ground. However, they can live there quite successfully with their cattle during 'wet' spells when the rain falls reliably for several years on end.

Previously the pastoralists achieved a balance with the wild animals that shared the semi-arid zone, for men and cattle were restricted to grazing areas within little more than a day's walk of the natural waterholes, while the wild stock, less dependent on water, grazed beyond. But the recently introduced technology that drilled more bore-holes and dug more watering places upset the balance. Now with cattle everywhere the wild animals lose both their water and their grazing grounds. Encouraged by abundant water and reasonable grazing through several seasons of good rains, the pastoralists allowed their herds to increase. This meant that they, their cattle and the environment were hit all the harder when the cycle of dry seasons returned, and the new forage failed to appear.

The four memorable drought years of 1969–73 affected some 8 million km² (3.1 million square miles) of semi-arid country and, according to some estimates, killed half the cattle in the Sahel. Nobody knows how many cattle there were or how many died – or indeed how many men, women and children in nomad camps died with them. But the damage to the environment was great: before the livestock died or were moved to wetter areas in the south, they overgrazed and killed off the sparse, soil-binding vegetation, letting in winds that swept the thin soil away. Much the same happened again in the recent cycle of droughts, degrading even more of the Sahel from semi-arid land to desert and making it impossible for domestic and wild stock alike to find a living there. On statistical evidence it is likely to happen every ten years or so, and each time another section of the Sahel will deteriorate further and be made unusable for generations to come.

If cattle are unsuited to desert living but addax, oryx,

Scimitar-horned oryx are heavily hunted throughout the eastern Sahel; oryx can be domesticated and are more efficient than cattle in semi-desert conditions.

and several species of gazelles grow fat on it, why should not human populations depend on the antelopes and gazelles? Some do: there are small tribal groups of hunters – the Azza for example – who hunt oryx and gazelles with nets and base their whole economy upon them. But nobody has recently tried to manage wild or semi-wild stocks of these animals, and here lies a possibility for the future – one which several IUCN/WWF-sponsored surveys have examined with great interest. Both addax and oryx were treated as domestic animals by early Egyptian farmers, and stocks have been reared successfully in zoos and game parks.

It was indeed ease of domestication that saved the Arabian oryx from extinction, and semi-domestication and stock management methods are being used to rescue other species of desert antelopes from a similar fate when they cannot be saved in the wild. Arabian oryx once lived in small herds of ten to fifty in the semi-desert scrub that extended throughout the Middle East from Jordan and Palestine to Iraq, and across the Arabian Peninsula. Hunted initially for meat, but later for their elegant horns (and latterly for fun by jeeploads of braves with automatic weapons) they gradually disappeared over the whole of its

Addax – heavily-built antelope of the Sahel and other desert areas, well adapted for living on scrub vegetation and surviving in almost waterless conditions.

range. The last wild specimen was recorded in the Sultanate of Oman in 1972.

By 1961, when it became quite clear that this luckless animal was heading for extinction, IUCN, the Faunal Preservation Society, and World Wildlife Fund combined with the Shikar Safari Club of Aden to launch a last-minute rescue bid, 'Operation Oryx'. With some difficulty two males and a female were caught in East Aden Protectorate and combined with six other captive animals to form a single breeding herd, and shipped to Phoenix Zoo, Arizona. Under excellent breeding conditions by 1969 stock increased to 100, distributed among six centres in Europe and the US, and the species was saved from extinction. Over the years WWF has maintained its interest in the Arabian oryx. It has recently been concerned with the reintroduction of animals from the breeding herd to the Shaumari Reserve in Jordan, and to Jiddat al Harasis, Oman, where the animals will be entrusted to the care of a nomadic tribe.

The Shaumari Reserve forms part of the Azraq Oasis National Park, one of several desert and semi-desert areas that World Wildlife Fund has helped to protect and develop over the years; now an important breeding centre

for gazelles and oryx, it lies within a basin of saline marshes and mudflats entirely surrounded by desert. In neighbouring Israel, grants from the British, Netherlands and US National Appeals helped to build a research station at the southernmost Hai-Bar Reserve, one of three reserves dedicated to breeding ostriches, gazelles, wild asses and other desert animals that were common in Biblical times but have now become rare or locally extinct. In Ethiopia's Danakil desert WWF supported aerial and group surveys of the Somali wild ass, finding it in steady decline in competition with domestic stock of local tribesmen, and helped to develop surveys that established reserves in several other wilderness areas of north-eastern Africa.

Then in 1975–6 WWF helped to fund a major IUCN survey of conservation problems in the Sahara and Sahel, with particular emphasis on the status of the two large antelopes, scimitar-horned oryx and addax, and associated species. These are of interest as desert animals of rare beauty and elegance; they have an additional interest as a possible source of protein, alternative to cattle, for the desperately poor Sahel nomads. Already desert-adapted, quick-growing, and producers of good meat from unpromising vegetation, their biology and status were well worth investigating.

The survey team found little wildlife of any kind left in the arid zone of northern Sudan, much better stocks of addax, oryx, dorcas and dama gazelles and ostriches in Chad, reasonable antelope stocks in Mali, a general decline in Niger, and a catastrophic recent decline in Mauritania, where ostrich, dama gazelles and oryx were hunted almost to extinction. The IUCN panel of consultants recommended the development of an overall strategy for dealing with the arid-land belt that extends from Mauritania through to central Asia, and draw up specific proposals for the immediate protection of addax and oryx. Special measures were recommended to reduce hunting, which was mainly a fun activity – target practice for trigger-happy soldiers, government workers and oil and mining company employees; their indiscriminate shooting was clearing large areas of legally protected animals. Oryx, more sociable than addax and favouring the better areas of grassland, were more at risk from the hunters, and already completely eliminated from several areas where they had once been plentiful.

Further reports recommended that strong support be given to the government of Chad for the Ouadi Rimé-Ouadi Achim game reserve, a huge area of 79,000 km² (31,000 square miles), where at least forty species of large

Overleaf Nyala does drinking at a waterhole in the Mkuze Game Reserve, Zululand. Bush-buck of the desert edge, their white stripes on reddish fur help to hide them as they browse among low vegetation.

Above Tahr, a goat-like grazer of high mountain deserts. The thick woolly coat gives protection equally against intense sun and extreme cold.

Right Gemsbok duelling. The long horns are important also as heat radiators.

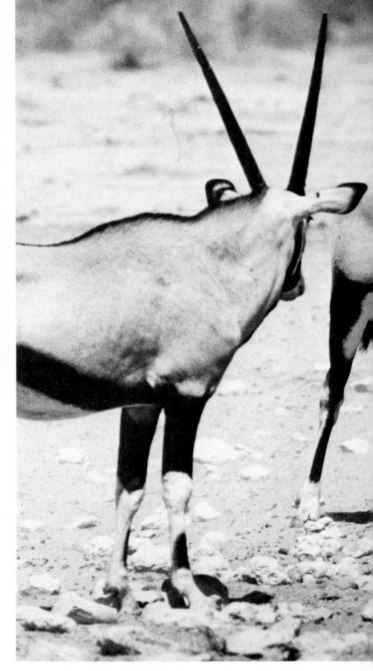

desert animals can still be found in relatively untouched semi-desert. The fauna includes about sixty-five per cent of the world's population of addax. With an area as big as Scotland, since its gazetting as a reserve in 1969 Ouadi Rimé-Ouadi Achim had proved almost impossible to administer – even patrol – with the slender resources provided by the Chad government, and help was urgently needed. The survey further recommended the establishment of a similar reserve in Niger, around the Termit Massif, where there were still good, relatively untouched stocks of many of the desert mammals.

World Wildlife Fund's response was an immediate grant of funds to Ouadi Rimé-Ouadi Achim in 1977, to buy fifty camels and a Land Rover that would allow the rangers to travel more frequently and efficiently about their business of protecting the stock against both casual hunters and organized meat poachers. This was a successful programme: by working the waterholes the guards were able to keep control and reduce poaching considerably. John Newby, the biologist who led the field work, living for six years with the Sahel nomads, began to look forward to the time when anti-poaching measures were less demanding, allowing leisure for the development of reserve management policies. High on his list of priorities was an educational programme to show the local tribesmen that the wildlife had a continuing value for them. He saw the need to develop the undoubted

economic potential of the antelopes and gazelles, exploiting to the full their capacity for sustained production of protein. 'Exploitation', he said in his report for the WWF yearbook, 'may well provide the nomads with the proof that wildlife is worth conserving and provide governments with incentives to look carefully at the value of wildlife.'

Regrettably, war has intervened. Since January 1978, civil unrest has stopped all work in the Ouadi-Rimé-Ouadi Achim reserve and put its wildlife at considerable risk from bands of armed marauders. Until the return of better times, WWF's effort has switched to neighbouring Mali and Niger. In Mali both addax and scimitar-horned oryx have been surveyed, and plans drawn up for their further protection. In Niger, World Wildlife Fund joined

with Direction des Eaux et Forêts (the responsible government department), the Zoological Society of London and Quest 4 Ltd (a tour and exploration group) to assess the conservation potential of the Aïr Massif, in the northern uplands.

Part of this area, the Takolokouzet Massif, was singled out as a possible centre for a faunal reserve of about 30,000 km² (11,700 square miles), where the country's desert and semi-desert fauna could be protected and studied. This proved to be an unusually interesting area with a wide range of habitats available, an outstanding fauna, and a bonus of archaeological sites recording earlier human occupation. A further reserve would be needed, possibly in the Termit region, for studies of the scimitar-horned oryx, the one important species missing from the

Takolokouset site. In the report recommending the formation of these reserves, two important possibilities for development were singled out – research into the economic potential of the wildlife, and the creation of national breeding herds of addax and oryx, for reintroduction of captive-bred animals to areas from which they have been extirpated by hunting.

While the Sahel and other desert and semi-desert areas can never support large human populations, they could conceivably provide better living for a small number, based on proper management of the wildlife, than for a larger number based on a marginal and very uncertain cattle economy. This is the suggestion arising from the preliminary IUCN and WWF surveys; the way is open for these interesting possibilities to be further explored.

Fallow deer, once widespread in Mediterranean countries,
are now mainly restricted to parks and reserves.

-ORESTS AND GRASSLANDS

MANAGING
THE DEER

STAY QUIET for a while in almost any forest of the Old or New World, and before long you may find you have deer for company. Mostly silent animals, solitary or sociable in small groups, they move through the forests like shadows, nibbling and browsing as they go. Some take to open country: reindeer and caribou often winter in the forest but move out on to the open tundra in summer. The red deer of Britain seem contented enough in our sour, sheep-ridden moorlands, though they too are forest creatures by choice, and seek the cover of woodland (if they can find it) in winter.

A thousand years ago our ancestors, creeping quietly through the forests of northern Europe or the Americas, might well have found more deer; five thousand years ago they would certainly have done so, for the forests were in their prime and deer were probably the commonest large herbivores throughout Europe, Asia and North and South America. Africa has always been relatively closed to deer; perhaps the deserts of the north were too great a barrier for them. Australia too was isolated long before deer spread into south-eastern Asia, and the deer that are there today were introduced in relatively recent times by man.

Since the early Pleistocene over a million years ago, both the deer and the forests have declined, mostly at the hands of man. Temperate forests especially have been reduced to a fraction of their former extent by cutting and burning, and whole populations of deer have vanished. Hunting too has taken its toll; deer are a handy size for man to kill, and both venison and deer skins have always been in demand. The deer that remain, in the forests that remain, keep their well-established relationship with man; timid and secretive, intensely sensitive to his sounds and scent, they try to stay out of his way, while he continues to hunt them for food and skins, or just for sport.

Père David's deer, now extinct in their Chinese home-land, but flourishing in European and American game parks.

The deer of the world form a small but significant branch of the huge mammalian Order Artiodactyla, the 'even-toed ungulates', most easily recognizable by their cloven hoof – two strong hoofed toes on each foot, usually with two lesser ones behind them. With cattle, sheep and antelopes they form the Sub-order Ruminantia; these are the cud-chewing mammals, with a powerful mill of grinding teeth, a complex four-chambered stomach, and a method of regurgitating and re-swallowing their food that promotes bacterial action in the gut as an aid to digestion. Deer belong to the Infra-order Pecora, the horned and antlered ruminants, a group which also includes the giraffes, pronghorn antelopes, true antelopes and cattle. From these they are distinguished mainly by their antlers – bony structures on the forehead that males of all but two species grow and shed at intervals, usually each year.

The family of deer, called Cervidae, includes about thirty living species, usually listed under two subfamily headings. The 'typical' deer of Europe and Asia – the red deer, axis and hog deer, sikas, barasinghas and sambars – form the subfamily Cervinae, which Europeans smugly call the 'true' deer. Rather more varied is the subfamily Odocoileinae, which includes many of the 'typical' deer of the New World – the white-tailed and mule deer of North America, and the marsh and pampas deer, huemuls (pudus) and brockets of South America. Moose and caribou of the New World, and their Old World equivalents elk and reindeer, also belong to this ragbag subfamily, and so do the roe deer of Eurasia and the musk deer, Chinese water deer, and tiny muntjacs and tufted deer of Asia.

Deer are mainly forest animals, derived from ancestors that evolved through the Middle and Late Tertiary – the last twenty-five to thirty million years – in the great forests of Asia. They spread early to Europe and rather later to the Americas; recognizable ancestors of many modern deer were present three to four million years ago on their appropriate continents. One kind of 'true' deer crossed from Asia to North America; the American wapiti is very closely related to the European red deer and shows its kinship clearly. Even later another group of red deer penetrated south by an unknown route into Africa, developing into an African subspecies among the mountain forests between the Sahara and the Mediterranean Sea.

How many different kinds of deer are there? Taxonomists cannot agree. Because so much of deer evolution has occurred relatively recently (and indeed may still be occurring today), boundaries between species and

Spotted sika or Japanese deer, a species that breeds well in captivity. The Manchurian sika is probably already extinct.

167

subspecies tend to be blurred. Most taxonomists recognize between twenty-eight and thirty-four species without agreeing firmly on any one figure. There is far less agreement on the number of subspecies – a point that becomes important when we are trying to decide whether a particular population is an isolated subspecies in need of conservation protection.

Wherever they spread, deer tend to form discrete local populations that, over many hundreds of generations, acquire distinctive local character; the differences are usually small points of skin colour or antler shape, but constant enough to show, for example, where a particular specimen has come from. How many of these local variant populations should be identified as distinct subspecies?

In every group of plant and animal taxonomists there are 'splitters' who like to emphasize variety, and therefore name many species and subspecies, and 'lumpers' who use stiffer criteria and distinguish fewer variants by name. Deer taxonomists include plenty of both, so different taxonomic accounts of deer can list as many as two hundred subspecies (among them thirty-nine separate forms of white-tailed deer alone) or as few as forty for the family as a whole.

The scientists who compile the Red Data Books tend if anything to be conservative in their listing of species and subspecies; their catalogue of animals at risk is not unduly swollen by dozens of doubtful 'subspecies', and an endangered population is not listed if very similar animals are known to be living in relative safety close by. Nevertheless some twenty-nine species or subspecies of deer are currently listed, nineteen of them on the red pages denoting 'endangered'. In practically all of them the prime cause of danger is deforestation. For deer this implies simultaneous loss of cover and food, and they can afford neither. Beset by poachers and other predators, loss of cover can be fatal to them: used to habitats of high seasonal productivity, they cannot switch easily to grasslands or forests improverished by loss of species and variety.

With many forms of deer facing a common problem, World Wildlife Fund is concerned to support research on the group as a whole, rather than helping them species by species. This it has done through IUCN's Threatened Deer Programme, which was launched in 1974 under the leadership of Dr Colin Holloway, after four years of preliminary enquiries and data-collecting in countries where deer were known or believed to be at risk. The programme, now incorporated in SSC's overall work on threatened species, aims to improve the status of threatened deer, both by ecological research and through long-term strategic management plans.

Ecological field work is usually an important starting point for any study of a threatened species. However, the survival of the species may ultimately depend far more on

Pudu or huemuls, among the smallest species of deer, are found in the rainforests of western South America from Chile to Ecuador.

finding a role for it in the community. This may involve convincing government departments and agencies of its importance and their responsibilities toward it, and showing local people (in whose hands the fate of the species may ultimately lie) that there is something for them to gain – food or employment perhaps – by its preservation, and something to lose by its loss.

Of the twenty-nine threatened taxa (species or subspecies) of deer listed, four are from South America, two from North America, and the remaining twenty-three from the Old World, notably Asia. Three forms (Bhutan's shou, China's Yarkand deer and Manchurian sika deer) are now almost certainly extinct, but studies of the remaining taxa develop as opportunities allow. Several of these forms at risk are mere subspecies, not full species, but money and time spent on any group of deer carry hidden bonuses. Firstly, deer are usually an asset to an area – easily managed, farmed, and able to provide good meat for local people. Secondly, they tend to live in rich habitats with a variety of other species; a reserve set aside for deer will almost certainly give protection to many other plants and animals – a point for consideration when funds are being allocated as economically as possible.

Investment to save the hangul, or Kashmir stag, certainly helped other threatened species of northern India. This was a WWF-sponsored project starting in 1975. An earlier survey had made it clear that the only remaining viable population of hangul existed, under

Axis deer or chital, common in the forests of India and Sri Lanka, disappear as the forests are cut down.

In much the same way, tiny Fea's muntjaks benefit from the inclusion of their rainforest habitat in Thailand's Operation Tiger reserve, and southern barasingha, a subspecies of swamp deer adapted for life in dry grasslands (p. 140), have found a haven in Kanha National Park, a reserve set aside for tigers in India's central uplands. Though a tiger reserve may not sound the safest place for a small population of near-extinct deer, barasingha had for long been declining over most of their range, due to loss of grassland, poaching and competition from domestic stock. Within Kanha they were relatively safe from man-made hazards, and with good cover, stood a reasonable chance against the tigers.

When in 1970 numbers of barasingha in Kanha were found to be dangerously low, the prime cause was shown to be human interference, not tigers. Dr Claude Martin, a Swiss ecologist called in by WWF to save the barasingha and develop a management programme, found that burning off old grass in winter (traditionally to lessen risks of more dangerous summer fires) selectively destroyed the rich perennial grasses on which barasingha depended. A secondary problem was the practice of feeding the tigers in a meadow where they could readily be seen by visitors: this encouraged tigers to congregate in an area that barasinghas favoured, and resulted in more kills than the limited stock could support. Changes of policy in these two small matters helped barasinghas to thrive once more, and almost treble their numbers by 1978.

From 1974 onwards World Wildlife Fund also supported a research and management study on northern barasingha, which are now restricted mainly to two reserves in India and one in Nepal. The Nepalese population, numbering about 1,000, live in the Sukla Phanta Reserve, a relatively small area of some 150 km² (60 square miles), less than half of which yields their preferred habitat of seasonally flooded grasslands. Here they compete for their forage with man (who uses the lush grasses for thatching and to feed domestic animals) and in the past have suffered steady losses to poachers. However, Indian tigers too have been found to live in the Sukla Phanta Reserve, and armed guards now patrol it to keep poachers of all kinds at bay. This can only be to the advantage of the northern barasingha, and help to ensure their survival.

Musk deer are small deer with tiny tusks and no antlers, that live at heights of 3,000 to 4,000 metres (10,000 to 13,000 ft) in the Himalaya from Pakistan to Bhutan, Burma, Tibet and China. They are hunted for their musk glands, small sacs of semi-liquid secretions that males carry on their abdomen for use in territory marking. The secretions have for long been valued in medicine and perfumery; in 1974 they were said to be worth more than four times their weight in gold as an export for the world

serious threat, in the Dachigam reserve of Kashmir. Originally a hunting preserve, Dachigam was subject to poaching, grazing by domestic stock, wood-cutting and burning – all the ills that overtake neglected reserves – and only about 170 hangul could be located in 1970.

A management plan, devised by IUCN/WWF specialists, that reduced some of the more destructive uses of the area, set the reserve on the road to recovery, encouraging the hangul population to increase to over 300 by 1978. Similar benefits would also have accrued to brown and Himalayan black bears, snow leopards, Himalayan langur, pig musk deer, serow, Himalayan fox, jackal, jungle cats, hog badgers and many other threatened species of the Himalayan foothills community, that share Dachigam with the hangul.

Similarly deer may benefit from inclusion in reserves set aside for other purposes. Corsican deer, another local subspecies of the ubiquitous red deer, have recently become extinct in Corsica and are now confined to three isolated areas in the neighbouring island of Sardinia. Here some 250 deer live under the surveillance of Italy's WWF, protected by law but constantly threatened by poachers. Their wild mountain habitat is covered with evergreen maquis vegetation; part at least of the deer population may benefit when a large area is gazetted as a Biosphere Reserve, the first aim of which is to protect the maquis scrub. The long-term aim of deer studies in Sardinia is to protect the remaining herds, build up a captive breeding stock, and in time reintroduce the subspecies to Corsica.

Sambar – forest deer of eastern Asia, ranging from India to the Pacific islands with many local variants.

market. Musk is traditionally collected by snaring and killing the deer: though males alone carry it, both sexes are taken indiscriminately, and persistent demand for musk has put the species seriously at risk.

In a WWF-supported project, the musk deer of Kedarnath Sanctuary, northern India, are being studied throughout the year by British and Indian ecologists. At the same time methods of farming the species are under investigation. Tough little animals, capable of surviving one of the harshest climates on earth, musk deer are already farmed successfully in southern China. From similar farms in India should come both a predictable supply of valuable musk, and a bonus of captive-bred animals for release in areas currently depopulated by hunting.

One of the world's rarest species of deer is the forest-living Bawean deer, with a population of 250 to 300 confined to tiny Bawean Island in the Java sea. This species, small, timid, and nocturnal, shares its island of 2,000 km² (75 square miles), covering no more than 15 km (10 miles) across, with a human population of about 70,000. Bawean is heavily wooded with natural forests and teak plantations. The Indonesian Directorate of Nature Conservation, concerned at the precarious status of Bawean deer, invited WWF to help them in defining a reserve on the island, and drawing up management plans to run it.

The result of this exercise, begun in 1978, is a projected reserve of 1,220 hectares some of mixed primary and secondary forest and the rest teak plantation. Under Raleigh A. Blouch, an American ecologist, and his Indonesian colleagues, an experiment is in train to manage the forest for the benefit of the deer – for example by protecting it from illegal cutting, thinning the plantations to reduce fire risks, creating grassy clearings and providing saltlicks – without inhibiting its potential for timber production. The management plan has several sensible recommendations – for example that softwoods be planted outside the boundary, so that local people can cut it for timber and firewood without damaging the reserve. There is hope, therefore, that room can still be found on this crowded, mountainous island for people and commerce – and also for a safe, continuing population of Bawean deer, tucked away in their forest reserve.

In April and May of 1975, Dr Hartmut Jungius conducted an exhaustive survey of South American deer, supported by WWF and on behalf of the Threatened Deer Programme. Four species listed as endangered by IUCN – marsh deer, pampas deer and northern and southern Andean huemuls – were his special concern. Southern

stocks of pampas deer were found to be most at risk, and a full study, supported by WWF, was begun in 1976.

That both northern and southern huemuls were threatened by hunting and deforestation had already been established during earlier field surveys of Chilean wildlife, supported by the University of Washington and the Peace Corps, with help from WWF. In 1974 began a more intensive study of the southern huemul, whose status seemed the more uncertain, in the cold rainforests of southern Chile. This is one of many species likely to benefit from the establishment of reserves, in an area that is rapidly being opened to exploitation by man.

World Wildlife Fund has been involved in many deer

management projects throughout the world, and is at present looking into one of the most interesting – the return of Père David's deer to China. Père Armand David, as Sir Peter Scott describes in his Introduction, in 1865 saw a herd of unusual deer in the hunting park of the Chinese Emperor near Peking. There were none like them in the wild, and their origins were unknown even to the Chinese. Père David bought skins of these animals for museum specimens, and later a few live animals were shipped to Europe, where they established breeding herds – notably in the Duke of Bedford's collection at Woburn Park. A series of disasters killed off the remaining stocks in China, so captive animals are now the sole representatives of the species. In the context of the agreement recently established between the Chinese People's Republic and the World Wildlife Fund some of these animals may shortly be returning to China, so that the species can be re-established in a suitable habitat in the wild.

BEARS AND PANDAS

AT ONE of the early meetings of the Committee that founded the World Wildlife Fund, the question of a logo came up. What was needed was a simple, eye-catching design that everyone, everywhere, could always associate with WWF. An animal? Yes; a rare or threatened species, perhaps, preferably a black and white one that would print clearly. They might have chosen an elephant, a lion or an antelope – any one of a dozen species of appealing African animals currently known to be endangered. But Dr E. B. Worthington, himself a specialist in African ecology, presented the Committee with a sketch of a giant panda, a rare, black and white bear-like mammal of eastern Asia.

It was an inspired choice, and not entirely outlandish, for the giant panda happened at the time to be one of London's favourite animals. The Zoological Society of London had in 1958 acquired Chi-chi, its first giant panda for several years, and she was currently drawing the crowds in Regent's Park Zoo. Already immensely popular, Chi-chi had everything a good logo needed. Peter Scott and Gerald Watterson redrew her in a design of intersecting curves, and the Committee looked no further. Chi-chi, the giant panda from Sichuan, China, became the official symbol of World Wildlife Fund. Soon her portrait was appearing on stationery, collecting boxes, lapel badges, posters, booklets, Land Rovers, aircraft and boats, in large format and small, wherever WWF was operating.

The millions who see the panda symbol and link it with WWF may assume that giant pandas were in some way early beneficiaries of the Fund. In fact they were not. Though they appear in the Red Data Book, listed as rare but not necessarily an endangered species, until recently

Polar bears spend much of their time on the sea ice, but there is food for them too on the tundra; here a mother leads her cubs in search of birds and their nests, berries, roots and carrion.

nobody outside China has known whether they needed help or not. Giant pandas live exclusively in the dense, dripping cloud forests of three of China's provinces – Sichuan, Kansu and Chensi – in wild mountainous country, and only the local people and a small number of Chinese biologists have so far had any true notion of how plentiful or endangered they are.

Recently there have been indications that giant pandas are in trouble, due to a failure in local stands of bamboo, their main food; 140 of them have died out of an estimated population of 1,000. So much was disclosed during the visit of an official WWF delegation to the People's Republic of China, led by Sir Peter Scott in September 1979. The Chinese have designated ten special reserves for their protection, and WWF is now, for the first time, financing a full programme of research into the ecology of its endearing mascot, led by George Schaller, a distinguished American biologist. WWF's visit to China was in this and many other ways an outstanding success, bringing the world's largest nation into IUCN and forging many other promising links with its conservationists and biologists.

Giant pandas are a biological anomaly. Though bear-like in size, form and temperament, they differ from typical bears in several points of anatomy and behaviour. They were first described for science in 1869 by Père Armand David, who discovered them in western China and was in little doubt that he had found a new species of black and white bear. However, anatomists in the Paris Muséum d'Histoire Naturelle, to whom he sent specimens, grouped it instead with the Procyonidae, a related family of the Order Carnivora, that includes such animals as the pandas, red pandas and raccoons.

Père David's mammal was thought to resemble most closely the red panda, a much smaller, raccoon-like animal well known from China and the Himalaya. So by comparison it became the giant panda. It can never in truth be more than an honorary panda, for serum tests have recently shown that Père David was right; Chi-chi and her kin are indeed bears, if slightly wayward ones, much closer to the bear family Ursidae than to the panda family Procyonidae.

The bears form a compact group of about eight species. Mainly forest animals, they originated from dog-like ancestors twenty million years ago, spreading north into the Arctic and south into the tropical forests and beyond. Heavy, bumbling animals with flat feet, pillar-like limbs and a stump of a tail, the bears have ceased on the whole to be chasers of quarry and taken to a quieter, more reflective

Restricted to the rainforests of south-western China and neighbouring Tibet, giant pandas may currently be at risk from a declining food supply.

life. Heavy-jawed, with blunt, crushing teeth, they seek a wide range of foods from carrion to grass, from leaves, shoots and berries to mice, fish and birds' eggs: for a hungry bear, almost anything will serve as a meal, and a hungry bear needs plenty to keep it going.

Giant pandas are among the most completely vegetarian: they live in mountain rainforests, and the leaves and succulent young stems of bamboos make up an important part of their diet. Their fore-paws are adapted for handling bamboos, with a curious thumb-like pad on the palm that helps them hold on to the slippery stems. But they also catch and eat mice and other small rodents that live in the forests, and have even been reported to catch fish and insects to supplement their bamboo diet. At the other end of the scale – mainly meat-eaters – are polar bears, which feed largely on seals and fish that they catch at sea among the ice floes. They in their turn come ashore in summer to feed on tundra shoots and berries, and forage for eggs, birds, lemmings and carrion.

Bears and men have seldom got along together. Wherever they meet there are conflicts of interest, and as man has advanced the bears have had to retreat. The brown bears of Europe were the first to feel the full impact of man. In early medieval times, while Europe was heavily

DISTRIBUTION OF GIANT PANDA

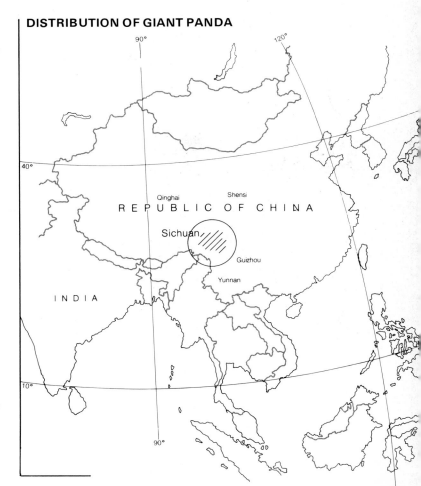

forested, large brown bears were frequent visitors to villages and small towns. Their size, persistence in searching for food and sheer brute strength (a brown bear, it was said, could fell an ox with one blow of his paw) made them unwelcome callers. In northern Europe and Asia they were worshipped, and throughout Europe they acquired a sympathetic role in heraldry and folklore. Many cities have bears in their coat-of-arms, and folk tales are full of bears wise, solemn, irascible, but often kindly. The Three Bears – clearly European brown bears – put up with a great deal from Goldilocks before chasing her out of their woodland cottage, and their diet of porridge, though sophisticated for bears, was characteristically vegetarian.

As the European forests were cleared for agriculture and cut for fuel the bears gradually disappeared, and few can have been sorry to see them go. In Britain brown bears were finally killed off during the tenth and eleventh centuries. They can still be found in continental Europe, restricted to small numbers in little-populated mountain and wilderness areas of Spain, Italy, France, Scandinavia and the Carpathian mountains, and the same species lives on in remote corners of the Middle East, the USSR and China. The biggest are from Scandinavia and the USSR, measuring 2.2 m (7 ft) from nose to tail and weighing 250 kg (560 lb) or more; the smallest are southern bears, measuring 1.7 m (5½ ft) and weighing only 70 to 80 kg (up to 180 lb). Mature males are usually bigger than females.

Where brown bears keep to themselves they are usually tolerated; however, they occasionally leave their wilderness and raid farms, killing stock and munching vegetables which mountain farmers can ill afford to lose. In 1969 World Wildlife Fund supported a study of European brown bears in the Abruzzi National Park, where a small population of 60 to 100 survives. Since 1967 the Italian National Appeal of WWF had helped to indemnify farmers against the bears' depredations; now a research programme was planned to see what else could be done to encourage bears and men to live peacefully together.

The Abruzzi study showed a flourishing stock with a healthy proportion of young. The bears were found to sleep for much of the winter from December to March, in wild upland areas well away from man. In spring they emerged to feed on bulbs, shoots and insects, moving gradually up-hill to spend summer in the high Alpine forests and meadows, and returning in autumn to fatten on fruits and berries. Sheep, goats, honey and cultivated vegetables – all at the expense of local farmers – supplemented their diet, especially in the hungry weeks of spring and autumn. The Park area was found to give the population only half the food required; for the rest the bears had to forage outside, taking their chances of being shot in the hostile world beyond the Park boundaries.

Local people were sympathetic toward their bears, and even proud of them, but dangers were foreseen from developments within the Park – more tourist facilities, wider roads with increasing chances of road deaths, and the incursions of ramblers and trigger-happy trophy hunters. The main conclusions of the study were the need for continuing alertness to the welfare of this small, highly vulnerable population, and a recommendation that the Park boundaries be extended to bring in all the land traditionally used by the bears.

The Italian National appeal also took under its wing an even smaller population of brown bears in the Trentino Valley of the Italian Alps. There only about a dozen survive. A guard was employed to keep poachers at bay, three critical areas of feeding were identified, and proposals were put forward to bring their area under National Park legislation. More recently World Wildlife Fund in France has begun caring for a similar remnant population of about a dozen European brown bears in the Pyrenees.

European emigrants who moved to North America in the eighteenth and nineteenth centuries found their old folk-enemies the brown bears waiting for them, larger if anything than the ones they had left behind. Typically huge, well-upholstered animals with tan or grey-brown tipped ('grizzly') fur, North American brown bears may stand over a metre (3¼ ft) tall at the shoulder and measure over two metres (6½ ft) from nose to tail. Biggest of all are Kodiak bears of the Aleutian Islands and southern Alaska. The smallest – a southern stock of grizzly bears formerly living in Mexico – have recently disappeared; a WWF-sponsored survey of 1968 showed that the last few, accused of raiding cattle ranches, were probably poisoned in the early 1960s. North American brown bears are restricted to the western mountains of Canada and the United States. Over most of their range they are thin on the ground, but endangered only where local populations come into too-frequent contact with man.

More widespread in North America is the black bear, a creature slightly smaller and less bulky than the brown, usually with a pale muzzle and chest. Black bears are darkest on the eastern seaboard, where they were first named by the early settlers. Inland toward the west they are brown or pale tan(some are called cinnamon bears); they can also be grey-blue, and the palest of all, living on forested islands of western Canada, are almost white. Like brown bears they live at relatively low densities. Males are usually solitary, rambling in huge overlapping ranges that cover many hectares. Females too keep to large territories where they wander in search of food, usually with two or three cubs dancing behind.

Meeting each other on well-worn forest tracks, bears are surly but seldom aggressive. There seems to be a simple

working rule that small bears give way to big ones – a rule that works well except in times of food shortage, or in spring when males may compete with teeth, claws and massive weight for the right to mate. Mothers defend their cubs vigorously against predators, which may include mountain lions, wolves and even other bears. Black bears are hunted under licence in some parts of the United States and protected in others; some local stocks are possibly endangered, but the species as a whole is plentiful.

Species similar and perhaps closely related to North American black bears live in South America and throughout eastern and southern Asia. In the high cloud-forest of the northern Andes live dark-brown spectacled bears, smaller and slimmer than black bears, with patches of pale fur on the chest and muzzle and white bands on the face, often surrounding the eyes like large sunglasses. Spectacled bears feed mainly on leaves and shoots, roosting in trees at night. A World Wildlife Fund survey of 1966, investigating its status in the five Andean countries of its range, found it a generally rare species, much reduced by hunting especially in Venezuela, Colombia and Peru. However, it has adapted to all kinds of habitats from near-desert in the foothills to Alpine scrub at 4,000 metres among the peaks, and was not thought to be in danger of extinction. The survey suggested the need for more Andean reserves and parks, which would

Spectacled bears, small brown bears of the high Andes: forest reserves will help to protect their small scattered population.

conserve whole areas of mountain habitat and ensure the safety of many species, including spectacled bears. One such reserve, the Equator National Reserve on the eastern chain of the Andes, was set up with WWF help in 1969, and others have been established since.

Asia has three species of dark-brown to black bears. All share the family characteristics of inhabiting upland forest (often the only kind left to them), living in grumpy solitude at low densities, and feeding on a mixed diet in which leaves, shoots and berries predominate. Malayan sun bears occur in the mountains of north-eastern India, Burma, Indo-China, Malaya and Sumatra. Smallest of all the bears, with short sleek fur, they have a tan-coloured blaze on the chest and brown face. Though harmless to man they are hunted and snared, and populations have fallen in recent decades: however, the species as a whole is not endangered. Nor is the Asiatic black bear of Kashmir, Nepal, China and Japan, except in one locality – Baluchistan – where hunting has reduced the population severely. Sloth bears of the Indian subcontinent have steadily declined in numbers during recent decades as the human population has increased. Forest destruction and

Brown bear cubs stay with their mother for over a year, learning the tricks of survival in their forest homes.

hunting are their main problems, though they remain in reasonable numbers where there are forests to hide them.

World Wildlife Fund has a long record of concern with polar bears, the great white bears of the Arctic. These are large animals, similar in size to big grizzlies and Kodiaks, and weighing up to half a tonne. Yellowish-white, with black nose, eyes and claws, they live throughout the Arctic, mainly in coastal regions where they divide their time between the coastal tundra and the sea ice offshore. Their immense white coat, with thick underfur and long guard hairs, protects them from cold on land or sea ice, and equally well in the freezing water. On land they move quickly with a shambling grace: in water they swim with a laborious dog-paddle that takes them long distances between coasts and icefloes. Emerging from the sea, their

greasy fur sheds surplus water readily – a couple of good shakes leaves them relatively dry.

Summer finds many polar bears ashore, leading solitary, nomadic lives in a constant search for food – birds, eggs, fish, carrion, berries – anything edible that the tundra will yield. Males keep out of each other's way. Females consort with them briefly for mating, but otherwise stay clear, and mothers with cubs at heel are aggressive in driving off all other members of their species. This behaviour fits well with their food supply, which is patchy and scarce, with barely enough in any one area of tundra coast to keep even a solitary polar bear in good shape. In autumn they move out on to the newly frozen sea, and winter is spent in searching the fast ice and floes for seals. These they catch by waiting at breathing holes, where they stun their quarry with a blow of the paw. Sometimes they stalk seals asleep on the ice: Eskimos say they hide their black nose with one paw as they creep up.

Polar bears mate in spring as the sea ice begins to break up and disperse. In the following October the pregnant female digs her way into a snow den, ashore or on the sea ice, and sleeps for several weeks protected by the enveloping snow. About December or January she awakens long enough to give birth to one or two tiny cubs, each the size of a half-grown rabbit, and starts them feeding on her rich milk. Then mother and cubs curl up together in a cosy ball, the cubs alternatively feeding and sleeping the winter away. About April they break out of the den, and the cubs, now the size of large chunky dogs, begin their life of nomadic hunting. They hunt with their mother for two years or more, learning the difficult craft of finding food – enough to keep a large bear going – in the harsh, cold world of the Arctic.

Left to themselves polar bears manage well. Many die young, especially during their first years alone, but they have few natural enemies and adults may live to a good age. Traditional hunting by Eskimos and other northern folk for food and skins depleted stocks of polar bears locally, but seldom seriously when both hunters and quarry were nomadic. Commercial hunting has always posed a more serious threat, for the market for fine polar bear skins was almost unlimited; little was known of the biology of the species, and licenced hunting could seldom be related to a real knowledge of the stocks available. In recent decades it became apparent that polar bears were disappearing from areas where they had previously been plentiful, and nobody knew enough about them to say whether or not the decline would continue. Were polar bears a disappearing species?

Arctic biologists of the several countries whose territories polar bears wander began to plan coordinated research programmes, meeting in 1965 at Fairbanks, Alaska, and in 1968 under IUCN auspices in Morges. In that year WWF gave substantial support to a long-term Norwegian programme of research, which since 1966 had been narcotizing polar bears in the pack ice off Svalbard and weighing, measuring, examining and tagging them with permanent markers. With similar research carried out in Canada, Greenland, Alaska and the USSR it gradually became clear that polar bears do not wander all over the Arctic: they live in discrete populations, circulating within relatively small areas. Any population could be wiped out completely by overhunting, or accidentally through oil spills and other man-made catastrophes that were likely to affect the Arctic Ocean in future years.

There was a further gathering of polar bear specialists at IUCN Headquarters, Morges, in 1970. The five circum-polar countries – USSR, USA, Canada, Denmark and Norway – were all represented, and the dangers affecting the species were discussed at length. The scientists

Polar bears, once over-hunted for their splendid furs, are now the subject of an international scientific research project. Tranquillized, this one is being taken aboard the research vessel for weighing and examination.

identified five separate populations of polar bears, and compared notes on many aspects of their differing techniques and approaches to research. The meeting, made possible by a WWF grant, was a remarkable example of international scientific cooperation, setting the scene for further research toward better legislation, to save what was now seen as a seriously endangered species.

Later WWF grants enabled Norwegian research workers to continue their field studies by aerial searches for breeding dens in the Svalbard area, and funded further conferences of specialists to discuss their most recent findings. As a result of a conference held in Oslo late in 1973 the five nations drew up an international 'Agreement on the Conservation of Polar Bears', severely restricting all forms of hunting and giving the species (and the ecosystems of which it froms part) almost complete protection. This agreement came into force in May 1976. The first treaty on any subject between the five Arctic nations, it was seen by optimists as a possible blueprint for further joint, far-reaching conservation action in the Arctic. There can be no doubt of its effectiveness in saving polar bears from the commercial over-exploitation that once threatened them.

LIONS
AND LESSER CATS

I N MATTERS of conservation for cats big and small, tigers have stolen the limelight. Biggest and most elegant of all the cats, the problem of conserving them was appropriately enormous, and took WWF's largest ever single-species campaign to solve it (chapter 4). Lions have been less of a worry; there are fewer races and correspondingly fewer problems. African lions are restricted by centuries of human interference to a fraction of their former range, but still quite plentiful in the savanna country south of the Sahara, maintaining their role of predator-controller of the game herds. Asiatic lions are less fortunate; the much greater human pressures have borne hard upon them, and there is only one small population left in the world.

Asiatic and African lions are closely similar in size and general appearance; Asiatic lions have a slightly heavier coat with a smaller mane, and a prominent ridge of skin and fur along the belly. Until the last century they were fairly common in savannas and thin woodlands of eastern Asia, Arabia, Persia and northern and central India. But throughout their range they fell foul of pastoralists, and in the grasslands and scrub they were easy targets for marksmen. By 1900 they were virtually eliminated from all but one locality – the Gir Forest, a region of dry, rolling hill country on the Kathiawar Peninsula of Gujarat, northwestern India. There they were declared a protected species. About 100 animals remained, in roughly 1,300 km² (500 square miles) of secondary teak and acacia forest, surrounded by semi-desert lowlands.

The hills were eventually gazetted as a reserve – the Gir Forest Wildlife Sanctuary. Occasional censuses indicated that the lions were holding their own, and might even have increased in number; a census of 1963 suggested that

Inquisitive lion cubs. The months after weaning, when cubs still wander with their mother, are an important period in their education.

over 300 were present. But in 1967 World Wildlife Fund contributed toward the costs of a thorough two-year survey to examine the habitat, count the animals, and estimate their chances of survival. The results were not promising. Accurate censuses indicated only between 160 and 175 lions, and they were sharing their relatively small 'reserve' with some 5,000 to 7,000 farmers. There were estimated also to be more than 50,000 domestic animals in the reserve, mostly water buffalo, domestic cattle, oxen, camels and goats, which between them were eating out the undergrowth and natural cover, and preventing regeneration of seedlings.

There were very few wild gazelles, deer, pigs or other ungulates that are the normal food of Asiatic lions, and the lack of cover (all of it cut or burnt by man, or eaten by his cattle) made it difficult for the lions to stalk what remained. Not surprisingly the lions were eating the domestic stock instead, and incurring the wrath of the farmers, who were trapping and poisoning them. It was not a happy situation for men or beasts, and clearly could not continue for long.

Paul Joslin, one of two scientists who completed the first survey for WWF, concluded that a long-term management programme for the Gir Sanctuary was needed, centred upon the lion and involving the development of the area as a National Park. In subsequent years the state government of Gujarat, helped by scientists of the Smithsonian Institution and Yale University, tackled the problem thoroughly, closing the area to cattle and building a stone wall around it. Farmers and graziers were gradually moved to other localities, allowing regeneration of the forest and making it possible for the natural browsers and grazers – potential food for the lions – to make a living for themselves.

These measures seem to have worked. The sanctuary, now a National Park, has become a considerable tourist attraction. Recent censuses suggest that the population of lions has increased, though they still remain a single, vulnerable stock. As a safeguard for the species, two have been transferred to Jersey Zoo, where it is hoped to start an additional breeding colony, and attempts may be made to settle other lions in reserves elsewhere in India as soon as numbers permit.

There are many lesser cats in the world. Smaller cousins of lions and tigers, they suffer human predation just as heavily and for much the same reasons – they are successful predators in competition with man, and many have beautiful skins that command a high price on the fur market. Several of them now stand in danger of extermination; their need for protection is just as urgent as

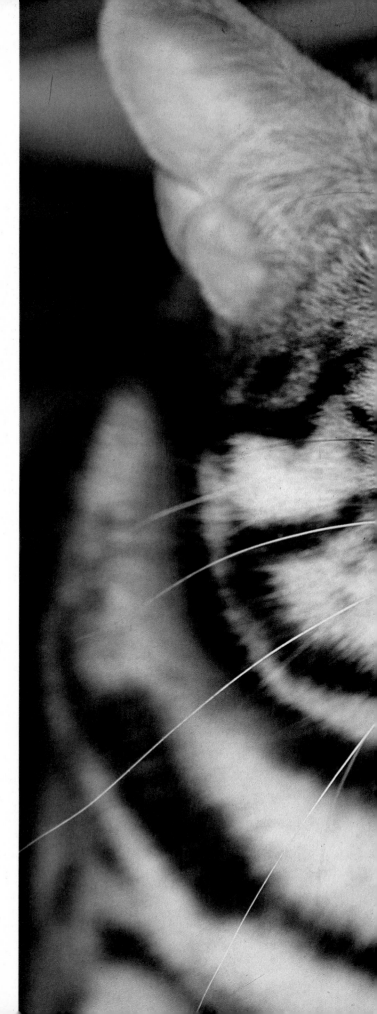

The leopard cat of India was once hardly worth hunting, but now is much in demand for its beautifully spotted skin.

that of tigers in the 1960s and 1970s. The lesser cats support an enormous international industry. In 1976 Britain alone imported almost half a million of their skins, West Germany more than a quarter of a million, and Belgium, France and Italy between them over 100,000 more. Most of the skins are those of the elegantly spotted and marbled lesser cats, and many of them are from South America.

Not surprisingly, local stocks of the smaller cats all the world over are showing signs of strain. IUCN's Red Data Book lists a dozen species or races as endangered, and several others are regarded as vulnerable. The status of many more is unknown; who can tell how many ocelots or pumas live in this or that corner of an Andean forest, and what pressure of hunting their stocks can stand? But the plight of the lesser cats has not gone unobserved: IUCN is helping their cause in several ways with lively and practical support from the World Wildlife Fund.

The cats of the world are a curiously uniform group: big or small, spotted, striped or plain, they are all easily recognizable as cats, and nothing that is not a cat could ever be mistaken for one. They form a family (Felidae) of the Order Carnivora, the meat-eaters; their closest kin are the civets, mongooses, genets and hyaenas. Lithe and slender, with short jaws, blunt faces, high cheek-bones and unmistakable eyes, they usually have a long whisking tail (lynx or bobcats are the exception), and all but cheetahs have retractable claws. Well-muscled and powerful for their weight, they sprint and climb (and some swim as well) with ease and grace. Knocking down prey their own size is no problem for cats. Most are solitary or hunt as individuals in twos or threes; lions alone are team hunters, with ploys like footballers for outmanoeuvring their faster-moving prey. Claws like steel hooks, and teeth for ripping, cutting and crushing make up a formidable armoury: from domestic pussy to heavyweight tiger, the cat is an animal to take seriously in a fight.

Zoologists distinguish about thirty-five species, with many local races and varieties. These are usually grouped in four very unequal genera. Lions, tigers, leopards, jaguars and snow leopards stand together in the genus *Panthera*; cheetahs (*Acinonyx*) and clouded leopards

Top Cheetah – fastest of the great cats, capable of stalking and running down antelopes. Thin populations remain throughout Africa south of the Sahara.

Opposite A yawn from a lion, largest of the African carnivores. African lions are still plentiful; only a few wild Asiatic lions survive in reserves.

(*Neofelis*) each have a genus of their own. All the remaining twenty-nine species, from pussycats to pumas, are similar enough under the skin to be included in the single genus *Felis*; some zoologists disagree with this, and divide them instead into ten or eleven genera. The cats live on all the inhabited continents in a surprising range of habitats from forest to savanna, desert and mountain snowfield. Invariably hunters, they take all kinds of prey including mammals, birds, reptiles, fish and insects, with strong preference for the living and moving.

Cats were well established as predators long before man existed, but his own inclination for hunting and his rapid spread across the world led inevitably to rivalry, conflict and enmity. As man has advanced, the cats have withdrawn; wherever our paths cross, relationships between us range from uneasy truce to open hostility – with avarice on our part for their splendid fur coats. We have seldom tamed them, and only the domestic cat has been clever enough to tame us.

Despite their basic uniformity, the cats both big and small have developed special roles – adopting particular habitats, evolving particular skills of hunting, concentrating on particular kinds of prey – that keep them ecologically apart and reduce or avoid competition between them. Tigers, as we have seen, are the large, solitary hunters of the poorer grasslands, savannas, desert edges and forests of Asia. Leopards, probably their closest kin, are much smaller animals: a lion or tiger may measure almost 3 metres from nose to tail and weigh over 220 kg (500 lbs), while a leopard seldom reaches $2\frac{1}{2}$ metres long or weighs more than 70 kg (150 lbs). Ranging through much of Asia and Africa, leopards are the solitary hunters of the open plains and savannas; they need trees or cover for their hunting, relying on surprise as much as speed for catching their prey. Antelopes and other small browsing and grazing animals are their main food, but rats, rabbits or even fish are quite acceptable to a hungry leopard.

Panthers and leopards were once thought to be separate species, but the names are now used as alternatives for the same species. Skin patterns vary enormously; the background colour can be almost white or rich yellow-gold, with spots large or small. 'Black panthers', which are simply melanistic (all-black) leopards, are fairly common in the forests of south-eastern Asia, but can appear anywhere, often alongside spotted ones in a litter of kittens. Because of the local variation many separate geographical races have been described. The species as a whole is listed as 'vulnerable' in IUCN's Red Data Book,

A leopard of north-eastern Asia, one of the many endangered varieties of a widespread species, hunted throughout its range.

187

and several races, notably those of north-eastern Africa and almost all that are found in Asia from Sinai to Korea, are considered to be endangered. Habitat destruction and hunting pressures are the twin causes of their scarcity; grazing domestic animals often replace their natural food species, and leopard skins command a fair price on the international market.

Snow leopards, or ounces, of the high mountains of central Asia are unusually beautiful animals with long silky fur. Closely related to true leopards, they are similar in size and shape; their silvery-grey fur is spotted with dark blotches and rosettes. Fierce hunting has reduced them throughout their range, possibly to no more than 500 to 600 individuals, and they are now listed as endangered. Clouded leopards are smaller, with yellow-brown coats banded and marbled in black. They range widely in mountain forests from Nepal through south-eastern Asia to Sumatra, Borneo and Taiwan.

Jaguars, the American counterpart of leopards, are one of the two large-sized species of cats on their continent. Heavy, thick-set animals, they roam through forest, grassland and desert from the southern United States (where they are now very rare) to southern Brazil. Despite official protection over much of their range, jaguars are extensively hunted; ranchers regard them as vermin to be killed on sight, and their range is declining steadily before the spread of agriculture. Their elegantly spotted skins are much in demand.

Similar in length but altogether lighter in build are the cheetahs; measuring 2 metres from nose to tail, they weigh up to about 55 kg (120 lbs). Long-legged and supple, with an immensely long stride, they are the high-speed hunters among the big cats, capable of sprinting at about 22 metres per second (50 miles per hour). They live alone or in small groups, stalking and then running down their prey – usually gazelles or antelope. Formerly widespread in Africa and Asia, they are now virtually restricted to Africa south of the Sahara; a few Asian cheetahs probably survive wild in north-western Afghanistan and Iran.

The remaining species of cats – those of the genus *Felis* – are mostly smaller. Pumas or cougars of the Americas are the largest, big males reaching the size and weight of a leopard; the smallest are the desert and forest wildcats from which domestic cats are descended. Felid cats differ from pantherid cats in several ways; they purr and yowl, but lack the convincing roar of a lion or tiger, and they seldom or never hold prey with their paws while they are eating. A few species are plain, but most have spotted or dappled coats, some of great beauty.

Plain sandy or dark brown felids with white underparts, pumas are big enough to have been mistaken for lions by early Portuguese and Spanish explorers of the Americas, who were the first Europeans to see them. Generations of

The long-legged serval, hunter of the African plains. As with other small cats, their skins have become more valuable as the larger cats have disappeared.

later settlers frightened themselves by calling these great cats panthers, mountain lions or even red tigers, and hunted them without mercy. Widespread from Canada to Patagonia, they live in forest, grassland or desert, hunting mostly at night; they eat anything from mule-deer to mice, taking readily to stock-rustling and being shot as vermin for their pains. Now they are mostly confined to wilderness areas and two races, the eastern puma of Canada and the US and the Florida puma, are listed as endangered.

The many smaller felids live in forests or open country, usually where they can hide among rocks during the day and emerge for nocturnal prowling. Few are well known or studied; the more beautiful ones – for example ocelots – are better known as fur coats than as live animals, and there are obscure species and races – jaguarandi, margay and Iriomote cat are examples – that gain little publicity except when their stocks are seriously endangered. WWF has been able to help some of these animals with grants toward special ecological studies. However, the most lasting benefit for them all will probably come from CITES, the international convention covering trade in endangered species (p. 32).

CITES offers some hope for controlling the trade in spotted cat skins – more, perhaps, than extra investment in anti-poaching patrols in the depths of the forest where most of the skins originate. The big cats feature in Appendix I, including tigers (except the Siberian race), the three kinds of leopard, and jaguar, cheetah and Asiatic lion; all except the last of these have attractively patterned skins, and have been in demand by the fur trade at some time. There are smaller cats too in Appendix I. Some are unspotted and virtually disregarded by the fur trade; others, for example the Indian leopard cat and some races of ocelot and margay, have beautifully marked skins that are much sought after for making into coats.

Enormous numbers of patterned skins are needed by furriers for the intricate matching involved in the production of a top-quality coat. When a particular species becomes scarce through overhunting, and a good selection of skins is difficult to obtain, the trade quickly shifts attention to other species that are similar, more abundant and more readily available. For this reason the big cats have declined one after another and the market value of their skins has decreased. The species of cats now in demand are the small ones, and the even smaller ones will be hunted when they have gone.

South American jaguars, which at over 1.5 metres (5 ft) long are the largest cats of the region, are now rare or absent over much of their former range and protected in many countries. Hunters have accordingly switched their attention to the ocelot, little more than half the size of the jaguar but far more abundant. It is possible that ocelots are still fairly common in the Amazon region, even after very heavy hunting during the last decade. But in some parts of its range, particularly in easily accessible areas, it has virtually disappeared and the similarly marked, somewhat smaller margay has been exploited in its place. Margays too have become rare in places, and now the even smaller little spotted cat is taken for the fur trade.

In Africa two large cats, the cheetah and the leopard, have both been severely reduced by hunting for their skins. Cheetah skins are less highly valued that those of leopards, and factors other than the fur trade have probably contributed heavily to the cheetah's decline. However, there are many fewer cheetahs than leopards, and their decline would certainly be slower if the demand for skins ceased. Leopards have declined severely in many areas: only a handful of countries now have buoyant populations. It is conceivable that leopards could in the future be exploited on a strictly regulated basis, but this would depend on the development of comprehensive management plans. Now that these two species of large cats are no longer so readily available to the fur trade, the smaller serval, with cheetah-like spots, has taken on their importance.

Asian tigers have been heavily hunted, but more for trophies than for fur garments. Asian leopards have declined over parts of their range as in Africa and, although completely protected, are still widely hunted for their skins – snow leopard skins are particularly in demand, despite their rarity and the animal's inaccessibility. The status of clouded leopards is poorly known, but the skins are now rarely seen in Eastern fur markets, either because protection has controlled the trade or because their numbers have declined through hunting. The much smaller leopard cat is now a favourite of the Asian fur trade, and some populations are sadly reduced in consequence.

Although there is some licenced hunting of the lesser spotted cats for their skins, there is also a deal of illegal hunting and smuggling, which can be prevented only by a proper enforcement of CITES. The wealthy consumer countries can readily implement the provisions of the Convention by strictly controlling all imports and reducing the demand for skins of protected animals. In Britain and the USA public pressure and legislation have made spotted cat garments unpopular, almost eliminating their sales. However, in West Germany, Japan and other prosperous countries, trade even in skins of big cats is flourishing. Recently the CITES Secretariat uncovered a West German smuggling racket in which forged documents were used to import hundreds of skins of ocelots and other animals from Paraguay. Many of the ocelot skins were probably smuggled out of Brazil, which has a wildlife export ban. The Secretariat is aided in its work by the Wildlife Trade Monitoring Unit of the Species Survival Commission of IUCN. TRAFFIC, which is partly funded by World Wildlife Fund, monitors international trade in wildlife, particularly the endangered species. The 1977 trade figures, for example, analysed for a meeting in Costa Rica, revealed an enormous trade in illegal spotted cat skins from South America to Europe; most passed from Brazil to West Germany, but several other countries, including Britain, were involved. Following this, World Wildlife Fund called for an immediate and complete ban on all imports of spotted cat skins into the UK, and a decision is awaited.

The fight to save the lesser cats continues in the field, in scientific meetings, and now in customs sheds and courts of law. Only when their skins are completely devalued will these beautiful animals be safe. Despite the best efforts of WWF and many other organizations, progress toward that happy day is slow and uncertain.

A blenny hides in brain coral in a Red Sea reef.

THE SEAS

THE SEAS MUST LIVE

I T IS a strange anomaly that most of the surface of Planet Earth is not earth at all: seven-tenths or more by area is sea. We who are land-bound often forget that life began in the sea, that it flourished there for hundreds of millions of years before the first specks of it emerged successfully on to land, and that life continues in the sea today in great diversity and volume. All the familiar creatures – tigers, elephants, gorillas, insects, slugs – these are just the land-bound minority that crowd with us on to the earth's relatively small dry patches. Within the sea is a completely different range of organisms – plants and animals by the million in all sizes and shapes, from tiny single-celled blobs of jelly to the greatest of whales. For the land-bound it is a new world full of surprising beauty, for marine organisms, virtually weightless in the sea, have evolved free from constraints of gravity in strange forms with magic of their own.

Deep as well as broad, the seas are deceptive in size. Their greatest depths far exceed the highest points of land. On a world scale they are merely a thin film: bring the earth down to a model of diameter 2 metres ($6\frac{1}{2}$ ft) and the seas scale down to a layer averaging no more than a millimetre (one twenty-fifth of an inch) thick. In real life this represents a lot of water. The oceans are on average five times as deep as the land is high, and their volume is fifteen times that of the continents above sea level. If we shovelled all the land into the sea (we may well do so one day, in a fit of technological enthusiasm) it would disappear completely beneath the waves, leaving a landless ocean over 3 km (two miles) deep.

This enormous mass of cool, salty water is the ever-changing, ever-circulating mobile home of the marine

The poisoned sea? Shoaling fish washed up on a beach in North Carolina, USA. Strandings can be due to natural causes, but man-made pollution takes an increasing toll in inshore waters.

Among the richest of marine habitats, coral reefs depend for their livelihood on clear, well oxygenated water; silting and other forms of pollution easily destroy them (Grand Cayman, Caribbean).

plants and animals. Like the land it has areas both of desert and riches. Tropical oceans tend to be deserts or semi-deserts; shallow-shelf seas and areas of upwelling (where submarine currents bring nutrients to the surface) are much richer, and polar seas in summer are richest of all in plant and animal biomass. Just as on land, the density of animals relates directly to the amount of plant life present, and this in turn depends on nutrients and sunshine. The plants make their living by absorbing the nutrients and fixing solar energy, and the animals live by eating – the plants or each other, according to taste.

It is mostly the near-invisible diatoms and flagellates – microscopic unicellular plants of surface waters – that count in these calculations; the seaweeds and grasses of the shore extend only into the shallows, and form only a fraction of the total plant life present in the sea. In a rich cupful of ocean there may be several thousand plant cells – too small to see but plentiful enough to tint the water – dividing rapidly and yielding food for hundreds of small-to-microscopic animals that swarm among them. These in turn are eaten by larger animals – shrimps and other crustaceans, perhaps, or larval fish – which in turn are gobbled up by the bigger fish, seabirds, dolphins, seals, whales, and other organisms that feed hungrily at the surface.

Density of plant cells in any patch of sea is usually determined by the amount of free nutrients – phosphates, nitrates and other useful salts – in the water, and this varies widely from place to place and season to season. Rich seas have abundant nutrients, washed in from the land, perhaps, or brought up from deeper layers by upwelling. Where nutrients are scarce the sea is a desert. Plant life at the surface (phytoplankton) is sparse, productivity is low, surface waters are steely blue and there are few fish, birds or mammals to be seen. Where nutrients are rich the sea comes to life. Plant cells abound and productivity is high. The sea changes colour to green or brown (according to the dominant plant cells), the small animals that feed on it (zooplankton) are plentiful, and so are the fish, mammals and seabirds. Hence the high concentrations of these larger predators in polar regions in summer, and over the rich waters of the Benguela and Humboldt Currents throughout the year.

Plants can live only at or close to the surface, for sea water absorbs sunlight and only the brightest rays penetrate more than a few metres – even less if the water is clouded with mud or plankton. Animals can live at any depth so long as there is food for them. Near the surface living food is plentiful and comes in all sizes. At depths an increasing proportion is made up of organic debris – tiny particles of living or once-living matter falling in a slow but constant rain from the well-lit layers above. Debris of this kind occurs everywhere – in the intertidal zone and at all depths; sponges, clams and other filter-feeders strain it from the water, anemones, corals and tube worms spread arms or sticky nets for the larger particles, sea cucumbers, snails and nemertine worms vacuum it from the carpet of silt and mud on the sea floor. The greater the depth, the more important this debris becomes as a food source, and many deep-sea creatures depend on it entirely. There are predators too on the bottom: lobsters, crabs, fish, starfish and a host of others hunt actively among the sedentary feeders, or scavenge for larger particles themselves.

Dredging and deep-water photography show a surprising abundance of living organisms in the depths of the oceans all over the world. At 1,000 metres (3,280 ft) sea anemones, sponges, delicate sea-fans, leathery sea-squirts, starfish and many other familiar marine animals jostle for space in the cold and permanent darkness of the sea floor. By 4,000 to 5,000 metres (13,000 to 16,500 ft) the ranks have thinned, for there is less food at greater depths. But mud-feeding sea-cucumbers, nemertine worms, sea-squirts, crimson shrimps, brittle-stars and molluscs are spread about the sea floor, with red or black fish and squid – some brilliantly illuminated with rows of tiny lights – moving like ghost ships among them. In the deepest waters of all, more than 10,000 metres (33,000 ft) down, there are still tiny fish, sea-anemones, sea-cucumbers, worms and crustaceans, all relying ultimately on the meagre rain of food from surface waters ten kilometres

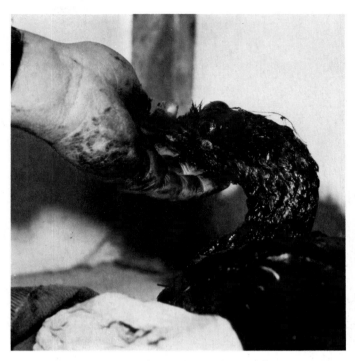

A cormorant smothered with heavy fuel oil from a leaking tanker. Thousands of seabirds are killed each year by oil; only a tiny proportion can be caught, cleaned up and released.

(six miles) above them filtering down into the abyss.

Man's main concern is with shallow seas and ocean surfaces. In them we bathe and sail our ships; from them we catch the bulk of our whales, fish, crabs, clams, and a host of other seafoods; and to them we entrust our sewage and toxic rubbish, in amounts that increase yearly. Most of our impact is felt close to the shore – on tidal flats, coral reefs, estuaries and coastal shallows – decreasing but by no means disappearing further out to sea. These are some of the richest areas for wildlife both above and below the water; the most valuable to us, they are also the most readily damaged if we fail to take care of them.

Enormous as it is, the sea accepts our insults with equanimity, absorbing what it can and spewing out the rest – insoluble plastic bottles, derelict tyres and oily scum – apologetically along the shore. Oil slicks it can absorb, though often – too often – only after the death of hundreds of sad, bedraggled seabirds. Toxic chemicals it dilutes or precipitates, metals it corrodes and dissolves, though fish by the thousand and shellfish by the ton may be poisoned in the process. Just occasionally we defeat it altogether. Enclosed seas like the Baltic and Mediterranean, and narrow arms of the sea like land-locked bays, harbours and sluggish estuaries are especially vulnerable. Where the load of wastes is locally too heavy the sea dies, leaving a foetid broth and poisoned sediments that take weeks, months or even years to recover.

Concern for the sea has grown steadily over the years as

man's effects on it have become more and more apparent. 'There are as many good fish in the sea as ever came out of it', said our grandfathers comfortably, but they were wrong. Already in their time stocks of herring, cod and many other commercial fish were deteriorating under man's impact; though fish were still plentiful, the good ones were getting scarcer. Since then our fishing effort has doubled and redoubled, stocks have deteriorated further, and fish is no longer a cheap and plentiful food.

There is concern too about our use of the sea as a dump for industrial wastes, for their bulk increases yearly as productivity rises, and we are clearly exceeding the sea's capacity for absorbing them. This is especially true of the continental shelf seas, on which we and much of our marine wildlife depend heavily for food. Pollution occurs too frequently these days; too many beaches are fouled, too many fish and shellfish poisoned, too many estuaries and tidal flats contaminated by oil, chemical sludges and sulphurous mud. We are overloading a willing system far beyond its capacity, and spoiling in every sense a valuable multiple resource.

World Wildlife Fund has for long been involved with problems of marine organisms, funding projects on turtles, seals, sea cows and other large creatures at risk from its earliest days (chapter 19). It helped with immediate and follow-up funds for the seabird rescue operation that was mounted in March 1967, when the oil tanker *Torrey Canyon* struck a reef in the English Channel. The 60,000 tons of crude oil spilling into the Channel killed tens of thousands of seabirds, and detergents used to destroy the oil slick devastated shore and shallow-water marine life. The WWF donation, channelled to the Royal Society for the Protection of Birds and other active organizations, helped in rehabilitating affected birds and keeping the oil away from nature reserves along the coast. More recently WWF funding helped France to clear its coasts of oil after the *Amoco Cadiz* disaster.

Oil pollution at sea has become an everyday problem; not only is oil drilled at sea, but enormous quantities of the stuff, crude and refined, are being transported in bulk about the world by sea. Tankers, often thin-skinned and underpowered, carry most of it. Even without accidents they manage to spill surprising amounts into the sea lanes; some leak, and some flush out their empty tanks illegally between cargoes. But every motor ship, tanker or not, carries bunker oil in bulk, and every collision or stranding brings hazard not only to ships, cargoes and crews, but to seabirds, seals and other animals going about their business in the world's great waters.

Pollution dangers increased enormously off the coast of South Africa in the early 1970s when, with the Suez Canal closed, a stream of tankers and cargo ships of all sizes took to rounding the Cape of Good Hope. Here runs the cold Benguela Current, rich in nutrients, plankton and fish, and the string of islands off south-western Africa supports huge colonies of fur seals and seabirds, including thousands of endemic gannets and jackass penguins. Intensive industrial fishing was becoming a further hazard to those stocks of marine birds and mammals, and in 1970 S.A. Wildlife, the South African WWF organization (now called Nature Foundation), mounted a three-year programme of research on their biology. This included a thorough investigation into the best methods of cleaning and rehabilitating oiled birds – now sadly a matter of urgent interest whenever sea lanes run close to seabird colonies.

Oil is a hazard we can see and legislate for; other dangers to marine wildlife are less tangible though no less deadly in their effects. DDT, produced industrially as a poison for insect pests in agriculture and used to excess, has washed off the land and into the sea. Now permeating the tissues of marine birds and mammals in every ocean from the Arctic to the Antarctic, its effects are not always known but likely to be detrimental. It has been implicated, for example, as a possible factor in the serious decline of Audouin's gull in the western Mediterranean; stocks of this species are down to less than 1,000, and DDT is an unwelcome component of their eggs. Compounds of mercury and cadmium, flushed as industrial effluent into Japanese seas, similarly accumulated in inshore shellfish during the early years of Japan's industrial expansion. The shellfish poisoned local fisher-folk and others further afield, with symptoms ranging in severity from sick headaches to permanent bone disease and brain damage. Again the effects on local wildlife were unknown, but would hardly have been beneficial.

Economic development may have many damaging side effects, most of them unmeasured, even unrecognized, until disaster strikes. Coral reefs sicken and decay when coral sand, valuable as a building material, is dredged from nearby. Whole areas of Australia's Great Barrier Reef decayed when predatory crown-of-thorns starfish increased explosively in numbers and rampaged; the cause is still unknown, but suspicion falls on over-ardent shell collectors, who market the attractive shells of the predatory whelks that normally keep the crown-of-thorns starfish in check.

Concerned with the growing problems of widespread dumping, pollution, destruction of coastal sites, and other insults to the sea both overt and insidious, IUCN in 1974 sought the help of WWF in preparing a full-scale programme of marine conservation. Work began with the identification of critical marine habitats – listed under five headings, these are (1) feeding, resting, breeding or nursery areas of marine animals; (2) major sources of nutrients for feeding areas elsewhere, for example, sea grass meadows and mangrove coasts; (3) coral reefs and similar habitats particularly rich in species; (4) highly productive habitats, such as estuaries; (5) habitats of special scientific interest – for example deep ocean trenches. Having identified the critical habitats, IUCN's task was to formulate plans to survey them throughout the world, assess their needs, and work toward the development of national parks, reserves, and comprehensive management programmes to protect them.

From these beginnings arose WWF's major marine campaign, launched in 1977 under the title 'The Seas Must Live'. Its largest campaign to date, with a target figure of US$10 million, this now supports a wide-ranging programme of marine conservation projects, within a framework drawn up by IUCN specialists in cooperation with UNEP and the Food and Agriculture Organization of the United Nations (FAO).

Announced at the end of World Wildlife Fund's Fourth International Conference, which was held in San Francisco late in 1976, this campaign declared 1977 the 'Year of the Seas'. Many of the projects that it supported were new; others were follow-on programmes derived from earlier surveys, for the marine conservation studies had already started and were well under way when the fund-raising began in 1977. Field surveys of the north-western Indian Ocean from the Red Sea and Persian Gulf to Sri Lanka, for example, were carried out under the 'critical marine habitats' programme early in 1975. Similar surveys of Caribbean, Pacific and Mediterranean coasts were completed later in the same year. Following conferences of specialists in Tehran and Tokyo, and the San Francisco conference itself, IUCN and WWF were ready by 1977 to announce their comprehensive Action Programmes incorporating the results of these surveys, and also pinpointing studies of whales, seals, turtles, sirenians, crocodiles, seabirds, shorebirds, coral reefs, mangroves, regional management, and legal and educational aspects of marine conservation.

The IUCN/WWF Marine Programme has developed along guidelines provided by the World Conservation Strategy (p. 217), with special subprogrammes for priority areas. For the Caribbean there has been emphasis on the development of an overall plan of management and conservation of marine and coastal reserves. In the Mediterranean the main problems tackled have been coastal wetland reserve management, and special studies of two endangered species – monk seals and Audouin's gulls. Islands of the southern Pacific Ocean too receive special attention: WWF/IUCN has prepared an overall South Pacific Action Plan outlining specific problems in Fiji, the Gilbert Islands, Tonga and Western Samoa, and suggesting that the Solomon Islands, Vanuatu and the Cook Islands may need advice and help before long. The recent

One of the few: a monk seal, once plentiful throughout the Mediterranean, now restricted to a handful of colonies on out-of-the-way islands and coasts.

discovery of a new (and of course threatened) species of iguana on Fiji underlines the world's ignorance of these islands, many of which, newly-independent, face hasty and possibly ill-considered development.

Within the marine programme IUCN and WWF have been particularly concerned for the stability of coral reefs under the impact of man. Surrounding many islands in the southern Pacific and elsewhere, coral reefs are living, growing walls that enclose a sheltering lagoon and protect the strand: many aspects of island economy from fishing to shore cultivation depend on their integrity. Formed continuously by coral polyps (like millions of small, stone-secreting sea-anemones), they are readily upset by toxins or stirred-up sediments: if the polyps die, the wall dies and breaks down, and its protection is lost.

On the Polynesian island of Moorea, close to Tahiti, where coral sand is dredged from the inshore lagoon for building, study has been made of the precise effects of the ensuing turbidity and disturbance on growth of coral and other reef organisms; similar studies are being made, with WWF backing, on the Caribbean island of Guadeloupe. With their wealth of expertise gained from reef studies in all the tropical oceans, IUCN and WWF have produced a comprehensive report and set of guidelines to encourage governments in the establishment of coral reef national

Though still plentiful on islands close to the Cape of Good Hope, jackass penguins are increasingly vulnerable to oiling as more and more heavy tankers are routed through their feeding grounds.

parks and reserves. The guidelines are being used in studying problems of coral reefs in the Red Sea, where the Sudan government is establishing marine reserves for the protection of the sea bed.

In the western Pacific Ocean, WWF has helped to promote an extensive IUCN ecological and economic study of the Palau Archipelago, where a development programme may seriously endanger both the ecology of the fringing coral reefs and the traditional ways of life of thousands of islanders. Currently a United Nations Trust Territory and scheduled soon to achieve independence, Palau possesses some of the world's finest coral reefs, and rich local fishing. There are plans to create port facilities there for Japanese tankers, and other shipping facilities which would seriously endanger the whole Palau marine environment. The study, organized by IUCN with WWF help, aims to inform the people of Palau how the development may affect local ecology and their livelihood, provide them with alternative suggestions, and ensure that the development does not start until they have been given the chance to make a fully informed decision about it.

Moving southward into temperate and polar waters, WWF is funding two linked projects concerning the Southern Oceans – the biologically rich waters extending southward to the shores of the Antarctic continent. One project models the distribution and abundance of krill – the major components of the zooplankton on which myriads of seabirds, seals and whales depend. The second project examines biological and management problems in the Southern Oceans, setting out alternative strategies for exploiting their resources, for the good of all mankind, in non-destructive ways. Sorting out the problems of the Southern Oceans is perhaps IUCN/WWF's greatest single challenge to date; answers acceptable to the community of nations will set many useful precedents in international law and resource management, as well as providing the world with a stable, sustained annual increment to its food budget.

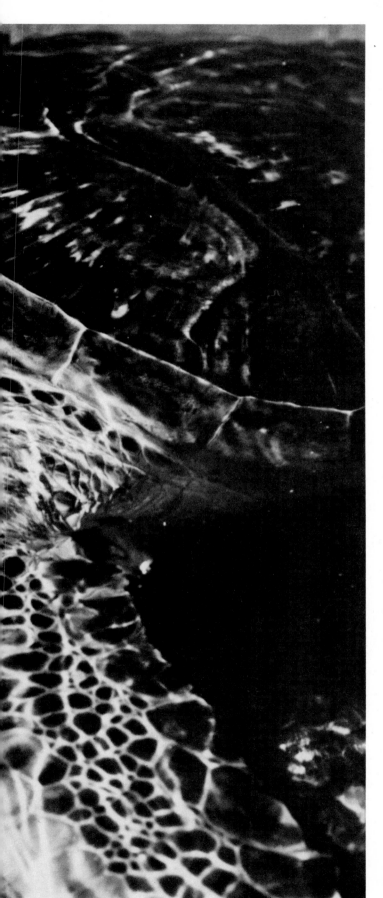

MERMAIDS
AND TURTLES

To landsmen the world over, oceans are vast areas of damp, heaving discomfort best left to sailors, and many sailors would agree with them. But seamen with naturalists' instincts can usually find plenty to keep them interested at sea, even on long voyages that take them halfway round the world. The slower their boat and the lower the freeboard, the closer they get to marine animals, especially the big ones – whales, dolphins, seals, turtles and game fish – that top the marine food pyramids. The layman sees one big ocean: to the marine naturalist no piece of ocean is quite like the last, and it is a poor four-hour watch that doesn't yield something new – anything from a shoal of plankton to a sea serpent – to ponder over on the next leg of the voyage.

Botanists have little to excite them at sea: apart from the narrow band of brown, green and red seaweeds, mangroves, and occasional patches of sea grass that line the shore, practically all marine plants are microscopic. Immersed in nutrients, unmoved by gravity or winds, there has been no call for them to differentiate roots, stems, branches, leaves, internal plumbing and storage, flowers and seeds – all the paraphernalia of complex plants ashore. So they have stayed small and simple, mostly unicellular, and the animals that graze on them are small and relatively simple too. The main bulk of grazing animals in the sea are invertebrates of the zooplankton and small fish, few of them longer than 30 cm (12 in.).

Two notable exceptions are the Sirenia, an Order of marine grazing mammals that sailors over the centuries have called sea-cows, and the marine turtles, sea-going kin

A green turtle of the Caribbean. Marine turtles, generally much larger than tortoises, may weigh over 200kg (440lb): they haul themselves ashore only to rest and lay their eggs.

Overleaf A Caribbean manatee mother (left) with suckling calf. Though they look like seals, manatees are herbivorous mammals that feed in coastal shallows, rivers and canals.

of the tortoises and terrapins, many of which are herbivorous. Most other large animals of the sea are carnivores.

The sea-cows – dugongs and manatees – are well named, if only because they often graze on sea grasses in underwater meadows of tropical and subtropical shallows. They do not look in the least like terrestrial cows. At first glance they might be clumsily-built seals, or overweight dolphins with perhaps a touch of elephant in their ancestry. This is zoologically less unlikely than it sounds: serum protein studies indicate that the Sirenia are probably more closely akin to the elephants than to any other group of land mammals, and certainly more closely than to the other sea mammals. They have lived in the sea for a long time – sixty million years at least. Now entirely aquatic, they are helpless if hauled out on to land.

There are two families of Sirenia, the Dugongidae (dugongs and Steller's sea-cows) and Trichechidae (manatees), superficially similar, with heavy head and tapering body. Both live in shallow rivers and estuaries, and along quiet coasts where there is plenty of sea grass and other fixed or floating vegetation. Almost hairless, with elephantine brown or grey hide, they have lost their hindlimbs altogether and converted the fore-limbs to flippers. For propulsion dugongs have a two-fluked tail like a dolphin's, manatees a flat spade-like tail; both can swim fast but prefer the quiet, ambling pace proper to a sea-cow. The head is heavy, the face walrus-like, thick-lipped and heavily bewhiskered, with small eyes and an aggrieved expression – fair comment, perhaps, on man's constant intrusions into sirenian lives, which are rarely to their advantage.

Both manatees and dugongs have lost their biting front teeth; lips and horny plates grasp the soft vegetation instead. There is a full row of constantly growing grinding molars on either side. On the Aru Islands of Indonesia, where about 1,000 dugongs are killed annually, human ingenuity turns the teeth into (of all things) cigarette holders for the export market. The hides too are tough enough to tan. Female manatees have pectoral mammary glands and are occasionally reported to stand upright in the water, tenderly clutching an infant to their breast. This is said to be the origin of the mermaid legend and possibly of the name of their order – Sirenia. That they sing to each other under water with squeaky, quavering voices may also have helped, though dugongs and manatees, charming animals as they are, would not be everybody's idea – certainly not every sailor's – of how a siren should look.

Dugongs live in the Indian Ocean and the central and western Pacific, usually in small herds that stay close to the coast. Only one species is alive today. Moderately sized animals 3 to 4 metres (9 to 13 ft) long, through most of

A leatherback turtle, almost two metres long, lays its eggs in a deep-dug nest. Studies on the breeding beaches show that females may lay over a hundred eggs per year in several different nests.

their range they are heavily hunted for their meat. A much larger species of dugongs, Steller's sea-cow, was formerly found in the north-western Pacific and Bering Sea. Over 10 metres (33 ft) long, they lived in herds and were hunted steadily by aboriginals along the Pacific shores for generations. The last 2,000 or so were exterminated by sailors on their final strongholds, Copper and Bering Islands, in the mid-eighteenth century. There are still occasional rumours of these huge beasts living on remote island shores of the Bering Sea, but the chances are slim.

Manatees are of similar size to dugongs, but restricted to the tropical and subtropical Atlantic region. Caribbean manatees live on the West Indies and mainland Caribbean coasts of Central and South America, in the Orinoco River and in Florida; South American manatees live in the Amazon River, its lakes and tributaries; West African manatees are found sparsely in rivers and coastal waters from Senegal to Angola. All stocks are hunted heavily, despite official protection in many of their haunts.

Both dugongs and manatees are quiet, inoffensive mammals that seek only to be left browsing in peace. This is not generally their fate; where man finds them, he usually kills them. It is their misfortune to be made of good, tender meat, and that most of them live in countries with expanding and hungry human populations. Almost all stocks of survivors have declined and their ranges decreased in the last few decades: all four species are listed in the Red Data Books. North American manatees are least at risk of being eaten, but most likely to be buzzed and even chopped by expensive outboard motors in their river, lake and canal haunts.

A Sirenian Specialist Group led by Dr Colin Bertram is looking after the interests of dugongs and manatees for IUCN. Dr Bertram and his wife have visited populations throughout the world with WWF support. They conclude that there are probably many regions where sirenians will never be effectively protected: their range will therefore diminish gradually. There are other areas, however, where conservation may well be effective, and there are possibilities too of farming them as grazers to keep canals clear, and perhaps for meat production. WWF is sponsoring research on Amazon manatees, among the most endangered species, in Brazil. In Florida and Australia too, local stocks are being monitored with a view to conservation. Manatee and dugong studies are coordinated under a worldwide WWF research programme led by Dr Sandra L. Husar, a US biologist, who is compiling monographs and bibliographies and assembling management data for every species.

Marine turtles form another group of large sea animals, often encountered on tropical shores and no less at risk then the sirenians. Turtles are aquatic tortoises, usually with flattened shells and fin-like flippers that allow them to fly in elegant slow motion through the water. Like tortoises they have a venerable past: they have swum the seas for 100 million years at least and probably much longer, confined almost entirely to warm tropical waters.

Turtles vary in the amount of time they spend on land; some are only partly aquatic, others mainly so. But the biggest turtles – the sea-going branch of the family – are all deep-water sailors that seldom come ashore, except for the few hours that the females need each year to dig nests and lay their eggs. There are seven species, most of them widespread and overlapping in range; five breed in the Caribbean alone. All are seriously threatened by human predation.

Green, hawksbill, loggerhead and ridley turtles have hard, bony shells like tortoises, with a casing of horny material that from some species is eagerly sought by trade. Leatherback turtles have a softer leathery skin that can be peeled off and tanned. But the main dangers to turtles arise from their meat and their eggs, both highly palatable to man. Sailors long ago found that almost any kind of turtle, caught at sea and hauled aboard, could be kept alive for several weeks in a cool corner of the deck or hold. Living on their fat reserves, they could be killed at leisure to provide fresh, tasty meat. Landsmen appreciated turtles too, catching them as they blundered up the beaches to lay. Turtles travelled far to satisfy gourmets: green turtles from southern Atlantic Ascension Island traditionally

Archie Carr – US scientist responsible for many turtle studies – adjusts a radio transmitter on the back of a green turtle: with it he will track the animal's movements in the open ocean.

provided the soup for the Lord Mayor of London's annual banquet. Just as tasty are the eggs, the size and shape of billiard balls with soft leathery shells. Laid by the dozen in nests dug deep in the sand, they take two to three months to hatch. Beach-combing folk throughout the tropics have learned to watch for the tell-tale tracks of the females coming ashore, leading them to an annual bounty of rich, oily, protein-packed eggs.

Marine turtles can be big animals; green or leatherback turtles may weigh over 200 kg and measure a metre from nose to tail. Other species are smaller, but it is only with difficulty that females of any species haul themselves up the beaches to lay. However big the adults, young turtles hatch at little more than matchbox size. Emerging in groups from the nests, often under cover of darkness, they cross the beach quickly with flippers flailing, like wound-up toys. Guided by the sound and vibrations of the surf, they head unerringly for the sea and swim out beyond the breakers. Bite-size for all kinds of predators from seabirds to small sharks, they are taken in enormous numbers during their their first week of life in the open ocean. The survivors grow quickly, however, undertaking long drifting migrations in the placid warm waters of the doldrums. Some turtles are carnivorous, feeding on floating plankton, including tropical jellyfish. Others – green turtles, for example – are mainly herbivores. Occasionally they drift out of the closed circulation system of the tropics and end up on the shores of Europe and North America, semi-torpid and helpless in the cold water.

Though individual turtles of all species are vulnerable to the hunter, the most serious damage to breeding stocks and species is inflicted by butchers and nest-robbers on the traditional breeding beaches. Coyotes, monitor lizards and other natural predators account for many, but the most systematic and therefore most dangerous predator of all is man.

For most stocks of turtles the problem is one of local rather than general extinction. Turtles and men can live together quite well for generations in a system of controlled exploitation. The turtles provide food and a subsistence livelihood for local villagers, who in turn protect the beaches against more serious predation from outside. Taking limited numbers of eggs and animals may be a long-standing tradition, evidence in itself that the stock is not over-exploited.

But growth of human populations, expectations of higher living standards, ease of transport and ever-ready markets elsewhere combine to upset these balanced relationships. Only too often a stock that has remained stable – even grown – under local predation may be destroyed in two or three seasons if commercial interests take charge. Organized lunacy may prevail when they do. Richard Felger, working on a WWF supported project on

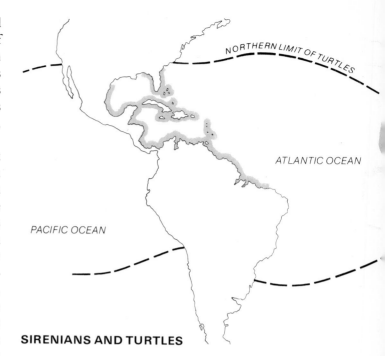

SIRENIANS AND TURTLES

Above Dugongs – widespread in Indonesian waters – are an important source of fresh meat for island communities.

Opposite Ridleys at a nesting beach (in Santa Rosa National Park, Costa Rica) during their 'arribada' or laying season.

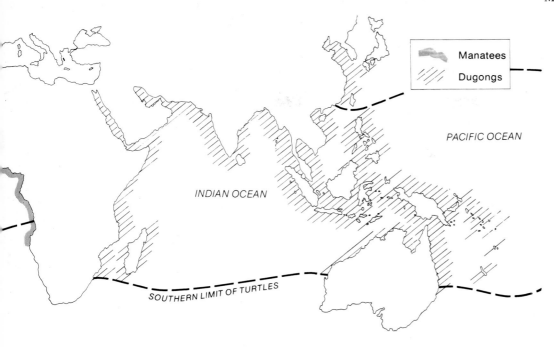

Manatees are found exclusively in the tropical and subtropical Atlantic region, while dugongs live in the Indian Ocean and the central western Pacific. Turtles may migrate long distances, but are helpless if they drift out of warm tropical waters.

the Pacific coast of Mexico, reports that 70,000 olive ridleys – almost half the breeding population, and nearly all of them gravid females – were killed on one Mexican breeding beach in a single season.

IUCN has a particularly active Marine Turtle Specialist Group which, first meeting in 1969, sounded an alarm for turtles. From a period of long, slow decline, stocks of all species were edging quickly toward catastrophic depopulation, due to incessant demands for turtle meat, leather, shell and oil. The greatest dangers lay on the beaches, where both turtles and eggs were under attack, and immediate action for conservation was needed by all governments that had turtle colonies within their territories.

Since then the Group has met many times and instigated valuable surveys all over the tropical world; WWF has supported conservation studies in the Caribbean, southwestern Pacific and Indian Oceans, Australasia, the Galapagos Islands and many other key breeding areas. Breeding seasons and habits, survival, migrations, growth rates, health, and other aspects of marine turtle biology have been studied, and monographs have been compiled on most of the species. This worldwide research now forms the basis of management studies, aimed ultimately at advising communities on how to conserve their stocks of turtles, and obtain from them sustained yields of meat, eggs and other useful additions to their diet and economy.

WHALES AND SEALS

FEW PEOPLE in the world have ever seen a whale; only those who spend time near a coast are likely to see seals. But these are possibly two of the world's most popular kinds of creature when conservation issues come up. 'Save the whale' is a splendid rallying call, and pictures of wide-eyed baby seals have done much to make people think again about the propriety of wearing animal-skin coats. So much to the good, and long may their popularity last. What kinds of animals are they, and how has WWF helped them to survive?

Both whales and seals are aquatic mammals, mostly but not exclusively marine; warm-blooded like the rest of us, they cannot live long without breathing air. Derived from completely different stocks of archaic mammals, they have approached the sea in different ways. Whales have been maritime far longer; fossils show that there were quite recognizable whales, already completely aquatic, in the sea over fifty million years ago. Seals have been recognizable only about half that time, and have never committed themselves fully to the sea in all their history. Both are superbly efficient in the water; if it is only a second home for seals, they are happy to spend weeks or months on end there without coming out on to land.

The ancestors of whales and dolphins were four-footed animals, warm-blooded and furry, and possibly akin to pigs. They may well have passed through a seal-like amphibious stage before finally giving up the land altogether. Now entirely aquatic, they are very much in danger if they accidentally run ashore. There are about seventy-four different species alive today, forming the mammalian order Cetacea.

Wonderfully adapted for their sea-going life, whales and dolphins have many special qualities that distinguish them from other mammals. Whether large or small, their

The elegant tail flukes of a southern right whale, a rare species of the southern oceans.

shape is that of an elongated torpedo, beautifully streamlined from tip of nose to slender, fluked tail. Despite their bulk they move easily through the water, undulating the tail in a steady, sinuous, up-and-down rippling movement that drives them forward with little turbulence or wasted effort; dolphins swim at about 30 km (up to 20 miles) per hour, big whales at 16 to 20 km (10 to 12 miles) per hour, keeping up their pace with effortless ease for mile after mile. Air breathers, they carry their nostrils on top of the head, 'blowing' or exhaling as they surface and taking a quick, deep breath before re-submerging. Most whales and dolphins spend most of their life at the sea surface or within easy reach of it; sperm whales and a very few other species are deep divers, able to hunt for long spells deep down. Whales see and hear well, and have soft, sensitive skins that ripple as they move through the water, thereby reducing friction. Most are completely hairless, relying on blubber – subdermal fat – for their insulation; a few have sensory hairs on their faces that indicate when they are passing through a shoal of plankton.

Within the Order Cetacea are two quite distinct kinds of whales – Mysticetes and Odontocetes – that probably evolved from different ancestral groups thirty to fifty million years ago. Mysticetes (also called baleen whales or whalebone whales) form a minority – there are only ten species of them – but they include most of the largest whales. Their names indicate that they carry whalebone or baleen, a stiff, bristly material that grows from the roof of the mouth and is used as a filter for trapping food. Odontocetes are the toothed whales; sperm whales and killer whales are the largest, and there are many others in descending size through to the smallest dolphins less than 2 metres (6 ft) long. Toothed whales all have teeth at some stage in their life, often in eccentric arrangements – lower jaw only in sperm whales, one or two pairs only in bottlenose whales, and deeply embedded in the gums – presumably functionless – in some females. Killer whales have a formidable double row of teeth suitable for biting and tearing prey of all kinds; dolphins and porpoises have small peg-like teeth that are right for catching and holding slippery fish.

Whales are found in every ocean of the world. The biggest ones, Mysticetes especially, tend to spend their summers in cold temperate and polar waters where the plankton is richest, and winter in the tropics, often without feeding for several months. They produce their calves in tropical waters; the shock of emerging into a sea close to freezing point would probably put a young whale off swimming for life, and in warm water the calf can survive with a relatively smaller endowment of fat from its mother. Blue whale calves measure 7 to 8 metres (22 to 25 ft) at birth and weigh two to three tonnes; they are said to double their birth weight within two weeks, entirely

A southern right whale breaching. Whales leap out of the water in courtship and play, falling back with a thump that can be heard miles away.

from their mother's milk. Most whales are sociable creatures, travelling in small groups of females, infants and young adults; males tend to be solitary or form bachelor herds. Dolphins often congregate in huge schools of several hundred animals, and gather in smaller groups around shoals of fish. Here they often fall foul of fishermen, who may also have an interest in the fish and regard the dolphins as trade rivals.

For well over a thousand years men have hunted whales for their oil, flesh, sinews, bone, whalebone and other components. Practically all species will have been hunted at one time or another, but in recent years the heaviest hunting pressures have fallen upon the largest whales – the right whales, sperm whales and fast-moving rorquals. The hunting has been good – good enough over the years to produce an enormous, highly capitalized, competitive international industry. It has launched fine ships, bred first-rate seamen, founded the fortunes of cities all over the world, and provided honest, often very hard work for thousands of men and women afloat and ashore.

Now the hunting is almost over. So efficient has the industry been, so competitive and so difficult to control in the absence of international laws for the high seas, that it has worked itself practically out of business. Since the 1950s it has been catching the great whales far faster than they could replace themselves, and the numbers remaining no longer justify large-scale, highly technological hunting expeditions. There may well be no industrial whaling left, except here and there on a small, local scale, by the end of the century – and few will shed tears for its end.

Fortunately there should still be whales, steaming busily through the surface waters of the oceans long after the last

Beluga, the white whale of the Arctic Ocean: small numbers are hunted each year by northern folk who value their meat, blubber, skin and sinews.

of the whaling ships has fallen to rust. Some are already on the increase, for whales breed young and often and live long when allowed to; reducing their numbers has left a vast surplus of food in the seas, and populations of animals usually expand to meet their food supplies. Unless seabirds, seals or man get there first, whale stocks stand a good chance of recovery once the hunting has ceased. Whale-watchers the world over will welcome the return of these huge, improbable animals, for those who know and care for whales care very much indeed.

Whales were not featured in WWF's early projects, but over the years they have insinuated themselves; now WWF is active in whale affairs, supporting whale biologists throughout the world. From 1972 onward the Fund has called annually, in association with IUCN and others at meetings of the International Whaling Commission, for a ten-year moratorium on commercial whaling, and in other ways made clear its strong anti-whaling stance. More practically it has sponsored surveys of several species of big whales of threatened or doubtful status – right whales off Alaska and Australia, for example, humpback whales in Hawaii, blue whales in the St Lawrence estuary, and sperm whales off the Azores Islands, Indonesia and Peru. WWF has funded research on narwhals and their role in Eskimo culture, and helped a

study of gray whales in Baja California; this species, once almost extinct but now recovered after forty-four years of international protection, faces a new hazard – boatloads of cheerful whale-watchers who come out to enjoy them and wish them well on their traditional Mexican breeding grounds. The Fund has also subsidized the development of a marking tag visible from ships and aircraft – a most useful aid to identifying individual whales at sea.

The Fund has also looked past the problems of the big and well-known whales to help some of the little ones, many of which are equally at risk. Some are hunted by inshore fishermen to provide food for local and distant markets, usually with little knowledge of how much hunting the stocks will stand. Some are killed by being driven ashore and clubbed, because they interfere with fishing in coastal waters. Many thousands of spinner dolphins and other species are destroyed each year by accident – caught up in nets set for tuna and other big fish, and damaged or drowned before they can be rescued. Though some of these species are plentiful, others are rare or of completely unknown status. WWF is helping by

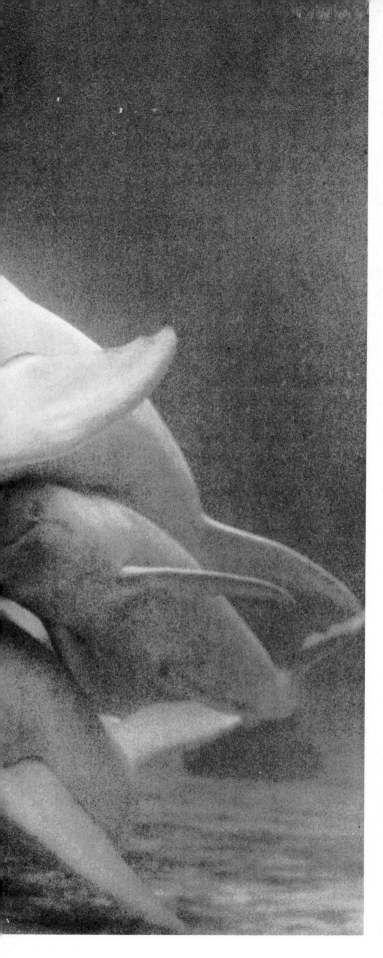

Amazon dolphins are found in the fresh waters of the river Amazon and its tributaries. The eyes are tiny and almost functionless: river dolphins hunt mainly by sound. Only small scattered populations remain after severe hunting.

drawing attention to the problems of particular species – dolphins of the North Sea, Black Sea and Baltic, for example, Indus River dolphins of Pakistan, and little cochito dolphins of Mexico – and helping IUCN to draw up general policies to conserve marine mammals. One recent development is the establishment of a chain of sanctuaries in waters all over the world where whales and dolphins will always be free of human killing and interference, a splendid ideal that will gradually be realized and extended during the next decade.

Seals, like whales, are carnivorous sea mammals, distantly related to dogs, bears and otters. Only quite recently evolved – in the last thirty million years or so – their sea-change has been less dramatic than that of whales and sirenians; they are still otter-like, bear-like or dog-like in many respects. Fur seal and sea lions have canine faces and teeth. Some bark like dogs, especially the pups, and they will chase you and tear your trousers like dogs if you wander too freely on their breeding territories.

All seals spend much of their life in water, hauling out on to land or sea ice to rest, court, sunbathe, moult, quarrel, scratch – seals lead busy lives. Some species mate in the water, some produce their pups on sandbanks and float them off with the next tide, but most mate, give birth and rear their pups on land.

Seals feed entirely in water, eating fish, krill, squid and seabirds. Nearly all take their food at the surface; just a few species, notably the bigger ones, dive well over 100 metres (330 ft) and hunt in the dim light far below; they have specially adapted eyes and probably use sonar to detect their prey as well. Walruses feed on the sea bed; their whiskers are bristles for detecting clams in the mud, and their huge tusks are rakes for digging them out.

Biologists divide the seals into three families – the earless or true seals (Phocidae), the eared seals (Otariidae) and the walruses (Odobaenidae). True seals have perfectly good ears and very acute hearing, especially under water; all that is lacking is the external ear flap or pinna. There are about eighteen species; derived from otter-like ancestors, they are in many ways the most sea-going of all the seals, and furthest evolved from their terrestrial ancestors. They include the common and grey seals of Britain and cool northern waters, harp and hooded seals of the polar ice edge, bearded and ringed seals of the pack ice, and beleaguered monk seals of the Mediterranean and Hawaii, and possibly extinct monk seals of the Caribbean. Most seals of Antarctic waters also belong to this group.

Eared seals and walruses, closely related to each other, are probably derived from bear-like ancestors. Eared seals fall into two closely-similar groups; there are about seven species of fur seals and five species of sea lions, and the most important difference between them – the quality of their fur – may literally be a matter of life and death for them. Fur seals have a smooth, velvety underfur which, properly processed, gives them a special market value, for tens of thousands of them each year meet an early death. Sea lions, like adults of most other species, have a coarse, bristly fur; their hides are sometimes taken for tanning, but not for the fine fur market. Juveniles of several species have fine woolly downy coats that cost them their lives within a few days or weeks of their birth – again in tens or hundreds of thousands each year.

Seals move clumsily on land or ice; true seals shuffle or crawl, sea lions and fur seals get up on their much longer flippers and can walk, run or even climb over rough rocks. All swim superbly, using their flexible hindquarters and hind limbs as a propellor; otariids use their fore-limbs as well. Mobility on land becomes important in the breeding season, when the cows haul out to produce their pups and mate again almost immediately, and the bulls guard them singly or in harem groups. In their big breeding concentrations on land or sea ice, seals are most vulnerable to attack by man; several species are hunted annually, usually under licence and during breeding times.

Curiously, the populations most heavily harvested by man are not the ones most at risk. Though nineteenth-century sealers wiped out stock after stock of fur seals and oil-bearing elephant seals, modern ones do not. Careful husbandry of fur seals in the northern Pacific, South America and South Africa, for example, has maintained breeding stocks despite a heavy annual kill; it is mostly young males that are taken, and many would never breed anyway. Some thousands of young harp and hood seals are killed for their skins each year under less carefully monitored conditions on the northern sea ice. Although the harp seal is one of the most numerous of sea mammals, WWF and IUCN have repeatedly advised the Canadian government that the annual cull is too great for the species to sustain.

In recent years World Wildlife Fund has supported conservation studies of several species that, reduced in numbers through hunting or disturbance in the past, are currently still at risk. Fur seals and sea lions of the Galapagos Islands, devastated by nineteenth-century hunting, come into this category; their populations seem now to be stable and possibly increasing slowly. Mediterranean monk seals by contrast are declining; shy

Grey seals on the Orkney Islands. Their population has increased under protection, and they are now subject to annual culling in order to protect the interests of the fishermen.

seals that seek isolation and solitude and breed in caves, their numbers are now estimated at 1,000 or less, scattered in widely separated groups from the Black Sea to the Canary Islands.

Throughout their range these seals suffer disturbance from tourists and harassment from fishermen. WWF has promoted surveys in Greece and elsewhere, regarding it as an important component in the overall programme of conservation for the Mediterranean area. Reserves are also being established for monk seals on the coast of Mauritania at Banc d'Arguin (p. 106).

Seals are sensitive to pollution and the disturbances created by sea traffic in enclosed areas. WWF has supported long-term studies of common seals in the Waddensee and of three species in the Baltic Sea, where populations are declining, to see if the causes can be pinpointed. In Korea it is preparing, on a smaller scale, for a welcome-home party: the Japanese sea lion, reported extinct there in 1960, may be trying to re-establish itself on offlying islands.

Fur seals of the Pribilov Islands: a bull surrounded by his harem of cows, some with newly-born pups.

POSTSCRIPT: WWF AND THE FUTURE

TRADITION HAS it that, just over twenty years ago, the first WWF projects were selected by a triumvirate – three newly-appointed Trustees of the newly-formed organization — one afternoon in a London office over glasses of sherry. Tradition may be right; there were knowledgeable people involved, the choice was in good hands, and their objectives were clear — they were saving the animals. Now times have changed; for better or worse the informality disappeared long ago as WWF grew, and everything has become more complex.

More schemes come up for selection each year, and more are selected. There is more – far more – money to be distributed; in 1980 it was over US$5 million, more than twenty times as much as in 1961, and the target figure grows yearly. Then the pattern of WWF-sponsored projects has changed. There was a strong element of emergency action – fire-fighting – among the early ones, and now largely replaced by long-term schemes and forward planning are also part of WWF's effort. Saving the animals is but one aspect of a much more broadly based approach to conservation that WWF has adopted over the years, resulting in more effective conservation of individual species.

This is consistent with subtle changes in WWF's image – in particular the way it has seen itself growing and developing as time has passed. It began unashamedly as a latter-day Noah's Ark, launched to save animals from the rising flood of human activities that was threatening to engulf them everywhere in the world. The first published report of WWF, edited by Peter Scott and issued in 1965, was called 'The Launching of a New Ark', and the second, produced three years later, was 'The Ark Under Way'. But as WWF grew in stature and certainty the Ark image faded; it is hard to believe that WWF for long saw itself sitting passively on the water and riding out the storm. 'Conservation in Action' was a suggested but unused title for the first annual report of 1969, and the livelier image

has persisted in untitled annual reports since that time.

Firstly and always a fund-raising body, WWF for long used the 'saving the animals' theme in its publicity, and many who support the Fund today still do so with the simplest of motives: they like animals or the idea of animals, and want to see them living on in the world. WWF has, however, always sought to get past the 'woolly animals' image into broader, if less immediately appealing, fields of conservation. Raising money for IUCN and other scientific organizations (ICBP and IWRB, for example) and supporting projects proposed by zoological societies, museums, local natural history societies and government departments has never prevented WWF from having its own views on conservation and how the work should be done. It has for long seen itself too as an educator and campaign organization, not only to raise money but, in its own words, 'to educate the public about the threat to the world's natural heritage and the action necessary to conserve it.' This, like so many other of its activities, it does internationally through IUCN.

In modern WWF thinking, education for action does not stop at travelling slide-shows for villagers, though it often very sensibly starts there. With large and now fairly reliable funds at its disposal each year WWF can enter a national or international controversy and pack a hard punch on the side of the conservationists. Opponents will find nothing meagre, for example, in its support for conservation interests in Palau (p. 199) and the Waddensee (p. 104). If this is a new Noah's Ark, it is an ark with a ram bow, torpedo tubes, and a formidable crew of conservationists below decks.

WWF's current attitudes to conservation are summed up by Dr Lee M. Talbot, until recently its Director of Conservation and now Director-General of IUCN, in his introduction to the WWF Yearbook, 1979–80. Whereas in the past conservation was seen by decision-makers as a luxury at best or an obstacle to development at worst, and clearly out of the mainstream of human endeavours, there is now explicit recognition that conservation is basic to human survival and welfare. Conservation and development are not mutually exclusive – they are interdependent, and conservation goals are becoming recognized as among the basic goals of humanity.

Following this recognition, conservation is under way in new directions – goal-oriented directions planned to achieve well-defined objectives. The new directions focus on causes of problems as well as effects, and on prevention rather than cure; they involve a professional approach based on sound science, and explicitly recognize the link between conservation and human welfare.

Will the new directions alter the WWF of the future, and will it still be saving the animals? Two recent publications help us to understand how the organization sees itself and its future on the eve of its twenty-first birthday. The first is *World Conservation Strategy*, a statement of global conservation priorities and plans for achieving them, drawn up by IUCN on behalf of the United Nations Environmental Programme. WWF helped to pay for its production, and also contributed strongly to its philosophy. The second is *A Conservation Programme for Sustainable Development 1980–82*, IUCN's comprehensive programme for the next three years, drawn up with the support and financial assistance of WWF, UNEP and others.

The *Strategy*, which in Dr Lee Talbot's words 'epitomises the new directions in conservation that WWF and IUCN will be taking', aims at helping to advance the achievement of sustainable development through the conservation of living resources. It starts by defining three main objectives of conservation – to maintain essential ecological processes, to preserve genetic diversity, and to ensure the sustainable utilization of species and ecosystems. It goes on to say why these objectives are important, and to be achieved as a matter of urgency.

Then it highlights six common obstacles to achieving conservation, which include lack of integration between conservation and development, lack of support for conservation, inflexible and destructive development, and lack of capacity to conserve – owing to poverty, inadequate legislation, lack of information or trained personnel, and a dozen other causes.

From there the *Strategy* defines conservation (rather wordily) as 'the management of human use of the biosphere so that it may yield the greatest sustainable benefit to present generations while maintaining its potential to meet the needs and aspirations of future generations', and then in six double-page spreads sets out more fully the three main objectives, establishing priorities for each. Priority is assigned for 'significance',

A mobile educational unit distributing leaflets to schoolchildren in Malaysia.

'urgency' and 'irreversibility', with highest priority of all arising when irreversible damage needs to be stopped.

Under 'essential ecological processes', for example, priority is given to reserving good farmland for crops and not building on it, maintaining croplands to high standards and soils intact, and ensuring that watersheds are properly managed. Under 'preserving genetic diversity', priority is given to preventing extinctions, preserving varieties of organisms, and preserving good mixed habitats in adequate reserves; under 'ensuring sustainable utilization', priority is given to determining productive capacities of stocks of fish and other exploited organisms, maintaining their habitats, reducing over-exploitation, and regulating the stocking of grazing lands.

Then the *Strategy* devotes seven spreads to 'priorities for national action' – essentially guidelines for communities embarking on conservation programmes – followed by five spreads recommending international action, stressing the need for better international conservation law, programmes to promote forest and desert conservation, programmes to preserve the international 'commons' – Antarctica, the open oceans and the atmosphere – and regional strategies to cover such shared resources as international river basins and seas. Finally the *Strategy* summarizes the main requirements for sustainable development, indicating general conservation priorities for the 'Third Development Decade' – the 1980s.

World Conservation Strategy is intended chiefly, according to its preamble, for government policy-makers and their advisers, conservationists and others directly

The Sahel – a tragedy for people as well as for wildlife. Soil erosion brings famine in its wake.

concerned with living resources, and development practitioners including aid agencies, industry and commerce, and trade unions. IUCN and WWF clearly base their own programme upon it; the second document, IUCN's *A Conservation Programme for Sustainable Development 1980–82*, published in December 1979 and subject to annual revision, is arranged systematically to match *Strategy* headings, making it easy to see which aspects will be dealt with in the near future.

The *Programme* is laid out in nine parts ('Programme Areas'). The first three, listed under the heading 'Incorporation of Conservation in Planning, Legal and Educational Systems', deal essentially with some of the obstacles to conservation that the *Strategy* defines. Projects covered in these sections include help from governments in developing national conservation strategies, planning departments of natural resources and resource development, and formulating conservation law. Strengthening the international conventions, revising the CITES appendices (p. 32) and many other legal and administrative projects are funded under this section. Educational projects include continuing support for African junior Wildlife Clubs, provision of mobile education units and advice on conservation education in schools.

Programme Areas Four to Six cover the objectives of conservation defined in the *Strategy*, under the heading 'Action to Conserve Ecosystems, Habitats and Species'. Here are listed projects on the publication of handbooks on mangrove management, establishment of national parks and marine reserves in Italy, Senegal and Sudan, publication of research on destruction of coral reefs and effects of oil pollution on marine environments. Under this section too come the projects on habitat destruction, especially of islands, rainforests, deserts and wetlands.

Here too are the new and the ongoing projects on threatened species – plants in Indonesia, the Caribbean Islands, Madagascar, Central and South America and Africa, and a host of animals from insectivores in Haiti to gorillas in Uganda. Humpback whales off Tonga are due for further help; so are monk seals in the Mediterranean and harbour seals in the beleaguered Waddensee. Project Tiger is still on the books, elephants and rhinos are not forgotten, and crocodiles, with a special priority rating, will be looked to in South America, the Philippines and Nepal. Whatever else WWF is doing, and however complex its programme, it is still in the excellent business of saving animals from extinction.

Programme Area Seven covers 'Comprehensive Area Based Conservation Programmes' and lists projects under such headings as the Caribbean, the Mediterranean, the Southern Ocean, Indonesia, Madagascar and the Galapagos. Areas Eight and Nine come under the joint heading of 'Programme Support and Development', and cover the

research and management of projects undertaken by IUCN and its associated bodies.

Finally, among the appendices at the end of the *Programme* is one that shows the criteria used in programme and project development – in sorting out, for example, the many hundreds of proposals submitted each year to IUCN and WWF for financial support. As might be expected, projects are favoured if they fall within the priorities and activities defined in the *Programme*, though others are considered. The project must achieve conservation – concentrating on factors that endanger species and communities and controlling them; research projects are welcome only if conservation is a clear objective. And there is a strong bias toward local involvement; acceptable projects will involve local organizations and benefit local people. Local experts should be brought in if they exist; if they do not, the project should include training local people as counterparts. Conservation and local involvement – these are clearly two very important features of the modern WWF image.

Programmes and Strategies explain to administrators and scientists how WWF sees its future, but what of the millions of WWF subscribers who have neither time nor inclination to puzzle a path through two tightly-crammed documents – how can they discover what WWF is up to? There is no single statement that shapes the future, but there is reassurance for them in every WWF statement. Within a larger and more complex framework, consistent

Emperor penguins of the Antarctic – the world's southernmost breeding species. Even polar species are at risk from the spread of man and his pollutants.

with its larger budget, the complexity of the tasks it is defining and the responsibilities it is shouldering – consistent with all that and a great deal more – WWF seems to be doing exactly what is has done so successfully for twenty years, what its best campaigns have been about, and what everyone hopes it will always keep on doing. It is saving the animals – putting down money efficiently to buy time for tigers and elephants, seals and whales, aye-ayes and nénés, gorillas and rhinos.

That it is saving plants, animals less well-known or likeable, and habitats as well, is entirely in its favour. Keeping the forests secure, the deserts intact, the seas alive and the coral reefs whole – these are things we all want and are happy to have WWF organizing for us – once they have saved the animals. If saving the habitats is the best way of saving the animals, so much the better. And if IUCN and WWF find they can stretch the concept of conservation every which way to involve education, administration and national and international law, and if this kind of stretching is more effective than other ways in achieving the main objectives, then WWF and IUCN are to be congratulated – they have found better ways of saving the animals. And so long as that is what they do, they will continue to have the blessing – and the money – of everyone in the wide world who can afford to give.

ACKNOWLEDGMENTS

The author and publisher would like to thank the following photographers, institutions and organizations by whose kind permission the illustrations are reproduced.

Heather Angel 80 *left*, 91

Ardea Photographics
26, 104 *right*, 180–1, 185; Dennis Avon and Tony Tilford 113; Leslie Brown 106; M.D.England 10, 39 *top*, 105; Jean-Paul Ferrero 100–1; Clem Haagner 16–17, 140, 141, 147, 149, 160–1; Eric Lindgren 39 *bottom*; Charles McDougal 52–3, 54–5, 63; David and Katie Urry 24–5; Adrian Warren 85; Alan Weaving 61

Gordon Carr 56–7

Bruce Coleman Ltd
42–3, 64–5, 74–5, 118, 125, 130–1, 169; Jen and Des Bartlett 26–7, 122–3, 188, 208–9, 210; S.C.Bisserot 98–9; Jane Burton 4–5, 66–7, 110–11, 116–17, 156, 182–3, 204; Alain Compost 195, 206; Eric Crichton 164–5; Gerald Cubitt 88–9, 158–9, 198–9; Jack Dermid 192–3; Nicholas Devore 78; Helmut Diller 89; Francisco Erize 168; M.P.L.Fogden 38–9; Jeff Foott 107, 112, 202–3; C.B. and D.W.Frith 108–9, 126–7; Jennifer Fry 86–7; Udo Hirsch 82–3, 83; Udo Hirsch and W.H.Müller 76–7; Carol Hughes 132–3, 134, 151; Peter Jackson 71; Jon Kenfield 190–1; Wayne Lankinen 172–3; Lee Lyon 148; Pat Morris 211; Timothy O'Keefe 194; Dieter and Mary Plage 29, 110; Goetz D.Plage 154–5; S.C.Porter 103; Mike Price 171–2; Donn Rein 128–9; Hans Reinhard 104 *left*, 166–7; M.F.Soper 160; Rod Williams 44, 70 *top and bottom*, 95; W.H.D.Wince 162–3; Gunter Ziesler 78–9; Christian Zuber 90–1, 94–5

Eric and David Hosking 28, 30–1, 92, 115

Peter Jackson 34–5

Behram Kapadia 174

Frank Lane
144–5; Lynwood M.Chace 121; F.Hartmann 18; Marineland of Florida 212–3; Leonard L.Rue 215; Irene Vandermolen 80 *right*

Magnum
14–15, 20–1, 48, 136–7; William Campbell 59; Peter Marlow 214; Alain Nogues 218; George Rodger 32, 142–3, 152–3

Marion Morrison 139

Bernard Stonehouse 219

World Wildlife Fund
97; Aquario Vasco da Gama, Portugal 197; Archie Carr 205; Georg Gerster 72–3; D.A.C.van den Hoorn 23; Howard Hughes 207; IUCN/Kenya Information Services 19, 146; Hartmut Jungius 177; T.Larsen 179; Bill Martin 157; Norman Myers 184; R.C.D.Olivier 150; U.Rahm 36–7; John Seidensticker 41; South African Nature Foundation 138; Fritz Vollmar 64; WWF Education Project 217; Christian Zuber 68, 92–3, 120

ZEFA
W.H.Müller 186–7; Hans Reinhard 178

The pictures on the back jacket are reproduced by kind permission of Bruce Coleman.

Maps by Terry Allen, Allard Studios

The publishers have taken all possible care to trace and acknowledge the ownership of the illustrations. If we have made an incorrect attribution we apologise and will be happy to correct the entry in any future reprint, provided that we receive notification.

FURTHER INFORMATION

Anyone with a continuing interest in international conservation, who wants to keep in touch and make a contribution, cannot do better than join the World Wildlife Fund. The world headquarters is on Avenue de Mont Blanc, Gland, Switzerland; they will supply the address of your own national organization. An annual subscription provides regular news bulletins and other information, as well as benefiting the Fund itself. For a small yearly subscription you can also give valuable support to IUCN and receive regular bulletins on its work; write to the main headquarters at the above address.

WWF Yearbooks, produced three-yearly during the first six years and annually from then on, provide excellent accounts of what the Fund has done since its inception; your public library may hold them, or be able to get them for you. New ones are obtainable from world headquarters or your national organization. IUCN has many publications on world conservation issues, written both for specialist and for general interest; a list of publications in print will be sent on request.

INDEX

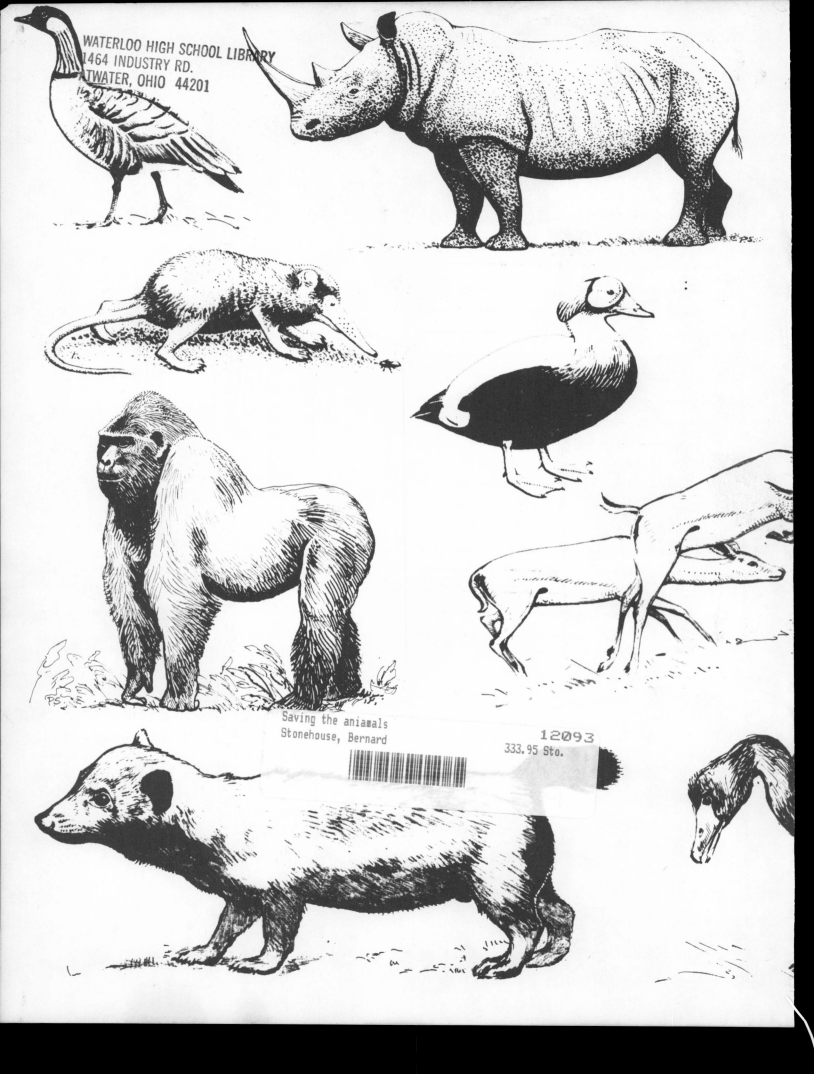